ITA BUTTROSE

Ita Buttrose AO, OBE, is one of Australia's most prominent women. Twice voted Australia's 'Most Admired Woman', she is a businesswoman, journalist, author, broadcaster and professional speaker. Ita Buttrose has held prominent positions with many of Australia's major publishing companies: Consultant to Fairfax Magazines and later Editor-in-Chief of the Sydney *Sun Herald;* Editor-in-Chief of the *Daily Telegraph* and *Sunday Telegraphs* and a member of the Board of News Limited Australia; and Publisher of Australian Consolidated Press Women's Division, controlling the *Australian Women's Weekly, Cleo, Belle, Bride* and *Mode*, as well as a member of the Board of Australian Consolidated Press. She has run her own company Capricorn Publishing Pty Ltd and edited its flagship magazine, *ITA*.

Currently, Ita runs her own marketing and public relations company in Sydney. She writes for *The Australian Women's Weekly*, is a regular panelist on the top-rating TV show *Beauty & the Beast* on Foxtel and Network Ten, and author of the best-selling novel *What Is Love?* One of Australia's busiest public speakers, Ita is patron to many community and charitable organisations.

ITA BUTTROSE

A Passionate Life

PENGUIN BOOKS

Penguin Books Australia Ltd
487 Maroondah Highway, PO Box 257
Ringwood, Victoria 3134, Australia
Penguin Books Ltd
Harmondsworth, Middlesex, England
Penguin Putnam Inc.
375 Hudson Street, New York, New Yórk 10014, USA
Penguin Books Canada Limited
10 Alcorn Avenue, Toronto, Ontario, Canada M4V 3B2
Penguin Books (N.Z.) Ltd
Cnr Rosedale and Airborne Roads, Albany, Auckland, New Zealand
Penguin Books (South Africa) (Pty) Ltd
5 Watkins Street, Denver Ext 4, 2094, South Africa
Penguin Books India (P) Ltd
11, Community Centre, Panchsheel Park, New Delhi 110 017, India

First published by Penguin Books Australia Ltd 1998
This revised and expanded paperback edition published in 2001

1 3 5 7 9 10 8 6 4 2

Text design by Cathy Larsen, Penguin Design Studio
Cover design by Nikki Townsend, Penguin Design Studio
Typeset by Midland Typesetters, Maryborough, Victoria
Printed and bound in Australia by McPherson's Printing Group, Maryborough, Victoria

National Library of Australia
Cataloguing-in-Publication data:

Buttrose, Ita, 1942–   .
Ita Buttrose: A passionate life.
Rev. ed.
Includes index.

ISBN 0 14 029902 5.

1. Buttrose, Ita, 1942–   . 2. Journalists – Australia – Biography.
3. Women journalists – Australia – Biography.
I. Title.

070.92

www.penguin.com.au

To Kate and Ben,
my two proudest achievements

CONTENTS

ACKNOWLEDGEMENTS

Books like this don't just happen and I am grateful to my friends who have helped me see it through to fruition. I'd particularly like to thank Craig Heilman for assisting me to sift through hundreds of articles and speeches. I have kept just about everything I've had published, as well as every speech I've ever given, so there was much to read. This was important research and Craig's enthusiasm and interest made the job more enjoyable than I thought it would be.

Ainslie Cahill kindly acted as a memory prodder whenever I phoned her and also read through the manuscript for me. Thank heavens she and I have worked together for more than twenty years. We had many a laugh over some of the things we both remembered, some of which are not in this book!

Thanks also to Jane North for volunteering to proofread the book. Every author should have such an eagle-eyed friend!

I also appreciated the advice of Professor Ron Penny, Jenny Ross and Allan Scroope. We all met through our work on the National Advisory Committee on AIDS (NACAIDS).

I have referred throughout the book to magazines and newspapers where I previously worked, such as the Sydney

Daily and *Sunday Telegraph*s, *The Australian Women's Weekly*, *Cleo*, the Sydney *Sun-Herald* as well as my own *ITA* magazine. I have also referred to the *Sydney Morning Herald*, the *Australian*, the *Good Weekend* and the *Bulletin*.

Thanks are due to the following for permission to reproduce extracts from several books: Hugh Mackay's *Reinventing Australia* (HarperCollins Publishers), Peter McDonald's *Families in Australia*, Richard Waterhouse's *Private Pleasures, Public Leisures*, Humphrey McQueen's *Social Sketches of Australia*, Peter West's *Fathers, Sons and Lovers: Men talk about their lives from the 1930s to today* (Finch Publishing) and Steve Biddulph's *Manhood: An action plan for changing men's lives* (Finch Publishing).

The Patterson Report or *Wooing the Australian Woman*, a publication produced by the advertising agency George Patterson in 1972, was also a useful source of information.

Thanks too to Bob Muscat, the former CEO of John Fairfax Holdings Ltd, for allowing me access to the Fairfax photographic library and for giving permission to reproduce some of the photographs in this book.

The Cold Chisel song lyrics from 'Ita' that appear on pages 77 and 78 are reproduced by kind permission of Universal Music Publishing/Rondor Music Australia Pty Ltd. Words and music are by Don Walker (© Rondor Music Australia Pty Ltd).

Finally thank you to the Executive Publisher of Penguin Books Australia, Julie Gibbs, for her continuing support and belief in this book.

PREFACE

There were days when I thought this book might never be completed. Reflecting on forty-plus years of my life's endeavours has been a huge undertaking as well as something of a cathartic experience. Occasionally it was impossible not to sit and muse for an hour or two over the consequences of some of the actions I've made, both personally and professionally.

This book like others I've written wasn't my idea. The Publishing Director of Penguin Books Australia, Robert Sessions, came to see me in 1994 not long after I'd closed *ITA* magazine, and told me it was time for me to write another book. 'A passionate book,' he insisted. 'Tell people how you *feel*.'

Over the years I've discovered much to be passionate about and my career has given me the privilege of sharing my passions with other Australians. This book allows me the opportunity to do so once again. I hope people who read it will agree that I have fulfilled my publisher's brief.

I want this book to encourage people, especially women, to dream dreams and never to stop trying to make them come true. I have never let the blinkers of others deter me from pursuing my dreams. Life hasn't always been easy but it has never been boring either!

As a woman with ambition, even when I was a teenager, I have sometimes felt very much alone. However I have never once felt the need to be anything less than the woman I am. I hope this is the important message other women will take away with them after reading this book.

When asked to write it, I said without thinking, 'This will be my goodbye book.' I've no idea why the thought even popped into my head, but now that my manuscript is finally finished, I'm convinced that it is indeed a goodbye book, marking the farewell to my past and the beginning of a new life's direction as 2001 takes me into the 21st century.

Maybe in another twenty years Penguin will ask me to write another book about this next journey I intuitively feel I am about to undertake. My gut instinct tells me it's going to be some trip.

1

STARTING OUT – THE FIFTIES
AND THE SIXTIES

Life's rewards appear at the end of the journey, not the
beginning.
There is no way I can foresee how many steps it will take me
to reach my goal.
I will perhaps meet failure at the thousandth step, and yet
success will be there
Hidden behind the last bend in the road.
I will never know how close I am to it unless I take one more
step.
If this doesn't work I will take another, and then another.
One step at a time is not so very difficult. I will persevere until
I succeed.

ANONYMOUS

When I began my career at fifteen I never thought that my
life would turn out the way it has. I thought I'd marry, have

children, stop working and live happily ever after. That was the way it was for girls in Australia in the late fifties and early sixties. My parents weren't the least bit worried when I announced I intended to leave school at fifteen without the Leaving Certificate, not something I would recommend to girls today. These days, knowledge is power and it will be even more so in this new century. But, in 1957, my parents were more concerned that my brothers were well educated. After all, men were the fundamental breadwinners and would need lifelong skills to feed their wives and families. That was how parents saw things back then and like other girls of my generation I went along with that kind of thinking in the belief that one day my prince would come.

I dreamt of falling in love with some gorgeous bloke who would love me too and, naturally, look after me forever. I had very little understanding about what marriage meant and it wasn't something parents talked about either. All I knew was that girls and boys grew up and married. Everyone said so, everyone expected it. Who was I to argue? No one told you that marriage was give and take, that parenting took a lot of effort, and that many women – and men – were unhappily married and didn't know what to do about it.

In the fifties girls did what they were told and rarely questioned. When I told Mum and Dad that I'd made up my mind to leave school, I guess I was signalling that somewhere deep inside me was an independent spirit, but I didn't know that then. I don't think my parents did either. If they did, they certainly didn't mention it to me. I was bursting to get out into the world and 'live'. My parents' marriage wasn't happy and hadn't been for years. There were constant arguments. Although my brothers and I knew our parents loved us, it wasn't easy being a teenager in a parental war zone. I figured that if I got a job and supported myself, I would be more secure. At least I would be earning money, and if my parents split as they kept promising each other (in voices loud enough for my brothers and me to hear, even in the middle of the night) I would be able to look after myself. I knew that I wanted to be a journalist – I had determined that when I was eleven.

I realise now how lucky I was to know what I wanted to do at such a young age, but then perhaps it wasn't all that surprising. After all, journalism is in my blood. My father was a journalist and, like me, started work when he was fifteen on newspapers. By the time I was born on 17 January 1942, he was working as a war correspondent on the *Sydney Morning Herald* in Java, in the Netherlands East Indies, now Indonesia. He didn't see me until I was two months old.

I suppose I became aware of what Dad did for a living when I was about nine or ten, and he was Editor of the Sydney *Daily Mirror*, then owned by Ezra Norton, one of Australia's most colourful and obnoxious newspaper barons.

Dad took a news conference every morning at eight o'clock directly he got into the office. It became my job to make him a pot of tea and get him breakfast before he left home shortly after seven. Mum got up later and cooked breakfast for the rest of the family. As he ate his eggs and toast, Dad would talk to me about the kind of day that awaited him and some of the things that would be happening at the paper. He had to go through both morning dailies – the *Sydney Morning Herald* and the *Daily Telegraph* – and listen to an ABC news broadcast before he left home. Sometimes he took or made phone calls between bites of toast about stories to be done for that day's *Mirror*. Those early morning sessions with my father and regular late Sunday afternoon walks we took together, which sometimes involved calling in on fellow journalists, impressed me. Dad's world seemed exciting. He and his friends always had opinions, debating and discussing the issues of the day with vigour. There didn't seem to be a dull thing about them.

I was even more convinced when Dad went from Ezra Norton to writing editorials for Sir Frank Packer's *Daily Telegraph*. At that time Australian Consolidated Press was staffed by some of the most competent journalists in the land. Not only were they brilliant craftspeople, but they were also personalities – entertaining, and rich in experience and knowledge of the world and its ways. Just about every Saturday night my parents either went to some journalist's place for dinner or we had a gathering at our home.

My brothers and I were allowed to stay up until the guests arrived for dinner when we were expected to shake hands with the visitors and have a few words to say for ourselves before being packed off to another part of the house. Later I would go to bed, but not to sleep. There were nights and early mornings when I listened for hours to the conversation coming from the dining room. Nearly all of it was about newspapers or magazines and the people who owned them and worked on them. I was fascinated. The talk was zesty and laced with humour. It struck me that journalists enjoyed their work. They were noisy, happy people with opinions on everything.

Because of Dad's work we moved about quite a deal in my early years. Towards the end of the war, in 1944, Dad had gone to New York and later to San Francisco to work in the Australian Government's News and Information Bureaus. After the war we moved back to New York where he was based as North American correspondent for Ezra Norton's organisation. My schooling began in the USA at the Bedford Hills School in New York's Westchester County.

When we returned to Australia in mid 1949 we had been away more than five years. I was seven. My parents loved living in the States, but they wanted my brothers and me to grow up and be educated in Australia. They were worried about our strong American accents, which, incidentally, we lost completely after only three months back home.

Ezra Norton had arranged for a house in the northern Sydney suburb of Northbridge to be leased for us for six months after our return. For awhile I went to the Northbridge Public School, but it was certainly a different place from the school I'd gone to in Bedford Hills. One day I bent down to pick up something I'd dropped in the playground, and my class teacher, a woman with dark hair, very thin and bad-tempered, kicked me in the behind. I went home at lunchtime and told my mother I didn't feel well. I never ever went back. I left my lunch of sardine sandwiches in the desk and hope they smelt the classroom out.

I went for a time to the Monte Sant'Angelo Convent in North Sydney. The nuns were shocked when they found out that I had not made my First Confession or Holy Communion. Mum and Dad had ceased to be practising Catholics and had not worried about my religious upbringing. The nuns, unintentionally I'm sure, made me feel as though I were a very wicked little girl and rapidly prepared me for the Sacraments. Dad's mother, Grandma Aggie (Agnes), after whom I was almost named (thank heaven they called me 'Ita' after Mum's mother instead), was also displeased when she found out. She lived in Adelaide and sent me my Communion veil and a strong lecture letter to her lost-soul eldest son.

When the lease of the Northbridge house ran out, Dad rented a house at Parsley Bay in Sydney's eastern suburbs from two eccentric writers and former Sydney journalists, Max and Maysie Murray. Both were extremely successful. While Max wrote thrillers, Maysie wrote romantic novels. They were such characters and liked nothing better than a gossip and a drink. Once they turned up for dinner at our place with a thermos of martinis!

Another time Maysie rang Dad in a terrible flap. We were having lunch and her distinctive voice boomed out over the telephone: 'Charles, I need your help! My heroine is stuck in a plane with the hero above Woomera and I can't work out how to get them down. Can you come over?'

Maysie and Max lived a few minutes away on the other side of Parsley Bay. Dad disappeared for several hours and returned home triumphant – and, I suspect, with a few celebratory martinis under his belt. He'd found a way for Maysie to land the plane enabling the hero and heroine to live happily ever after. He dined out on the story for months and from then on Maysie often rang him for advice when she had a problem with one of her plots.

Our change of address also resulted in my attending yet another school. I finished the year out at Monte's sister school in Rose Bay, before being enrolled at Barat-Burn, the junior school of the Sacred Heart Convent on the Rose Bay hill. The three years I spent there were some of the happiest of my school days. Unfortunately, in the senior school, under the convent rules then applying, I would have had to become a boarder despite living only about a kilmometre from the school. Neither my parents nor I thought much of the boarder idea. More to the point, the fees involved in the change were higher than my father could afford.

I was sent to what then was called the Dover Heights Home Science High School, now Dover Heights High School. From having been in a class of eleven at the convent I went into a class of forty-five. As a I recall there was something like eight first-year classes at the school and a total of 360 girls in first year. At the outset I was very unhappy. Parents tend to believe that 'children will get over it', but I resented my parents paying for my brothers' education while I went to a free school. I thought this indicated that they considered my brothers' education more important. I cannot recall my parents ever seriously discussing the subjects I should study. I'm not bleating but admitting a resentment that still rankles a bit. It annoys me that I still feel irked – I should have outgrown such feelings by now, but this particular change of schools was a significant turning point in my life and required a certain maturity to cope with it. As I was only 11, this was something of a challenge.

After the convent, I found Dover Heights overwhelming: it was so big and impersonal. Very few of my girlfriends from the convent wanted to have anything to do with me after I'd changed schools either. (I know now that this is insignificant, but it was hurtful then.) Those first early months at Dover Heights were lonely ones indeed. Thank heaven for a wonderful woman called Phyllis Desmond, the school's singing teacher. At my first choir session I removed my blazer after we'd sung a few songs. This was apparently a good sign as far as Mrs Desmond was concerned. I was giving my singing all that I could – she liked girls who made that kind of an effort. It wasn't long before I was taking part in the school's annual Gilbert and Sullivan production and making friends with other girls, who like me, loved music. I had had piano lessons at the convent, but Dover Heights did not run to a piano teacher, so I continued lessons with a private teacher not far from home.

Looking back, going to Dover Heights was probably one

of the best things that ever happened to me. At the convent
I had little difficulty in being a class leader in most subjects;
school life for me was sweet and easy. At Dover Heights
the going was testing and I had to work very hard because
the competition, principally from diligent, ambitious girls
from migrant families, was intense. I specially enjoyed
English and debating and once again was fortunate to have
a terrific teacher, Mrs Enfield, who encouraged my journalistic ambitions. She was disappointed when I left school
early, but I can clearly remember her telling me that she
was sure I would succeed in my chosen profession. When
she wished me well, I knew she meant it.

Our time at Parsley Bay was the longest period we ever lived
together as a family in the same house. It is still one of the
most picturesque and least spoiled spots on Sydney Harbour.
Our street, Parsley Road, was full of kids. We all led a wonderful healthy, natural life. Peter Weir, the film director,
whose family lived next door to us, always said that ' Parsley
Bay was Camelot for kids'.

We made our own fun. We swam most of the year and
my brothers Julian – the eldest of us – and Will were champion swimmers of their school. Boys and girls played
together in the ground between Parsley Bay Park and the
Harbour. Cowboy and Indians, cops and robbers, hide-and-
seek, rounders, cricket, football . . . we played them all. In
picking competing teams, boys and girls were equal – all men.
To my regret, my mother stopped me playing football when

I was eleven. My bosoms had begun to grow and Mum decided that I should no longer be subjected to tackling by boys. For the same reason she stopped me wearing my cotton one-piece Speedo swimming suit. Girls whose bosoms were becoming obvious were not considered to be decently clad in a one-piece Speedo in the 1950s. Mum also forbade me to play hockey, declaring it to be unladylike – though it looked like a lot of fun to me.

By today's standards we were strictly brought up and by 'we' I mean all the kids in the street. None of us considered our parents oppressive nor ourselves unduly unrestricted in what we wanted to do. We did as we were told. Our parents expected us to do so and we respected their authority. The standing rule at our house was that when we came home from school we changed out of our uniforms into more knockabout clothes, had something to eat and a glass of milk (Mum made us each drink at least a pint of milk a day; I'm sure my calcium-enriched bones will be grateful in my old age) and did our homework. We were not allowed to go out and play during the school week.

Mum was working by the time I was nine, but had to stop when my youngest brother Charles was born in September 1952 when I was ten. She went back to work not long after his arrival and we had a succession of what Mum called 'housekeepers', who were usually unmarried mothers. They were young and often from the country. Mum taught the girls how to look after their baby and tried to get them together with the child's father. Several of our housekeepers' marriages were due to Mum's tactful matchmaking. I hope the marriages turned out well.

Mum trusted us to behave when we came home from school while she was at work and we usually did. She did publicity work and fundraising for good causes: the Family Welfare Bureau, UNICEF, the Spastic Centre, and the Royal Prince Alfred Hospital. My mother was a kind, softhearted woman and often came home distressed about some sick little boy she'd seen at hospital or a little girl with cerebral palsy who had to undergo surgery.

Some evenings when Dad was able to get home for dinner – as a newspaperman he worked irregular hours – he took us for a swim. That was special. We were expected to make our beds and keep our rooms tidy, help with the washing-up and lend Dad a hand in the garden most week-ends. We usually ate dinner at seven in the evening when the ABC radio news began. We were not allowed to speak or to interrupt in any way while the fifteen-minute broadcast was on and then the conversation started. Meal times were not rushed as they are today. We often didn't leave the table until after 8 p.m. When I learned to cook, it became my job to make a cake, usually a sponge, for Sunday afternoon tea. By the time I was thirteen I could cook just about anything on the family menu and often prepared a whole meal if Mum were unable for some reason to do the job.

If there was little luxury in our lives, we did not know it. We could not afford a car, although we had owned one in the United States, and were the only family in the street without one. Nobody seemed to care about that – certainly not us. We never went away for a holiday, but there was nothing hard about that since we had Parsley Bay and all it offered for fun and games right on our doorstep. Other kids in the street were congenial. We were all friends and many friendships still endure. Most of us have done pretty well in life, too. There was a special camaraderie between us. Even if the family exchequer could have run to it, finding a better place for a holiday than where we lived would have been difficult.

Most kids in the street collected stamps and coins. Book-swapping was a major activity. My longtime friend, Trish Byrne, whose family lived next door (the Weir family were on the other side of us), and I tried to start a lending library. We failed because the other kids wanted to take the books without paying. We had a cubby house in which we made lemonade using lemons from trees growing in the garden of the man who lived behind us. One tree hung over Patricia's garden and another over mine. Our neighbour did not approve of our 'borrowing' his lemons and complained to our parents. They were always apologetic and spoke harshly to us, but did not cease their practice of sending one of us 'up the back' to get a lemon to go with our fish on Friday nights. The family's last relic of religious observance – no meat on Friday – thus was tainted by petty larceny!

Trish had the most beautiful plaits I'd ever seen and I immediately wanted to grow my hair so that I could have pigtails, too. My mother said no – I guess because she knew that she'd have to plait them!

We would get the bus to school together and on weekends and in school holidays played together. Somehow we got to calling each other Maud and Myrtle, although neither of us can now remember how it all started. Whenever one of us wanted the other, we would lean over our respective front verandahs and yell out 'Maud' or 'Myrtle'. I often remember her mother calling out to her: 'Ita wants you, Trish'. Our brothers thought we were both quite mad. Our parents were what could best be described as quietly amused. Even today, I still call Trish 'Maud' but my Myrtle has fallen by the wayside – Maud calls me 'Ite'!

At night we played card games, draughts and chess. My brothers' fiercely competitive spirit rubbed off on me. I always played to win. Whatever the boys did, I wanted to do too. My brothers now take much credit for my career success, claiming they taught me how to think like a man! God bless them – but to be honest, I did learn a thing or two from them that has stood me in good stead. We loved listening to the radio in the way kids enjoy TV today, but except for the 'Goon Show', which fascinated us but which my parents said they could not understand, Mum and Dad chose the programs and decided the times when the radio went on and off. Our listening was restricted largely to the news and classical music from the ABC, but on Sundays we were allowed to listen to plays on the commercial stations. Sometimes though, when Mum and Dad weren't around, we'd listen to the 'Lone Ranger' or some other popular afternoon serial.

Parsley Bay kids were pretty well behaved even by the strict standards of the 1950s. Peter Weir was always organising concerts and plays. When any of us went to his house, he would conduct imaginary interviews with us. We did magic shows, send-ups of radio commercials and put on theatrical performances for which we wrote our own scripts. Some of the boys may have tried puffing a cigarette behind a bush in the park, but to my knowledge none of the girls did. Trish and I once tried smoking her father's pipe and were so sick we never tried a second time. As for drinking, even when we were fourteen or fifteen, we never gave it a thought. Occasionally, on some day of celebration, my father poured us a small glass of whatever wine was being drunk, but never more than a few tablespoonfuls. The idea of going into a pub was unthinkable. I don't want to give the impression that we were all good little children who never entertained a naughty thought for we were as normal as bread and jam.

Naturally the older we got, the deeper became our interest in the opposite sex. We girls began to see our boy playmates in a different light and got the message that the boys had begun to see us as something other than 'men' in one of the game's teams.

We were less disposed to try sex than later generations, if for no more virtuous reason than that the contraceptive pill was not yet available and also possibly because of the ghastly step-ins (girdles) that girls had to wear. To the extent that they were difficult to get off, these acted like chastity belts. These things apart, I think the real reason for our being slower than today's kids to begin having sex was that we were allowed to be kids. There was no pressure on us to grow up too quickly and abandon our carefree, childish way of living. We were allowed to be uncertain, to make mistakes. Our parents were there when we needed them. We had our meals together and, with no television to inter-rupt conversation, they listened to us speak about things in which we were interested. We did not object to a firm parental hand steering us towards adulthood. Therefore, we were able to assume responsibility when it came.

From our early teens Parsley Bay kids and my other friends all talked about what we were going to do when we left school. The girls all expected to work temporarily before we got married. Ah, the dreams of young girls! None of us visualised life-long careers.

Fortunately for me, in the fifties it wasn't considered necessary for a journalist to have higher education. In fact, the feeling among older journalists – my father included – was that the school of life was the only education for aspiring journalists. A person with a university degree who wanted to be a journalist was viewed with suspicion. That attitude prevailed well into the seventies. Scores of well-educated young men and women were turned away from newspapers simply because they had made the error of getting a university education!

Getting a serious education wasn't much of a priority for any girl in the fifties. Our days were not filled with much deep thinking. A look at the women's pages in newspapers shows that we were interested in clothes, fun, parties and travel. Perhaps some of us were beginning to wonder if there was more to life.

I remember once, when my mother was telling me how happy I would be as a housewife, saying I was worried I might get bored. 'Oh, no, you won't,' she assured me, forgetting that she was a working mother herself. It didn't occur to Mum that she was a part of changing times, and that the fact that she was combining motherhood with a career would be a strong influence on me.

My parents hoped that one of my three brothers – Julian, Will and Charlie – would follow in Dad's footsteps and have as distinguished a career in journalism as he did. But it was me who followed in his footsteps and if, at times, I seemed in a hurry, it was no doubt because I was also following in Mum's footsteps. Two sets of footprints are a lot to live up to!

Woman's role and women themselves began to change during World War II when Australian men went overseas to fight in the forces and women took their place in factories, offices and on the land. As Eli Ginsberg said, 'How are you going to keep them down on the farm after they've seen Paree?' Ginsberg, the distinguished professor of economics at America's Colombia University and a well-known specialist on human resources, calls the employment of women outside the home the most important social change of the twentieth century. The long-term consequences are absolutely unchartable,' he says. 'It will affect men, women and children and the consequences of that will be revealed only in the twenty-first century.' I suspect that we're seeing signs of that already, especially as far as men and boys are concerned. There's no doubt that the changing role of women which began in World War II was the beginning of a brave, new world for women, but few realised it at the time.

There has been a revolution going on in Australia, and even now few people, women included, comprehend the significance of what has happened. We are reaping today the harvest we sowed over the last forty years, both good and bad. It is high time modern Australia was examined in light of the massive social transformation of the last forty years. This transformation has been precipitated and intensified by the changing role of women. It follows, then, that to understand where we are today we need to look back to the place from which we have come. I've been a part of the journey and my career in the media has enabled me to witness first-hand what I call the feminisation of Australia.

I managed to get a job as a copygirl on *The Australian Women's Weekly* after completing four months at business college learning shorthand and typing. (The *Weekly* was then a weekly, not a monthly as it is today.) My parents had impressed on me the need to have skills – if you have skills you can be useful. The same advice still applies today, perhaps even more so.

Although the *Weekly* was owned by Sir Frank Packer (father of Kerry) and the founding editor had been a man, George Warneke, when I arrived at the *Weekly* all the senior editorial positions were held by women – an extremely unusual situation in the fifties, not that anyone at the *Weekly* thought so. It seemed perfectly natural. Why wouldn't women be running Australia's biggest and most successful magazine? In the book, *The Weekly*, published to celebrate the *Weekly*'s fiftieth anniversary in 1983, and which I commissioned when I was Publisher of the magazine in the late seventies, its author Denis O'Brien sums up the *Weekly* and the fifties.

The emancipated woman had almost disappeared from the pages of the magazine. 'What makes an ideal wife and mother?' it asked in a 1955 contest. Judged by the advertising of the day, she was the woman who washed with Persil or Rinso, bathed with Lux, cared for her hair with a Richard Hudnut home permanent, gave her husband a mug of Horlicks at night and her children glasses of Milo throughout the day and looked 'young and beautiful all the time' in Spenderpants, Cotton Dinkies, panty girdles with 'the Stay-Up Top' and a Hollywood Maxwell Bra with 'Whirlpool' cups.

If the *Weekly* had lost sight of the cause of women's rights, it was not alone. In the social climate of the time, only a brave or foolish editor would have contradicted a society apparently contented with the way things were. A 1959 article headed 'My wife works and I hate it' drew thousands of letters – most supporting the husband.

Such matters did not concern me. I was thrilled to be working on the *Weekly*, soaking up the atmosphere of the place. As for working after marriage – it wasn't something I'd ever considered. All nice girls knew that when they married and had children they were expected to give up their jobs.

If the *Weekly* was hesitant to even consider that a woman might find happiness outside the home, as Denis O'Brien suggests, there was one working woman of whom they did approve – the Queen. Like most girls who read the *Weekly*, and lots of us did, we soaked up every line written about the Queen and the royal family. After all, they were the stuff of which fairytales were made and in the fifties we believed in happy endings.

Kay Melaun, who was a very no-nonsense Features Editor when I became Editor of the *Weekly* in 1975, probably winces even now when she reads what she wrote about the Queen back in the fifties in the *Weekly*'s Youth Series column.

She has a job; it's a regal job, but nevertheless a job. She has a husband and children. She is Queen, wife and mother to perfection – yet she is completely feminine. She is monarch yet she is as real, as natural, as sunshine. Paramount among her attributes is a sort of shining good sense that irradiates her every action. Why, she even had the good sense, as someone observed, to have a boy first.

Given Prince Charles' behaviour since, the Queen might have other views about that. What would a mother think about her married son who told his married lover that he wished he were a tampon?

I left the *Weekly* and went down one floor of the ACP building in the heart of Sydney, to the *Daily* and *Sunday Telegraph* Women's Section, where I worked as secretary to the Women's Editor, Micky McNicoll, before getting my cadetship in 1958 at the age of sixteen. Everyone told me that I hadn't a chance of getting my cadetship at sixteen, but I didn't believe them. I came in on my days off to work with the senior journalists, I submitted paragraphs for publication and ideas for stories to Mrs McNicholl. I think I wore Micky out with my enthusiasm. I can still recall the absolute joy of being told that I had been granted a cadetship. It was one of the happiest days of my life.

My first assignment wouldn't even rate a mention in the papers these days. I was sent to the change-over lunch of the Rotary Club of South Sydney and noted that all the women guests at the lunch received a small bouquet of either orchids, camellias, roses or carnations to pin on their lapels. Perhaps that says something about women's roles in the fifties. The story ran to nine paragraphs and was published on 1 July 1958. As far as I was concerned, it could have been a page one story and worthy of some grand prize.

As I look back upon newspaper and magazine articles in the fifties and sixties, I get the strong impression that life was somewhat less pressured for the average woman. We seemed to smile more. We had more time – for ourselves and for others. We were interested in fashion, cooking and household tips. We could cook, sew and knit. We could clean a house well. We were polite and respectful. And young women in their teens, like me, stood up for older people (anyone over thirty) and pregnant women on buses and trams. We didn't mind because in those days people always thanked you and made you feel good. There was time in the fifties and sixties for politeness. Time to say hello. Time to talk to one another. In these time-strapped days, one can only wonder whether we really have our priorities right.

Five days after the Rotary lunch I wrote my second piece, about a polo carnival. Two things strike me about just how different things were in 1958. I listed every woman by her husband's name. That probably seems very quaint today but it was the accepted form of address for a woman in the fifties. Having a husband was like wearing a badge of honour. The only name that was important was your husband's. A woman was not a person in her own right, no indeed. I am reminded of how upset my grandmother would become if people referred to her as 'Mrs Ita Rodgers' and not 'Mrs Bill Rodgers', even after the death of my grandfather in 1953. A woman without a man's name had no real identity, and all women knew it.

The second anomaly is the article's heading, 'Country atmosphere at gay polo carnival'. Granted, not a particularly racy title in 1958, but it again illustrates the dramatic changes which have taken place in Australia since that time. In March 1959, I was sent on what I've recorded in my scrapbook as 'my first away job' to cover the Goulburn Picnic Races in southern New South Wales, and I wrote that 'Beach umbrellas were popular at gay picnic race meeting'. A title like that would mean something altogether different today. It makes me smile even more to read the opening paragraph: 'Fashions at the Goulburn Picnic Races on Friday were "a little each way"'. I did a follow-up the following year with 'Picnic racegoers did a quick-change act', but that pales in comparison to my 'Gay, informal scene at Canberra picnics' in March 1962. Those were simpler times indeed!

The obsession – or so it appears all these years later – we had with identifying women through their husbands comes through again and again in the pieces I wrote. On 8 July 1958, I wrote a piece about the Australian opera singer, Rosina Raisbeck, who had returned home from overseas. What strikes me as odd now is that I felt compelled to quote her married name, and to explain to the readers that her husband would soon be following. It suggests to me how in the fifties not only were women very much identified with and through their husbands or primary male relationships, but there would have been eyebrows raised about a woman

flitting around the world by herself, especially a woman travelling with her three-year-old son. Consciously or unconsciously, I was reflecting the mood of the era.

Of course, women had interests of their own and none
more so than fashion. It was expected that women would
be interested in clothes and would always dress like ladies,
with gloves and hats. When prominent Australian women
(most of whom owed their 'status' to their notable husbands,
usually corporate business leaders or wealthy landowners)
returned from overseas holidays, I would be sent to interview
them and sooner or later the conversation would get around
to fashion. A *Daily Telegraph* article from 20 March 1959 says
much about what fascinated us. 'Pastel ski pants, apricot,
lemon and white, were the latest fashion statements on the
slopes in Switzerland', my interviewee reported; while in
New York the look was 'little hats and wisps of veiling with
glamorous gowns and nothing but minks for first nights,
especially at the Metropolitan Opera House'. Indeed, many
of my articles from this period discussed fashion issues. The
French couturier Pierre Balmain arrived in Sydney in May
1959 to present his designs and declared: 'Wool is wonderful'. Sometimes fashionable terms were used that would be
extremely unfashionable today. For instance in the fifties,
French couturier Nina Ricci showed a coat in 'nigger brown
and off-white check wool'. Another designer, returning
home after a fact-finding trip, told me 'dark nigger brown
stockings were "in" on the Continent'. Who would dare talk
about 'nigger' anything, and rightly so, nowadays?

During this time, women became more and more concerned with their image. In April 1961 I was sent to interview Shirley Docket, a specialist instructor and hair colourist with Clairol, when she returned from a three-month overseas trip studying 'the latest hairstyles and colours in London, Rome, Paris and Hong Kong, as well as America, where she attended an advanced technical course in hair colouring'. In keeping with the times, I wrote that 'Miss Docket was, in private life, Mrs Robert Ennor, of Bellevue Hill'. I told the *Telegraph* readers, 'Fourteen-year-old American girls are following so closely in their mothers' footsteps that they're changing the colour of their hair as often as the mood takes them', and about 'the amazing improvement that a change of hair colour could do to a woman. Sallow skins become healthy and suntanned while pale coloured eyes become vividly alive'.

Around the same time, I wrote about the new look coming from the French fashion salons of Nina Ricci and Lachasse, and the need to be 'Slender and Sophisticated', perhaps foreshadowing ominous things to come for women. Preoccupation with beauty was an ever-present reality. In an interview with a Double Bay woman, just returned from six weeks in Spain, I quoted, 'There are so many servants to help in the home that women have nothing else to do but look beautiful'.

The sixties also saw another important influence on the lives of women – the introduction of the Pill. The Pill had nothing to do with image, but ultimately it was going to give women the kind of sexual freedom they'd never envisaged. It began to be routinely prescribed to women in Australia in 1961, but like most things to do with women's bodies, there was very little information for women about it. Sure, women — well, some women — knew there was something called the Pill, but it wasn't openly discussed, and very few doctors talked to women about such intimate matters as contraception. It's incredible when you think about it. Contraception as efficient as the Pill changed the lives of women not only in Australia of course, but in other countries around the world, and yet governments (whose members were predominantly male) forbade the advertising of contraceptives.

We can only wonder why. What were they frightened of? Did they think women might actually say no to sex? We'll never know the answer to that one. Women might have hoped that the medical profession would have kept them up to date with contraception. That certainly wasn't so in my case. No doctor ever talked to me about the Pill until the mid-seventies, after the birth of my son — my second child. I am sure I wasn't an isolated case. There were articles about the Pill in the press from time to time, but more often than not, they were scare articles about how the Pill could cause thrombosis, for instance. The frank and honest reporting about women's health and bodies that *Cleo* pioneered in the seventies was not very evident in the sixties.

There were signs of other change in the sixties, and again I suspect the significance of most of them was overlooked. On 1 July 1962, I wrote a piece about 'image' for the opening page of the *Sunday Telegraph* Women's Section. It was titled: 'Are you a living IMAGE?' The first paragraph read: 'Pick up a magazine, a book, a newspaper – and ten to one you will come across the word IMAGE'. Perhaps the invention of TV, and the shrinking world around us, had made us much more self-aware, but as I look back now I see surreptitious change happening – exemplified in the word 'image'. Were women beginning to emerge from the shadows of their men? Was this the genesis of superwoman?

That article observed portentously: 'If you want to keep up with the times, it's smart to talk about image'. I continued with, 'But the most fascinating thing about the whole image idea is the fact that almost everyone has been caught up with it – and generally completely unawares. Images are much like dreams, they reflect us as we think we are – or would like to be'. The article seems somewhat Orwellian now, as I reflect on how I described the 'Brisk Young House-wife Image'.

She dresses with casual elegance, is surrounded by a gleaming washing machine, a huge refrigerator, and every other labour saving device. She has whiter than white children who play in a neat back garden. She's seen on TV, and in magazine ads – unflurried, efficient, and always pretty. You know just by looking at her that her home is neat, her cooking good, her children happy, her husband blissful. She is the housewife image for a million housewives. Gradually as the picture of the perfect housewife image is formed, more and more women try to achieve the ideal of THE IMAGE.

If Image One was Orwellian, Image Two, the 'Career-Wife Image', surely describes superwoman.

A cool, poised woman balancing her precarious life perfectly between home and career. She does her job superbly, wearing a simple but exquisitely expensive suit and a mink hat (her status symbol). She organises her working life like clockwork. Then she goes home and, peeling off her long suede gloves and changing swiftly into a little black dress, whips up a perfect dish – something casseroled in red wine – and becomes the charming, witty, sophisticated hostess to her husband's important guests . . . the hit-or-miss career-wife can strive towards the IMAGE. And it's a good idea for her to keep it in mind so she knows what she's striving for.

I wonder if the roots of the superwoman image, which gained prominence in the seventies and eighties, lie just here. Few of us in the sixties had any inkling of the role that lay ahead of us. I had never thought about my own image, or been on a diet until I started work. It never occurred to me that there was something wrong with the way I looked. I was seventeen when Rosemary Wilton, one of the tall, glamorous senior journalists, said to me: 'Do you realise how much sugar you put in your coffee? Two teaspoons. You have two cups a day, that's twenty teaspoons of sugar a week. Sugar is fattening. You'd lose weight if you gave up sugar. You'd look better, too.'

I figured Rosemary, being older and wiser, knew what she was talking about. I stopped putting sugar in my coffee. I sometimes ate only a carton of yoghurt with honey for lunch. I know I've been conscious of my weight ever since. But Rosemary was right – when I gave up sugar in my coffee I did lose weight!

Even without sugar, however, life was good. I was doing work I loved. I was earning money. I could buy nice clothes on lay-by from David Jones, my grandmother's favourite store and where so many special things in my life have been purchased. When I reached my teens, my grandmother announced that she would buy me a winter coat every year ('All young women who want to be well-dressed need a winter coat', she declared). My father bought me my first ballerina (a mid-length evening dress) at David Jones for a formal dance at Scots College in Sydney. And when, at seventeen, I was sent by Micky McNicoll to Queensland to cover the tour of that State by Princess Alexandra, my grandmother bought me my first full-length evening gown at David Jones, a wonderful chiffon creation in varying shades of soft green. Even in the sixties, there was no other store – for me – like David Jones!

That royal tour was an important break. It was a big

assignment for a teenager but, as Princess Alexandra was only nineteen, Micky and her husband, David, who was then Editor-in-Chief of Australian Consolidated Press, thought a young person should cover the tour. It marked Queensland's Centenary, and I spent a month travelling with the Princess all over that vast State as well as Canberra. It was fabulous fun. I wore my David Jones evening gown to at least nine formal balls.

In those days women reporters were expected to dress the part and look as though we 'belonged' among the invited guests. I didn't mind at all. There was a gorgeous private detective in the Princess' party – his name was Norman Chorley and he was (to my young eyes) very distinguished and handsome. He explained to me that it was easier for him to keep an eye on the Princess when she was on the dance floor, if he was dancing too. He would be grateful, he explained, if I would be his dancing partner. I felt a bit like a princess myself, swirling around the dance floor with Norman. I was in seventh heaven. All the hard work of the tour was well worth it to dance with Norman Chorley.

I got my first byline on that tour, too. Bylines were hard to get in the fifties and sixties. Most of my stories from Queensland were acknowledged as being 'From our special representative'. But at the end of the tour, I wrote a piece for the front page of the *Sunday Telegraph* Women's Section on how 'The local slang fascinates our Royal visitors' and reported that Princess Alexandra's doctor, Wing Commander Brian Kelly, had admitted he was fascinated with the term 'a bit crook' and that the next time he issued a medical report he was going to say his patient was a 'bit crook, but not as crook as he was'. I summed up the tour as one of the friendliest ever and told the paper's readers that Princess Alexandra was beaut! To my great delight, Micky gave me a proper byline – 'From Ita Buttrose, who toured Queensland with the Princess'.

When I returned to Sydney, Mrs McNicoll told me she was very pleased with the work I'd done, and a few months later told me she was going to recommend a promotion which resulted in me completing my cadetship in three years rather than the usual four.

They were happy, carefree times. I doubt that I worried about much at all. What's more, Sydney was a safe place to live. As a cadet I worked shiftwork – some days from ten in the morning until seven at night, other days from two in the afternoon until eleven at night. When I had the two-to-eleven shift I often went surfing at Bondi Beach in the morning before starting work. At night, it was safe to walk across Hyde Park and catch a tram from Queen's Square to Rose Bay, where I'd wait at the bus stop for the bus to take me to my home at Parsley Bay. I'd walk down the dimly lit street to our house, arriving home just before midnight.

It's something I wouldn't dream of doing today. Sydney is a particularly unsafe place for a woman on her own. Now I wouldn't even consider walking across Hyde Park at seven, let alone eleven at night, by myself. I'd be too frightened. I sometimes feel apprehensive just hearing someone walking behind me when making my way down one of Sydney's main streets in the early evening. Women may have gained freedom in a great many things, but we have lost our independence in other ways. Towards the end of the nineties one of Sydney's main city streets, George Street, was declared a 'high risk area' because of the increasing number of street gangs and violence. Businesses began employing security guards with German shepherds to protect their businesses and customers. With the 2000 Olympics on our doorstep, authorities quickly promised all kinds of things to make the city safe. Criminal activity did decrease while the Games were on, but by January 2001 New South Wales Police Commissioner, Peter Ryan, warned that gang activity in Sydney was rising and that the city was on its way to becoming an international money-laundering hub. Ironically, it seems the Games indirectly promoted the affluence of the city and its potential for crime. A special police report revealed that hoodlums of Russian, Vietnamese, Chinese, Malaysian and Lebanese extraction were forming gangs and fighting to control Sydney's heroin, extortion and prostitution market. As for George Street – it remained as dangerous as ever with gang members threatening to stab victims who refused to hand over their money. Do these activities suggest that the time has come for a rethink about Australia's great experiment with multiculturalism? Many Australians, including me, think so.

At the end of the fifties it would have been impossible to imagine Sydney reduced to such a sad and sorry state of affairs. When I worked the two-to-eleven shift, safety was never an issue, but today many firms send their female workers home by taxi if they have to work late. All things considered, I liked night work not only because I could enjoy a morning swim, but also I could go shopping or meet a friend for a coffee, and there was always a convivial hour for our tea break at 6.30 p.m.

We'd head for 'The Greeks', the name we gave the restaurants around the corner from the *Telegraph*. These were run by 'new Australians' who, like many of their countrymen and women, settled here after World War II. You could get a huge serving of sausages, gravy, mashed potatoes and peas downstairs for just 1/6 (about 15 cents). If you went upstairs, where traditional Greek dishes were served, you could get a plate of rice pilaf, also with gravy, for just 1/- (about 10 cents). This was a pretty useful meal as cadets were always broke, especially on Wednesday, the day before payday, and rice pilaf was good and filling as well as cheap. More often than not, we'd borrow the shilling for Wednesday's tea from one of the senior journalists.

Sometimes our photographic colleagues, several of whom were also cadets and the right age for us to flirt with, joined us. For some reason that was never made clear to me, my parents did not approve of photographers and they did not encourage me to form friendships with them. But of course I did. Forbidden fruit is always the most interesting. Naturally I liked the opposite sex and as I was so young, most boys my age were still at school. Photographers were, and as far as I'm concerned are, fun people. As a young woman I enjoyed their company and still do today. As cadets, we talked the same language; we dreamed similar kinds of dreams: getting the best story or the best photograph, that kind of thing.

Journalists of my father's generation often looked down on photographers – not unkindly, but in a professional way. They simply didn't think they were as good as journalists and saw photographers as adjuncts to their creativity, not as creative people in their own right. Things have changed, and rightly so, since then. Photographers are as important to a good story as the writer is.

I learned a lot from photographers, and not only what makes a good picture. They taught me, at various stages, how to drink beer, gin and Scotch; and, most importantly, how to do the perfect expenses claim! Ah yes, my photographic colleagues taught me a useful thing or two. When I became an editor and had to approve expense claims, many would wonder at the uncanny skill I had in detecting a claim that wasn't legitimate.

It would be wrong to think that some women were not questioning their role in the sixties. They were – but what they had to say didn't seem to be taken too seriously by many people. However, 10 June 1962 saw the publication of my article, 'Women lack voice in politics', in the *Telegraph*'s women's pages. Here I observed, 'Mrs H. Jefferson Bate, a former president of the Country Women's Association [and at that time the second wife of Federal MP, Jeff Bate] is a strong and determined advocate for the rights of Australian women in public life, but she says the biggest obstacle in the way of their advancement is the Australian male'.

Mrs Bate said: 'Australia is a predominantly male country, and there has never been willingness on the part of men to allow women to take their place in public life.'

Her attitude was hardly radical by today's standards, but it was in 1962. I remember returning to the office full of excitement. It was, I think, the first time I'd been exposed to such a challenging line of thought. Of course, women had the right to be heard. Mrs Bate was absolutely correct. She denied being a 'feminist who runs around waving flags', or that she believed in 'women entering public life simply because they are women'. What Mrs Bate wanted was a fair go: 'I think that if women have ability and merit they should at least be given a chance and the opportunity to show their capabilities.' She was looking for equality, not affirmative action.

She took part in a panel discussion set up by Sydney University to examine the non-participation of women in Australia's public life and what might be done about it. The pendulum for change was already swinging. I noted that 'Mrs Bate put forward a strong case and was undaunted by her opposing panel members, who included the then general secretary of the New South Wales branch of the Liberal Party and the assistant general secretary of the New South Wales Labor Party'. Her arguments were intriguing from a sociological perspective. She insisted that women were becoming a larger force in the Australian workplace, which illustrated the movement toward economic autonomy on the part of women, and thus would become 'a pressure group creating interference in the government'.

Mrs Bate's remarks hit me like a thunderbolt. All kinds of possibilities of what I might do in the future went through my mind. She'd probably have been amazed had she been aware of the effect her remarks were having on me. She argued that women could not be ignored: 'These women's organisations are too big and powerful', and she said, 'I'm sure more women would be encouraged [to enter public life] if Australian political parties showed more interest.' In 1962, as a university graduate with a BA degree, she also seemed to epitomise the beginnings of superwoman. (Some years later, Zara Holt, the widow of Prime Minister Harold Holt who drowned at sea in 1967, became the third Mrs H. Jefferson Bate.)

Like most girls of my generation I married young – when I was only twenty-one, in 1963. A husband was not only the person you loved most in the world, he was also an important status symbol. Girls who were still single in their late twenties were to be pitied. It was a fate to be avoided at all costs. My husband, Alasdair 'Mac' Macdonald, had been a friend of my brother, Julian (older brothers do have their uses as far as meeting prospective husbands is concerned) and Julian introduced us. It wasn't love at first sight, but it was certainly instant attraction. Mac is British and had followed his father into the shipping business, but he yearned to be an architect. Being an adventuresome kind of man, he decided to see the world and ended up in Sydney working in a shipping company. Julian, an accountant, did the company's audits. One Christmas he asked Mac what he was doing, discovered he had nowhere to go for Christmas dinner, and asked him home. I was eighteen and still enjoying my work on the women's pages. Mac was twenty-three. It wasn't long after that his desire to be an architect became stronger than continuing in shipping. He applied, and was accepted, as a student at Sydney University's Faculty of Architecture.

Our courtship didn't begin until I was twenty. Once again, big brother Julian turned out to be useful. He suggested to Mum that Mac rent our downstairs room (as a university student he wasn't exactly flush with funds) and that the money would be a useful addition to her housekeeping budget. It didn't occur to me to think of him as future husband material. And when friendship turned to love it was just one of those magical things. Out of the blue, he had asked me out to dinner at a smart city restaurant – I think to thank me for doing his ironing. We had a wonderful time eating and dancing. Mac drove me home and as I thanked him for a nice time and went to get out of the car, he said, 'I was just going to kiss you'. He did, and Bingo!

Our courtship went along happily – I was busy learning my profession, he was absorbed with his architectural studies. We still managed to have fun, though. On Sundays we'd often meet up with friends at the beach along with an Esky of beer, and later play cricket at Balmoral Beach Park. Other times we'd go swimming at Bondi Beach and then adjourn to one of the local pubs, sit in the beer garden and eat fresh prawns and drink beer. Sundays were strictly for pleasure.

My shiftwork suited Mac's timetable. He would pick me up at eleven, after studying all evening, and then we'd go to the Platypus Coffee Shop at Kings Cross and drink cappuccinos and eat raisin toast. It was the trendy thing to do. Raisin toast was a new taste sensation in the sixties. It had to be cut thick and drip with butter as you ate it.

Once we realised we were in love, Mac moved from the downstairs room and took a flat in Surry Hills. It would not have been 'proper' for a young girl's fiancé to be living in her mother's downstairs room! (By now my parents had separated after twenty-five years of marriage.) Mac and I hadn't planned to marry until he finished his studies, but our desire to share our lives made the long wait too frustrating for us both. Consequently we married in the middle of his studies, by which time I had transferred back to *The Australian Women's Weekly* to become the magazine's Social Editor. By now I was a D-grade journalist and I thought the *Weekly* would be good experience as well as an opportunity to learn from some of the best women journalists in the business.

Being Social Editor meant Mac and I got invited to parties and balls, first nights – we thought all this was just marvellous, and even though we had only my salary to live on, we managed. Of course, no one drank as much as people do today, and girls like me drank nothing much at all. But of course in deciding to continue working – not that I had much choice about it, we would have starved if I hadn't – I had unknowingly taken another important step. I had married, but unlike some of my friends, I had not stopped work. I was enjoying life so much that I never gave the possible ramifications of that decision any thought at all.

As Social Editor I wrote a column for the *Weekly* called 'Social Roundabout', and a look back at the pages sees that word 'gay' cropping up again and again, just like it did in the *Telegraph*'s women's pages. The homosexual community has robbed us of a word which so well described the way we were in the fifties and sixties. I wonder if they realise that?

The *Weekly*'s approach to the social life of Sydney and the well-heeled areas of the New South Wales countryside was very genteel. It was never nasty or in any way unkind about anyone. I wrote about women travelling, women going to balls, women organising their daughters' weddings, women having babies. I wrote about gay trios at formal events and gay times being had by all. The word 'lovely' was used in abundance, too – people were lovely, homes were lovely, and everyone always had a lovely time. And when Mrs Igor Oistrakh (under her maiden name of Natalia Zertsalova) arrived in Sydney from Russia with her violinist husband to accompany him on the piano, I told the *Weekly*'s more than three million readers that she wore (God help me, there was *that* word again) 'a nigger brown calfskin full-length coat that her husband had bought for her in Paris'.

Life might have continued on its lovely, gay path at the *Weekly*, but ambition tempted me. The Women's Editor of the *Telegraph* Women's Section (Loma McDonald had succeeded Micky McNicoll over the years) announced her resignation. I'd been on the *Weekly* for about eighteen months and, while I was happy enough, I found the pace a little slow. I was only twenty-three, and the *Weekly* seemed to me somewhat old-fashioned and stuffy. I decided to apply for the job of Women's Editor and dropped a line to David McNicoll. 'It is the dream of every cadet,' I wrote, 'to one day run the department in which she started her career. Could I please be considered for the position of Women's Editor?'

There was a silence. Then a few days later Sir Frank Packer rang.

'Hear you've applied for the Women's Editor's job,' he said.

'Yes, Sir Frank.'

'But you're married,' he said. 'You might be going to have babies.'

'Not at the moment Sir Frank.'

He hung up.

Next day I got word that the job was mine. Mind you, no one thought I had a chance of getting it. I was considered far too young. When my appointment was announced, half the staff on the Women's Section thought the same. They quit. I sat in the somewhat spartan office of the Women's Editor, with its compensatory, fabulous view across Hyde Park to St Mary's Cathedral and the Harbour and wondered what the hell I had done. What had possessed me to put my hand up for this job? I knew it was sink or swim time and I certainly wasn't in the mood to sink – not then, not ever. The staff quitting just made me more determined to succeed and they probably did me a great favour. When things are at their toughest I somehow seem to find an inner strength that helps me get through. But, as so often has been the case throughout my career, I knew I was well and truly on my own.

There was so much to learn and to think about that it worried me. I tried not to let the anxiety show. I also had to look after the needs of my husband and run our home. His parents had given us the money to buy a house in the inner-city suburb of Paddington. It was what is now called a 'renovator's delight', but we loved it and renovated to our hearts' content. We were there at the beginning of the trend to inner-city living, which now is taken for granted. My father, however, thought our terrace house was 'awful'. Whenever he'd call over to see how we were progressing, he used to tell me I was nuts. 'This place is just a dump. Why didn't you buy a decent apartment somewhere?' he'd ask. Our first home cost just under $10 000. In 1997 it was up for sale and valued at around $650 000. If we'd had any idea of how Sydney's property market was going to escalate, Mac and I might have thought of borrowing to buy the houses on either side of us.

I know now that at this point in my life I was fortunate to have had Mac as my husband, because he was so supportive of my working and, as it developed, of my career. He was proud of my achievements and genuinely interested in what I was doing. He was also better educated than I was – in fact, I think that I fell in love with his mind long before I discovered the man behind it. He encouraged me, without being bossy about it or making me feel like a dill, to read some of the great writers like Somerset Maugham, Graham Greene, John Galsworthy, Ernest Hemingway, J.D. Salinger, Gore Vidal and others. I loved them all, and still have them in my bookcase and consider them 'treasured friends'.

When I'd come home, quite worn out by the long nights that working on morning newspapers demand, he was supportive. He didn't cook the dinner nor do the laundry and ironing, as some men do today, but as men went in the seventies he was way ahead of his time. And he was thoughtful enough to buy me a dog to keep me company in the evenings, which he had to spend studying for his degree.

In retrospect, I'm sure it must have been a pain in the neck for the staff to have a twenty-three-year-old as boss, not that I worried about that at the time, although I was aware of the need to be tactful. I know I dressed to look older. In a note to Dad in 1966, I said: 'I've sent you a couple of pictures of me at the races. If you are going to keep one in your office make it the serious one. I think it looks very sophisticated!' The thing that most concerned me was to produce women's pages that were different and stimulating and that pleased Sir Frank and Mr McNicoll. I knew that a call on a Saturday night at around 10 p.m. was the one all Women's Editors sweated on. If he and Sir Frank were happy with the paper, Mr McNicoll would ring at that time, and say 'good section tonight, Ite', and I would go home happy and enjoy the rest of the weekend. It took some months before I got that first call but there were many, many more after it.

I was happy with my lot. I adored my job. Mac and I were settling into married life successfully and his studies were going well. We had plenty of friends with whom occasionally we'd share a meal either at their place or ours. Entertaining was usually done at home with the wife doing the cooking, of course. But sometimes four of us would go to our favourite BYO and share the cost of a bottle of claret – you could buy a bottle of Coonawarra for about 9/- – and have a glass of wine with our dinner. Drinking wine was new to us, but we thought it did add to an evening out and considered ourselves very fashionable.

Most of my women friends were married and working. When the first of our group had a baby, several of us were over at her flat admiring her son and having a cup of tea, when she told us she was thinking that she'd go back to work once her baby was old enough to go to kindergarten. That got the rest of us talking and thinking about what we might do when we had children. Go back to work after having a baby? Would it be possible? I think I still thought I'd stop work when I had children but, looking back, I wonder if I really believed it. I was blissfully unaware of the revolution that was under way, but I was most definitely a part of it.

The pace quickened for me quite unexpectedly in 1966 when the fickle finger of fate struck. I was at the Australian Jockey Club's autumn race meeting at Randwick in Sydney writing about the fashions worn by women racegoers. As I was going about minding my own business studying the fashion form, I became aware that a woman was trying to catch my attention from outside the Members' Enclosure. I went over to see what she wanted.

She invited me to enter the *Sydney Morning Herald*'s fashion contest to find the most elegant woman at the races. I couldn't believe it. The *Telegraph* had run the fashion contest in conjunction with the Millinery Manufacturers' Association for several years. In 1966, they gave us the flick. For some reason they had decided to run the contest with the *Herald*, our rival newspaper. Sir Frank Packer was not amused.

In 1966 I was not well known like I am today, but some people were familiar with my name. I looked at the woman, smiled and told her I would love to be in the fashion contest – and whatever we may think nowadays, to be 'Mrs Alasdair Macdonald', instead of 'Ita Buttrose', was a real plus. She told me where to be at a certain time for the judging. Unbelievable as it may seem, I won. Stunned, I returned to the *Telegraph* and went to see Mr McNicoll. I was clutching my prize – a Cyclax beauty case valued at twenty-six guineas (about $57) and containing thirty-six guineas (about $76) worth of Cyclax cosmetics. A lavish prize for someone earning only £26 (about $52) a week.

Dad was working in New York at the time, running the North American office of the ABC. I wrote to him about my triumph: 'When I got back to work I told Mr McNicoll. He didn't believe me at first and then he started to laugh like everyone else did when they heard. King Watson [the Editor of the *Daily Telegraph*] was almost hysterical. The *Herald* has told the Millinery Manufacturers' Association that if I win the Grand Final they will publish nothing.'

Sir Frank was beside himself to have scored such a victory against 'the enemy'. A *Sydney Morning Herald* executive rang and said I should withdraw, that having won a heat I should not go on to the final. Sir Frank would have none of it. 'Miss Buttrose will continue to the final,' he said. He ordered me to be photographed in my prize-winning outfit and the *Telegraph* published a huge picture of me on page three, with the heading, 'Right Filly but Wrong Stable'. I was reliably informed that Sir Frank wrote it! Of all the things I did during my time and his at Australian Consolidated Press, I am sure that winning the *Herald*'s fashion contest was the thing that pleased Sir Frank most.

In my letter to Dad I told him: 'Next Saturday I have to go to the Grand Final and if I win – which somehow I feel I won't – I get a trip to Montreal [for Expo 67] with spending money.' That particular Saturday in October 1966, I found out that miracles do happen. I won the Grand Final! Mac and I decided to turn the return trip for one into two one-way tickets, go to Montreal, and then on to London to live and work.

It was called 'Swinging London' then and it was very different from Sydney. I thought London was fantastic. We were there for three years and I well and truly broke the umbilical cord. My education continued – I went to concerts, opera, ballet, theatre, European movies and art galleries. Mac introduced me to the great masters and modern art. We'd been in London for only six weeks when I landed a job as sub-editor on the best-selling British magazine, *Woman's Own*. 'We like Australians,' they told me, 'because they work hard and are well trained.' I hadn't been there for long before I put aside my white gloves, took the French pins out of my lacquered, beehive hairdo, let my shoulder-length hair down, and took up my hems to show my legs in the carefree miniskirt.

I look back at my years in London as a kind of finishing school. I learned so much at *Woman's Own*, especially about production and marketing, all of which have been invaluable to me in my career back in Australia. I learned, too, that near enough is never good enough, and that no matter how big or how small the task, a 100 per cent effort is required. It's something I've never forgotten. It applies to everything I do.

This period in London was one of the happiest in my life and when in 1968 I became pregnant, it was the icing on the cake. Mac and I moved to Wadhurst in Sussex, a very pretty part of England, about an hour from London by train. He commuted to his job as an architect with a company in London, whose offices were just behind the department store, Selfridges, while I looked after baby Kate. I knew no one in Wadhurst and was lonely but I enjoyed watching my beautiful daughter grow. I wrote letters home and attacked the long-neglected garden, turning it into a showpiece with vegetables, raspberries, rhubarb and anything else I could lay my hands on. I grew flowers, too, and to this day remain remarkably proud of my splendid lupins. I made clothes for Kate and subscribed to a weekly cookery magazine and polished up my cooking skills. Mac was delighted – his sweet tooth enjoyed several special treats! I may have been isolated but I had no intention of sitting on my bum feeling sorry for myself. Occasionally some of my former colleagues on *Woman's Own* would come down for the weekend and I'd serve them up homemade sponge cake topped with cream and my home-grown raspberries.

It was great catching up with all the gossip from the magazine too. I had enjoyed my time at *Woman's Own* and was very pleased when the Editor, George Rogers, told me I could return whenever I wanted. I might have done so but fate intervened again. A telegram from Sir Frank arrived offering me my old job back as Women's Editor of the *Daily* and *Sunday Telegraphs*. It was totally unexpected but it helped Mac and me to determine our next step. We would go home. Our parents and families were there (his parents had retired to Australia when Mac's brother also married an Australian) and we agreed that Australia was a good place to raise children.

There was one other deciding factor for me. Sir Frank had told me before I left for overseas that he had me in mind to run the *Weekly* one day. During my time in Wadhurst, I had realised that being a housewife was not enough for me. I wanted to do more with my life. Once Mac and I had decided to return to Sydney, I knew exactly what I wanted: the editorship of the *Weekly*. For the next five years I worked hard to make sure that when my time came I'd have as much knowledge as possible to do that well.

2

CLEO AND THE SEVENTIES

Where did you get that information that kissing a man's armpits turns him on?

It doesn't!

SIR FRANK PACKER, AFTER READING *CLEO*'S 'WHAT TURNS A MAN ON?'

As I cruised into Sydney Harbour on 24 December 1969 –
Kate's first birthday – I was completely unaware that anything
remotely like *Cleo* awaited me. I was coming home after three
years away. The only thing on my mind was to introduce
Kate to Mum and my brothers and to Mac's parents and his
brother, Euan. Dad, who was now running the ABC's North
American Office in New York, had met Kate the year before,
when he came for a holiday in Wadhurst.

It was a glorious Sydney summer day. The sun was
shining, the sky was blue, the harbour sparkling, and a light
southerly was blowing. Most people were on their annual
holidays. It was customary for Australia to 'close down' over

the Christmas–New Year period up until the end of January, something that continued until 'the recession we had to have' (according to former Prime Minister Paul Keating) in the late eighties and early nineties. Many Australians now work as hard in January as they do in the other months of the year. However, back in 1969, Mac and I were in a mood to celebrate not only Kate's first birthday but also Christmas and just being home.

Two things immediately struck us – firstly, how much everyone drank, including women. In England, where everything was so expensive and we had to live on one wage after Kate was born, we couldn't afford to buy alcohol, especially spirits. Sometimes we lashed out on a bottle of rough Spanish red, but that was about it. When Mac came in late from the office I'd make him a cup of tea. Drinking wasn't really all that important and it certainly wasn't a way of life, as it appeared to be in Australia. Sydney people never seemed to have a glass of something out of their hand.

We noticed, too, how well-off everyone was. They looked it, dressed it and talked it. People discussed money ad infinitum, too, especially their shares. A look at the stockmarket of the day illustrates what was going on. It was boom time. Poseidon nickel shares had captured everyone's attention. Only a few months earlier, they were valued at just under $7 each, but were going up so rapidly that by February 1970 they were worth $280 each. People were making money in sums they never dreamed of and in record time, too. No one could believe it. Everyone was trying to get rich quick. Like all booms, it didn't last. By 1971 it was over.

A Senate inquiry into the share market followed not long after. In his book, *Social Sketches of Australia*, Humphrey McQueen says the committee found 'crooked dealing to be so widespread that only a few cases could be written up. Brokers had used inside information to make their fortunes, while journalists praised companies in which they owned shares'.

No one seemed unduly perturbed. Making money and having a good time were the priorities of the day. However, it marked the birth of what I call Australia's greed society, which continued more or less unabated until the eighties. The 1987 crash unveiled the true treachery of the corporate cowboys. They were not the heroes we imagined but just a bunch of spivs and crooks, obsessed with making money and acquiring assets like paintings, boats and fancy cars, regardless of the consequences and with no thought at all for the men and women who sometimes lost all their savings, because they had believed in the cowboys and their schemes.

But we knew none of this in the seventies. Most people just wanted to have fun. Life and work were much more joyous than they seem to be for young men and women nowadays. The seventies were a time of significant change, especially for women, but my contemporaries and I didn't seem to fear it as much as most Australians seem to fear change today. In the seventies, we weren't frightened of anything really. We not only wanted our cake, but also expected a second helping. We worked hard and we played hard. We wanted to make a difference, felt sure we could, and nothing was going to stop us.

We were fuelled by a sense of patriotism that many of us had never before experienced. Sure we knew we were Australians and that this was 'the best country in the world', but it took Gough Whitlam to make us feel truly zealous about our birthright. I've often thought that this was Whitlam's greatest contribution to Australia. In 1972, the Australian Labor Party won Government after twenty-three years of being in the wilderness, and on becoming Prime Minister Gough Whitlam promised us an Australia of which we would all be proud. No one doubted him for a second.

Cleo made its debut soon after Labor's victory and represented my first significant publishing step. I was excited and determined to make my mark. *Cleo* broke lots of new ground and reflected perfectly the changing role of women. It's difficult, no it's just about impossible, to imagine today's executive woman having a conversation with her boss about the sexual merits or otherwise of men's armpits – it simply wouldn't be the politically correct thing to do. But in the early years of *Cleo* there were few taboo topics of discussion. It wasn't long before all of us working on the magazine became matter of fact in talking about subjects that would have made us shy. Sometimes we floored Kerry though.

He developed an almost paternal interest in *Cleo* and called into my office frequently with his one question, 'How are things going?' One day however, he saw me editing some copy, and asked: 'What are you doing?'

'I'm working on this article about how masturbation can help female frigidity,' I replied. I was not prepared for his reaction. With a groan he sank in a chair and said, 'Oh, no . . . not masturbation. What will I tell the old man?'

'Tell him it's medical,' I proffered. We laughed and Kerry did as I suggested. Sir Frank did not object and shortly afterwards the story ran in *Cleo*.

Originally, the plan had been for us to launch the Australian edition of *Cosmopolitan*, the highly successful women's magazine that *Sex and the Single Girl* author Helen Gurley Brown had revamped in America. The deal fell through – one of the competitors edged us out at the last minute. Kerry Packer was furious. We'd been double-crossed. An angry Packer is not pleasant, as I would discover myself in the years to come.

The decision to launch *Cosmopolitan* had coincided with Sir Frank selling his beloved *Daily* and *Sunday Telegraphs* to Rupert Murdoch in 1972. As Women's Editor of the *Telegraphs*, I'd been told to keep some of the best people at ACP for the new magazine project. Everyone else moved to Murdoch's News Ltd. To fill in time while we were waiting for the contracts to be finalised, we worked on dummies for new magazines – just to see if we were any good, as few of us had much magazine experience. We called one of them *Cleopatra*.

When Kerry got word that we weren't going to get

Cosmopolitan, he asked me what we'd been working on. I told him about *Cleopatra*. 'Let me see it.' He flicked through the dummy, looked up, smiled and said: 'This is it. We'll do this one. I want it out on the streets six months ahead of *Cosmopolitan*'. *Cleopatra* was shortened to *Cleo* and the rest is history. *Cleo* sold out in two days and became one of ACP's most profitable titles.

Cleo's triumph was important for Kerry. It was his first big test. Sir Frank didn't really understand the new woman of the seventies although he did his best, which is how he and I got to discussing the sexual merits of men's armpits. In an effort to understand the 'new woman', Sir Frank insisted on reading the copy for the new magazine. When he got to an article called 'What Turns a Man On', he rang and asked me to come down to his office. 'Where did you get this information that kissing a man's armpits turned him on?' he asked. Before I could answer, he said, 'It doesn't!' I wasn't going to argue. I was prepared to take his word that he knew more about such things than I did.

As far as Sir Frank was concerned *Cleo* was Kerry's baby. In fact, Sir Frank was not at all confident that *Cleo* would prosper. He was overseas when the first issue was due to go to the printer and sent me a somewhat pessimistic telegram saying: 'Good luck with this venture. I think you'll need it.' Hardly the kind of message to inspire a new, young editor and her team!

He needn't have worried. Australian women couldn't get enough of *Cleo*. In the first five months of its existence, the magazine kept selling out. Within five years it was the fifth largest-selling magazine in Australia with a circulation in excess of 250 000 copies. *Cleo* was a symptom of the seventies, a sign of the transformation that was taking place among women. Their new aspirations, which *Cleo* understood, coupled with hard work, and a talented editorial team with lots of creative genius – especially Art Director, Andrew Cowell – guaranteed its success. Andrew was (and still is) a brilliant man. He had come to see me to ask for a job and refused to take no for an answer. 'I want to be art director on your new magazine,' he insisted, listing all sorts of reasons why he was the one! It was my lucky day. Art directors like Andrew were rare in 1972, nor, as yet, were artists held in high regard in Australian publishing. I had worked with several talented artists at *Woman's Own* in London and knew how essential they were to the 'new' kind of publishing. Andrew was from England. He and his wife Carol, a journalist, were seeking fame and fortune Down Under. My gut instinct, which rarely gets it wrong, told me Andrew was exactly the person I was looking for to give *Cleo* style and pizzazz. We used to worry the life out of Kerry though. He was never sure what we'd get up to next – especially with the male centrefold.

One day he came across us excitedly planning a centrefold with a minister's son as the star. Kerry assumed we were talking about the son of a man of the cloth. 'Who is it?' he asked. 'Jon Lewis, Tom's son,' I told him. A look of horror swept over Kerry's face. Tom was the Minister for Lands and Tourism in the New South Wales Liberal Government, and became Premier in 1974. Kerry used to have regular discussions with him about developments he wanted to make to the company's holdings in the valuable Perisher Valley snowfields. He could see that Andrew and I were pretty pleased with ourselves to have 'got' a politician's son for the centrefold. He had to handle us with care – but at the same time, he was more concerned about his ski-resort plans for Perisher than he was about our centrefold! 'Look,' he said, 'I don't think Tom would be happy for Jon to be a centrefold. It could be embarrassing for him. You can't use Jon.' He could see how distraught we were. We'd lost our centrefold and they weren't easy to come by! 'I'll make it up to you,' he said. 'You can have a holiday at Perisher.' As he left the office he turned back, and chuckled, 'in summer'.

Cleo pioneered the nude male centrefold in Australia. Originally, it was only going to be a one-off, but the first one created such a storm that Kerry insisted that we keep it going. In these modern times, something like a nude male centrefold probably doesn't seem like all that much, but in the seventies it was ground-breaking. The *Cleo* centrefold was always modest – considerable time was devoted to coming up with creative ways to hide the penis, although occasionally we slipped up. For instance, it was difficult to keep an eye on every penis in our football team centrefold. We didn't even notice one that had slipped through our safety net. The readers did however. 'Thank you for the wonderful surprise of the player in Seat 14,' wrote a Queensland woman.

Our first centrefold was actor Jack Thompson who has gone on to make a distinguished international career for himself. He said 'yes' after we'd had a great many knock-backs from other well-known men. Aussie men used to become strangely shy whenever I suggested they get their pants off for the women of Australia. Jack told me the centrefold changed his career for the better. Film producers felt that if he was considered gorgeous enough to pose for the *Cleo* centrefold, then he was definitely romantic lead material.

Andrew came up with the brilliant idea of reimposing Jack's body over Venus in Titian's masterpiece *Venus of Urbino*, which enabled us to use Jack's hand to cover his vital parts in a way we thought most tasteful – but not tasteful enough, as it turned out, for the Queensland Literature Board of Review, a group of men and women who determined what the people of their State could and could not read and see in their magazines. Without even asking to see our proposed centrefold, the Board decided it sounded a bit risqué and doubted Jack's hand was up to the job. To keep them happy we put a slightly larger, elegant gold square over Jack's hand – there was no chance that anyone could possibly glimpse what was underneath. Fortunately, the women of Queensland didn't feel deprived. *Cleo* sold out there, too.

Cleo wrote about sex as though we had discovered it. A look at the contents of the magazine's first twelve months gives an idea of what was on our minds – 'How to Be a Sexy

Housekeeper', 'Women's Sexual Fears', 'Are the French Lousy
Lovers?', 'Female Fantasies', 'Would You Let Him Have a
Vasectomy?', 'All You Need to Know about Sex Aids', 'All
You Need to Know about Group Sex', 'What Every Couple
Should Know about Sex', 'Diary of a Virgin', 'Sex and Your
Son'. We even profiled Mike Willesee as TV's 'Reluctant Sex
Symbol'. Mike hadn't let the latter go to his head though.
'Sure women get a thrill when they see me,' he told *Cleo*,
'they also get a thrill when they see Humphrey B. Bear.'

But there was actually more on our minds than just sex.
The magazine's contents also illustrated the extent to which
women were changing. Their world was getting bigger and
there was much they wanted to know. We looked at
motherhood (we were for it); ways to save a marriage (we
believed in it); the loneliness of old age; the rise in female
alcoholism; the fear of flying (something that seemed to
worry women more than men); premenstrual tension (it did
not have to be 'endured'); Irish women and their fight for
equality; and Russian women and their battle for Women's
Liberation. We worried about the over-population of the
planet and what it would mean to our children. We declared
Don Dunstan (then the Premier of South Australia) to be
the bright young man of politics. We carried ads for Formfit
panty girdles both short and long leg, with copy that said
that panty girdles were 'a fashion investment that took years
off your figure'. Our Food Editor, Alan Nye, who suggested
such daring culinary advancements as sprinkling nutmeg
over Brussels sprouts before serving, had the nerve to

complain in 1973 that he'd had to pay $7 for a bottle of Penfold's Grange! We talked to the people who influenced Australians in the seventies, like playwright David Williamson who told *Cleo* that 'the Australian male still tends to show a lot of chauvinism, mistrust and fear of women. The rugged individual thing is a myth'.

Cleo was never anti-men. As early as 1973 we signalled our concern about changes that were occurring which we believed might not be in men's best interests. It seemed to us that men were beginning to do themselves out of a job. We published an extract from a British book, *Strip Jack Naked*, that carried what might now be considered a 'red alert' warning: 'With artificial insemination techniques now available the male's physical presence is no longer needed. Any number of virgin births is now possible by this means – if society is willing of course'. As we know now, society is indeed willing. The same article also said: 'Male and female sensuality and awareness are counterbalanced. If the one is imperilled, so is the other.' Could any of us have imagined how far things would go? How much the male/female roles would alter? Is this why there are indications that today's boys are taking on feminine traits and girls are becoming aggressive and violent? Perhaps, in the seventies, none of us was listening.

Perhaps we weren't, but the politicians were. They couldn't help but hear. The Women's Electoral Lobby (WEL) made sure they did. It was formed in 1972 to keep pressure on politicians about women's issues. As Eva Cox, the sociologist and 1995 Boyer Lecturer, says, the seventies were a very important period for women. Important professional gains were made. WEL was followed by equal pay for women, anti-discrimination laws and the view that women should be accepted into public life. At the time, there was not one Australian female politician in the Federal House of Representatives. Now there are record numbers of women in our Federal Parliament, but still nowhere near enough.

It seems hard to believe that as little as twenty-five years ago Australian women were as repressed as they were. I'm sure a great many women – and men – have no idea what life was like for Australian women in the seventies. Why, in the past, did so many Australian women accept their lot without questioning? Perhaps some clues can be gleaned from the *Patterson Report*, 'Wooing the Australian Woman', put out in 1972 by Australia's then largest advertising agency, George Patterson Pty Ltd. In the foreword the agency's boss, the late Keith Cousins, explained the rationale behind the *Report* was to 'capture a little of the Australian scene as perceived by women in the 1970s' and, 'if nothing else, should demonstrate that the women in Australia are a lot smarter than they have ever been encouraged to think'.

The *Patterson Report* explained that the average seventies woman is 'a mother and her whole life revolves around this basic role. As a good mother, she must also be a good wife and, basically, a good homemaker. Her home and family are the basis of her life; they are her domain. They are the justification of her existence; they are her full-time job'.

In the chapter on current affairs, the *Report* tells us that

Australian housewives' knowledge and involvement in current affairs seems to depend largely on how closely the current social issues relate to her own little isolated kingdom of the home. A family holiday, a bit of money in the bank, a bigger house, her own car, getting the kids a good education and just being happy and normal – these are the things that really count. Current world affairs are too far removed from everyday living to matter at all.

As long as living remains stable and affluent and the present Australian way of life persists, most housewives will not be motivated to think deeply at all about the majority of social issues; the housewife's main concern (and this is probably not unique to her sex) is simply to 'give us this day our daily bread; and occasionally let us afford butter instead of super poly-unsaturated margarine'.

On the subject of education:

Although almost all mothers are interested in education, very few of them are happy with the way they see it going. Education is confusing; they know it is a big and important part of family life but they have problems understanding what's going on. Here is this thing in their lives and they can't influence or control it. Almost every mother wants her children to have a better education than she had – or her husband had. For boys it is vital, and for girls 'well, they should have it just in case'.

The seventies' mothers wanted their daughters to be more independent than they had been, and to be equipped to escape the humdrum of life if they ever felt constrained by its limitations. Yet at the same time

most mothers agree that the ideal is for a daughter to be a housewife and mother all her life. If she doesn't get married, or has to go back to work later, it's good for her to really have something she can do well and be respected for it. But it's a terrible thing to think that a daughter might finish up as Chief Justice of Victoria – that's too much. It's a reflection on the mother, particularly if the daughter is a spinster to boot. Success must have the right pattern.

And what about Women's Liberation? 'A lot of housewives feel that they would be better off without Women's Lib. They feel it is like a tide overtaking them and beyond their control.' In fact, many Australian women included in the *Report* said they resented Women's Lib because they considered it a threat to their right to find fulfilment as housewives and mothers. But women were stirring, even if the *Patterson Report* didn't make much of the fact.

For some housewives, particularly those tied down by young children, the idea of having a job is appealing. Bored with being housebound and with the conversation of children and other women in the same position (all they talk about is Johnny's bowels), they feel it would offer them needed stimulation. The financial independence is also important; with an independent income, they can spend money on personal things such as make-up and clothing without feeling guilty.

Germaine Greer, having written *The Female Eunuch* in 1969, came to Australia in the early seventies on a lecture tour. We, and by that I mean women only, gathered at an Italian restaurant somewhere in Sydney's George Street. Tables and chairs had been moved back against the walls to enable us all to sit down on the floor. One woman actually swigged red wine from the bottle – daring stuff indeed! It was a memorable day. Women questioned out loud their role in life and spoke about their dreams, for all to hear – something most of us had never done before. Germaine told us the world was ours and we should go for it. We believed her.

Women taking part in the *Patterson Report* said that Germaine Greer and Women's Lib had made them question themselves and the satisfaction that they had hitherto accepted as part of being a housewife and mother. The very thought of Women's Liberation had made them feel discontented. They felt they had suffered a loss of security and contentment, that life had become more complicated, making many of them unsure of which road to tread. 'They are not sure whether they will be better or worse off when they get there. Deep down, they feel that Women's Lib might be more destructive than beneficial.' They worried, too, about combining motherhood and working. The children would have no 'Mum' to come home to, and the working mother has neither the time nor the energy to 'listen to their little problems' and 'help with the homework'.

This was a big worry for many women in the seventies, myself included. I became pregnant with my son, Ben, some two months before we launched *Cleo*. I didn't know how I was going to tell Sir Frank and Kerry. I knew they would not be pleased. Like most men in those times, I think they considered pregnancy as some kind of illness. I suffered from the most awful morning sickness in the early months and often disappeared to the Ladies to be ill. No one working on *Cleo* seemed to notice my absence. I don't think it occurred to anyone that I would get pregnant at such a time. But I wanted this baby and I was overjoyed to be pregnant again. Finally my condition was becoming apparent and I had to tell the Packers. They took it well enough, but were worried that my pregnancy would prevent me from seeing the job through. They should have known better – after all, I was superwoman. I did laugh though, when Kerry rang to say he and 'the old man' reckoned I should have read more closely one of the articles in *Cleo*'s first issue, 'How Much Do You Know about Contraception?'

It was a time of conflict for me. When I had Kate, I stopped work six weeks before she was born and did not return to work (on the *Telegraph*'s women's pages) after much soul searching – until she was fifteen months old. There was no question of my stopping work at *Cleo*. It was assumed that I would keep on working although it was uncommon then for a pregnant woman to do so. Companies discouraged it. A colleague at the Murray Magazine Group, one of the Packer subsidiaries, told me that when she became pregnant not long after I'd had Ben, the only reason she had been allowed to keep working was because she used me as an example.

In fact, Mac and I hadn't planned to have such a large gap in years between our two children but getting pregnant was never easy for me. As the years passed I told my gynaecologist that I was concerned about not becoming pregnant again. I had all kinds of tests but no major reason could be established for my seeming non-fertility. I was considering taking fertility drugs when, thank heavens (as I could have had a multiple birth on the drugs), I became pregnant. God does sometimes move not only in mysterious ways but also slowly. Mac and I persevered during these trying times with charts and thermometers trying to determine effectively my most fertile time and discovered it wasn't at all romantic making love this way, as anyone else who has shared our predicament would know. However, we did not want an only child. I was also getting older and I wanted to be young enough to enjoy my children and handle their adolescent years comfortably. Because there was four and a half years between Kate and Ben, we worried that perhaps she would find it hard to adjust to the new baby. As it turned out, we had nothing to fear. Kate loved her brother from the moment she set eyes on him and happily took on a protective role. Ben's big sister is a pretty special girl and he knows it.

My male colleagues at ACP took a genuine interest in my pregnancy. At one board meeting Ben decided to start kicking. The man next to me – I think it was Rob Henty, Kerry's cousin and then general manager of ACP – was fascinated. He couldn't help gazing at my stomach, which was bouncing up and down. It wasn't long before all the other men were doing the same thing. One of them asked if he could feel the movements. Always happy to help educate the opposite sex, I, of course, said yes. He put his hand on my stomach – the look on his face was magic.

I worked until the day Ben was due and was back at work within six weeks – too soon really. Sometimes I used to have to ask Kerry if I could leave a meeting and go home – Ben needed his six o'clock feed. Kerry was a very undisciplined man with other people's time. He would run meetings haphazardly. He would take phone calls that sometimes went on for ten minutes or so, while you sat and twiddled your thumbs. He would often want to talk about a million things other than the reason he had called you to his office. As a result, his meetings always ran over. He

played havoc with my keeping to schedules – and in publishing, keeping to timetables is vital. Later, when I became
Editor of the *Weekly*, I often had to work back late in the
evening or get up at five in the morning to catch up with
jobs not done because of Kerry's inability to run a meeting
on time. It wasn't something he did deliberately; it just didn't
occur to him and no one was courageous enough to suggest
that perhaps he would have benefited by taking a time management course.

Like a great many (perhaps, all) working women in the seventies, I felt guilty about leaving my children when I went to
the office. Mac was always accommodating and never
complained about my long hours and never once suggested
that I should quit. Indeed, on the couple of occasions when
I hinted that perhaps I should retire, he told me he thought I
would regret it and that I would be bored. But women who
didn't work and had children added to my guilt. At parties
they would inevitably ask: 'Who looks after your children
when you are at work?'

My mother used to take great delight at ringing about
six in the evening, usually when I was cooking dinner and
talking to the children or playing with them.

'Hello dear, how are you?'

'Fine, thanks Mum.'

'Is that the children I can hear? Aren't they in bed yet?
I always had you and your brothers in bed by 6 p.m. so
your father and I could enjoy a quiet dinner together.'

'Yes Mum, but it's different now.'

'Those children should be in bed!'

Mum never rang for any other reason at that time but to give me a lecture. It seemed to give her some kind of pleasure. It just made me mad.

Her calls added to my guilt feelings. There were few childcare facilities in the seventies. I spent most of my pay on getting women to come to my home to look after the children. When I had only Kate, the job was shared between two women – one coming two days a week, the other for three. When I had Ben, we hired a live-in mothercraft nurse. It was expensive, but I remember reading somewhere – and I have no idea where – that it was important for children to have someone caring for them who remembered what had happened yesterday. I felt that by having carers for Kate and Ben in our home as opposed to sending them 'out' to be cared for, which is a common practice these days, they would be better off. It seems to have worked well for us, but I know I was fortunate to earn a good salary that enabled me to do this. Many Australian women didn't have that choice then and don't now either.

At the end of the day there's not much women can do about guilt feelings except live with them. I knew my children were in good hands – they were healthy and happy and much loved, as they well know. I have always done my best for them and wherever I am, whatever I am doing, they have always known that they are my priorities in life. I took my holidays to coincide with their school breaks, so we could do things together and enjoy each other's company, and we had some memorable times together.

My secretaries knew that if the kids rang, it didn't matter what I was doing, I was to be interrupted. There was to be no exception, ever. Kate and Ben knew that too. If they needed me they could always find me. Even as adults, as they are today, they still know that I am here for them and always will be. I consider them my greatest achievements and they have given me much joy and happiness.

Cleo's editorial indicated that the age of the single-income family was over. Women had disposable incomes and genuine interests. They were also beginning to question their status. The *Patterson Report* may well have convinced women they were smarter than they thought they were, but it also flagged some of the changes that were going to come. As is often the case with information that relates to women, however, Australia's political leaders and decision makers didn't take time to consider fully what the research was telling them.

The seventies revealed that Australian women had very strong feelings about many areas of inequality. In the *Patterson Report*, they spoke out with feeling about being regarded as inferior in Australian society. They were angry that because women were regarded as second-class citizens, a signature from 'the male gender was necessary for a woman to obtain a loan, to open a charge account, to join a club'. Clubs would not admit women to full membership and, as for hotels, 'they shouldn't call it a public bar if it is only for men'. Many agreed that abortion should be legalised: 'It is a personal decision that should be made by women.' They felt that the Pill should be free, and that child-minding facilities were needed to help the women who must work and also to let housewives have a day away from the house if they wanted to.

The last two sentences in the *Report* said: 'Women hope that their daughters will not fall into the humdrum pattern of life that trapped them. Education is the key, not only will it open up attractive job prospects, it will alleviate any feelings of inferiority.' This is now becoming a reality.

A look at the second issue of *Cleo* brings home forcibly the incredible turnaround that has taken place in female education. We carried the findings of a survey by Dr Don Edgar, who went on to head the Australian Institute of Family Studies, but was then a reader in sociology at La Trobe University, Melbourne. In 1971 he surveyed children from a wide range of social, religious and ethnic backgrounds on adolescent attitudes and drew the conclusion that 'the Australian education system produces women who lack ambition and self-confidence; who consider themselves inferior to men; and whose level of achievement is desperately low.'

Don Edgar said:

Being a girl in Australia [in the seventies] is like being a Negro in the United States. Their place or station in life is well defined and backed by historical facts. They are stigmatised by their appearance; they don't assert themselves in the company of their superiors; they drop out of school earlier; only certain jobs are suitable for them; and they are expected to stay where they are put. But they form roughly half the population and are not a minority. Only some massive effort planned or unconsciously implemented could explain the vast discrepancy between women's potential and their performance.

The education system is one of the major institutional bases for the social production of incompetent, dependent, self-denigrating females. And the Women's Liberation movement has a lot of work to do in demystifying and changing the situation.

I am sure that back then Don Edgar could not possibly have imagined the changes that would occur in Australia between then and now. For example, in the seventies Dorothy Drain and I led the way for women when we accepted our directorships on the Australian Consolidated Press Board. When you think about it, our appointments were of some consequence, but no one seemed to notice. To be honest, I don't think Dorothy and I quite realised it either, but we were among the first Australian women ever to be appointed to an Australian public company. We were proud of that fact but we didn't make a song or dance about it then. Like all women of those times, we knew our place.

It's no wonder *Cleo* appeared like a breath of fresh air in the Australia of the seventies. It was part of the push to get the worth of women recognised, and it supported women who wanted to make more of themselves in the public arena. The magazine played an important role in getting the message across because it spoke to, and reached, the middle ground in a way that some of the more vocal feminists never could. We were breaking new ground, and at the same time were delicately treading the fine line of balance needed to produce a magazine that spoke frankly about women's health and sexual desires without being offensive. As I look back, I am amazed at some of the things I got away with. *Cleo* was a real break from tradition for such a conservative company.

But it was fun. There was a great deal of merriment at *Cleo*. Even Kerry, who is more renowned for his bad temper, used to laugh a lot at some of the things we got up to. *Cleo* always had a sense of humour, something I thought the early feminists lacked. They often criticised us for not being feminist enough. But I think their aggression sometimes frightened women and terrified men. It turned the word 'feminist' into a dirty word for many Australians. At *Cleo*, we often made our point without being shrill about it. We interviewed anthropologist Margaret Mead in 1973 and, in a story titled 'The First of the Libbers', asked her views on Australian women.

Women in Australia have a long way to go. The key
to the problem is in the question of bosses versus

71

husbands. A man doesn't want his secretary answerable to her husband. He wants to give the marching orders. And a man wants his wife at his disposal. This rivalry exists in America but not nearly so intensely. In America I have heard bosses complaining about a secretary who is preoccupied with her children. But I have never heard the overt comment, as I have in Australia, that 'I'll be damned if I'll have a girl working for me who takes orders from someone else'.

We explored the influence of talkback radio in 1973, too. It had then been around for only six years and was called talk-in radio. 'One Sydney talk-show compere, who does seem to be there predominantly to solve people's problems,' said *Cleo*, 'is silver-tongued heart-throb John Laws, probably the smoothest operator on the air. His show is pure soft-touch schmaltz with special appeal to the sentimentalists and romantics out there in radio land.'

Almost thirty years later, John Laws is still doing talkback. His show is syndicated around Australia to more than two million people and he is consistently Number One in his time slot. Back in the seventies he told *Cleo*:

I don't think the plight of the Australian woman is exaggerated. I can tell from the ones who ring me up that the problems they face are more serious than most people probably imagine. Isolation and the pressures of life today are forcing the suicide rate up.

Just listening to other people talking about their problems helps, it makes a lot of them feel they're not so badly off in comparison. The Australian woman is neglected by her husband and by society. What she really cares about is love, marriage, children, people . . .

Cleo looked at 'Jesus in the Seventies' and spoke to the Very Rev (and highly original, so *Cleo* said) Dean Hazlewood of Perth's St George's Cathedral, who later became the Bishop of Ballarat. We asked him about women in the church.

There appears to be no theological ground for excluding women from the priesthood, but this is still being studied. We are up against the old difficulties of what to do about children. I know men should take much more of the responsibility and if they were married to a clergywoman they would have to – it can be a twenty-four-hour a day job. My wife is a doctor and I know the problems we have getting organised. Still, as one Catholic bishop said, 'I will await the decision of the theologians'.

In the same article, *Cleo* included the following information in brackets: 'A vibrant group of interdenominational women in New South Wales is examining the position of women in the church and finding it dismal. They have been instrumental in instigating a Commission on the Status of Women by the New South Wales council of the Australian Council of Churches.' The advancement of women in the hierarchy of church life is still a major issue for women and generally an area where they are still not welcomed. Perhaps ultimately this continued rejection will lead to women starting their own church – anything is possible.

I often talk to my daughter and her chums about how it was in the seventies and before for women, and they look somewhat disbelieving. It's hardly surprising, I suppose. There were so many things that women were ignorant about. For instance, in that article on contraception in *Cleo*'s first issue, we included a report on a survey of 2652 Melbourne women, all under sixty and once married that revealed 31 per cent of them had never heard of the diaphragm, 18.5 per cent had never heard of the condom, and 67 per cent had never heard of modern chemical contraceptives. In the seventies, although the Pill had been around for ten years, many Australian women were reluctant to take it because of side effects like headaches, nausea, depression, loss of sex drive and weight gain. Scare stories in the media, that women could drop dead taking the Pill, didn't help. Neither did the fact that it was difficult for women to discuss such matters with their doctors, who still have a well-deserved reputation for being poor communicators.

I'll never forget the poor chap who rang me during the early days of my editorship of *Cleo* seeking information about hysterectomies. His wife, he told me, was going to have one, and they had been unable to find out from her doctor what it would mean to their sex life. Could I help? I invited him into our office, sat him in our one and only armchair and gave him a couple of books on the subject. He read for a few hours, thanked me very much indeed and departed. I assume everything went okay for him and his wife, as I never heard from him again. But can you imagine an Australia where the only place a man could find information about his wife's hysterectomy was from a sympathetic magazine editor?

I can't leave the seventies without mentioning the other significant happening of the decade – the introduction of the *Family Law Act* in 1975 that made it possible to obtain a divorce after a marriage breakdown and a year's separation. This was to have a huge effect on women. It freed many of them from an unhappy marriage, but it also allowed men to walk out and, in some cases, not bother supporting their children. It has resulted, too, in fewer marriages. Why bother to marry if you can get a divorce so easily?

In the seventies, 20 per cent of people didn't marry, which was a big change from the previous two decades when almost everyone married. And in the seventies divorce figures, not surprisingly, began to increase – one in three marriages ended in divorce. *Cleo* asked Margaret Mead whether she thought marriage could be saved.

Maybe, but it needs a heavy injection of flexibility

and individuality. I went to a Roman Catholic marriage recently and one of the lessons was from Gibran's *The Prophet*. Directed against too much togetherness in marriage it said: 'Eat together but do not eat from the same loaf of bread' and 'Do not turn your love into a bond'.

Cleo also asked broadcaster Caroline Jones what she thought about marriage in 1972 when she was the anchor for the ABC-TV's 'Four Corners'. 'It seems terribly irrelevant somehow,' she said. It appears a great many modern Australians agree with her. A national survey of Australian values, released by the Australian Institute for Family Studies in March 1997, revealed that 62 per cent of Australians believed it was all right for a man and woman to live together without planning marriage, while 45 per cent thought it was all right to have children without being married. In September 1997 figures were released that showed one in three children were born out of wedlock. The Sydney *Daily Telegraph*'s front page headline put it another way. It declared Australia to be 'A Nation of Bastards'.

My life changed enormously during the seventies but I was not alone – other women made the journey too, although perhaps not at quite the pace I did. I seemed to have been in one hell of a hurry! I came back to Australia at the end of 1969, took up my old job as Women's Editor in 1970, became Founding Editor of *Cleo* in 1972, gave birth to Ben, in 1973, became a director of Australian Consolidated Press in 1974, and the following year was appointed Editor of *The Australian Women's Weekly* in 1975. No wonder I often felt exhausted!

I also became a household name through the national TV commercials I presented each week telling viewers what stories were in *The Australian Women's Weekly*. Then in 1980, much to my delight, the top group of the day, Cold Chisel, wrote a song about me simply titled 'Ita'. I was amazed that an editor advertising the attractions of her magazine could inspire someone like band member Don Walker to be so creative. What memories his words bring back . . .

Every night when I get home
I settle down to prime time limbo
When all the boys are gathered around
Shouting Ita's on TV
And though the roaches are thick on the ground
Somebody goes to close my window
Keep the noise of the city down
Get a dose of integrity

Every week, in every home
She's got wholesome news for the family
I believe, I believe, in what she says
Yes I do
I believe, I believe, at the end of the day

Ita Buttrose

Her magazine'll get me through

Ita's tongue never touches her lips
She could always be my godmother
And though the desk-top hides her hips
My imagination's strong
She's the sweetest thing I've ever seen
I'd like to take her out to dinner
But when I think about the places I've been
I'd probably hold my fork all wrong

Every day and every night
She's the only one we can depend upon
I believe, I believe, in what she says
Yes I do
I believe, I believe, at the end of the day
Her magazine'll get me through

To every housewife through the land
There is no one else they can depend upon
How could I not believe, when Ita tells me to.

The song still gets reasonable airtime today. When my
children were old enough to have a good idea of what I did
for a living, it was Cold Chisel's song that impressed them
the most.

3

THE AUSTRALIAN WOMEN'S
WEEKLY AND THE SEVENTIES

Mate, sometimes I think you have more guts than brains.

JOHN SINGLETON'S MESSAGE ON HEARING I WAS GOING TO
WORK FOR RUPERT MURDOCH

The year 1975 was a momentous one, not least because it
was the year in which the Whitlam Government received
its marching orders from the Governor-General Sir John
Kerr, and Malcolm Fraser became Prime Minister. Colour
television also arrived that year and I became the youngest-
ever Editor of the *Weekly*. The magazine was forty-two years
old, heading towards middle age and in urgent need of a
face-lift.

The same feeling of euphoria that I'd felt when Micky
McNicoll told me I'd got my cadetship swept over me the
day I officially became the *Weekly's* fifth editor. It was the job
I'd wanted most in the world. What's more I had all sorts of

plans for the magazine and I couldn't wait to get started. I had no idea that changing the *Weekly* would be as tough as it turned out to be, but it is often said that the toughest jobs are given to women. In my case, that was certainly true.

Of course, I knew that the *Weekly* was in trouble, but I didn't know the full extent of its problems, which were rarely discussed in full detail at the company's monthly board meetings. Dorothy Drain, the then Editor of the *Weekly*, and I had joined the board not long after Sir Frank's death in 1974 when Kerry had become Managing Director. I liked and respected Dorothy. She was a long-time friend of my parents and, when I was a girl, had often come to our house for dinner. I felt awkward in her presence after Kerry told me I was going to run the *Weekly* but hadn't yet said anything to Dorothy. Before it could happen there were things that had to be done, such as finding a new Editor for *Cleo*, which by now was making ACP handsome profits. We appointed a South African woman, Vicki Wright, who has since gone on to make a name for herself in Australia as an author. While we were searching for her, I was ordered to attend future planning meetings for the *Weekly* at the offices of its advertising agency, J. Walter Thompson. Understandably enough, Dorothy was not happy about this.

When Kerry finally did announce my appointment as Editor, I know Dorothy was sad, but I suspect she also had been secretly relieved. The *Weekly* was a demanding taskmaster, as I was about to discover. Dorothy and I used to meet sometimes in the elevator when we were going home late in the evening. She always looked worn out and was never without her large bag of 'homework' to do after dinner. She was by then well into her sixties and I'm sure there must have been days when she wished for a less stressful life.

If Dorothy wasn't pleased at the thought of my appointment, neither were most of the staff. To them, I seemed so young. Most of them were in their fifties and sixties and to me they seemed so old, although I did respect their knowledge and experience. Even so, they were very negative about the changes I was about to initiate. I am sure they knew as well as I did that the *Weekly* needed an overhaul, but it's one thing to know that change is needed, and quite another to be brave enough to admit it. As far as they were concerned, they were the *Weekly* – I was just a newcomer. No matter if I'd worked on the *Weekly* in the sixties, that was then and this was now. What would I know about running a mighty magazine like the *Weekly*? But what they didn't know, and I did, was that if the *Weekly* didn't change, it wouldn't survive. This was crunch time for the *Weekly*.

I understand far better now, more than twenty-five years later, that many of the older *Weekly* staffers must have been terrified they would lose their jobs. No one likes to think they have passed their use-by date. This is a very real problem today, when men and women forty-five and over frequently are told they are too old to employ. No doubt that attitude will change. We are, after all, an ageing society and in a few short years forty-five, even fifty-five, will seem young.

As I took my seat in the basic, no-frills office of the Editor, I was reminded again of how alone I was. I had taken this huge step and now everything rested on my shoulders. It was not only crunch time for the *Weekly*, but for Ita Buttrose, too. Would I be able to turn the magazine around, inspire the staff, communicate with the readers and keep the advertisers happy? Would I be able to cope with the workload and still have time for my husband and children? I kept my doubts and fears to myself. I didn't sleep well in the first few months and I lost weight, too. But I kept telling myself: 'You can do it, Ita.' I began by taking a good look at the *Weekly*'s circulation figures. They were terrible. The *Weekly*'s sales had dropped to the low 700 000s, but somehow ACP had managed to keep the figures hidden and people thought the magazine was selling more than 800 000 copies each week, which is what it claimed. Only a select few had any idea just how perilous the *Weekly*'s situation was.

My first task was to change its size. This was to happen in August 1975, six months after I had taken the Editor's chair. More was at stake than just a fortune and the future of a magazine. This was a social institution which was about to undergo major plastic surgery. It was like tampering with the Melbourne Cup, moving it from November to April!

The *Weekly*'s size was similar to that of a tabloid newspaper. In the seventies there was a world paper shortage and the cost of paper rose dramatically. Not only was the *Weekly* losing circulation; it was also losing money. Australia did not produce the quality of paper required for a publication like the *Weekly*. Its paper had to be imported. Production costs were too high. Other publishers around the world faced a similar problem and had solved it by reducing the size of their publications. Kerry decided the *Weekly* would follow suit and be reduced to the standard size that it is today. But, having made the decision, he worried about it. The *Weekly* was a powerful magazine and the queen of the Packer publishing stable. It was part of the national fabric. As an advertising medium, it was without equal. What if the size change didn't work? What then? No one had the answer to that one.

Now that it's a monthly (this happened in January 1983) the *Weekly* has lost much of its influence; but in the seventies, the *Weekly* was strong and authoritative, held in high esteem throughout Australia. It had the ability to sway people's minds, and often did.

In 1975 the *Weekly* going monthly was the last thing on our minds. All we wanted was to make sure it survived as a weekly, but in a smaller format. We were about to downsize it by 33 per cent, and, in so doing, test the loyalty of our readers, built up since 1933. The new design may have been forced on us by the economics of publishing but it was, nevertheless, a revolutionary departure in a business noted for its conservatism.

Market research had predicted success, but what if the research was wrong? I knew from my *Cleo* days that research didn't always get it right. I had taken a bigger gamble with *Cleo* than most people suspected. The advertising agency,

J. Walter Thompson, was in charge of *Cleo*'s advertising launch and had pressured Kerry to have the *Cleo* dummy researched. I think they were somewhat uncertain about 'the progressive woman' we said was the *Cleo* market. When they brought their findings back to us, it was with the advice, 'Don't do this project, it will fail'. It was a bleak day for Kerry and for me. We both had a lot riding on the future success of *Cleo* and now research was saying don't do it. Kerry didn't let it worry him for too long. 'Take the research upstairs and hide it,' he told me, 'and don't tell anyone, especially the old man.' I did as I was told. Sir Frank never knew about that damning report.

But the *Weekly* wasn't *Cleo*. It was unique, a magazine that many Australians regarded as a kind of 'bible'. As Founding Editor, George Warneke wrote in a letter to me before his death in 1981: 'Pretty well every woman over two generations in Australia has been touched by the influence of *The Australian Women's Weekly*. It does what it does better than any other paper.' Not only were the readers counting on me not to fail, so were a great many other people, especially Kerry. He had given me a free hand with the editorial side of the magazine and the fact that he trusted my judgement explicitly gave me confidence, but he had moments of fear that could reduce me to terror. Like all of us, he was well aware that the magazine was a cherished family heirloom and he didn't want to go down in the history books as the man who 'fucked up the *Weekly*'.

On one of his visits to Conpress at Mascot, where the

Weekly was printed, he came across a transparency that we were using in a pictorial souvenir album. He didn't think its quality was up to scratch and drove back to 54 Park Street in record time. He rang me on the Hot Line (a special system which he'd had installed so that he could get hold of his executives in a hurry) and summoned me to his office where he abused me for ten minutes or more – it seemed like hours – for having had the stupidity to select something so inferior. Even when I finally managed to get a word in to point out that the photograph was an historic one, the very best available and that it captured the mood we wanted to convey, he was hard to pacify. Somehow I managed to calm him down, but when I got back to my office I was completely unnerved. Not for long, however – I had no intention of being remembered for screwing up the maga- zine either. As far as I was concerned the *Weekly* was the greatest magazine in the world and it was going to remain that way.

There was a corporate sigh of relief when the new-look *Weekly* passed through its metamorphosis without losing read- ership, prestige or face. In its new garb it gathered strength and garnered new readers. Just before the first issue hit the streets Kerry sent me a note which I still have. It read:

Ita,
Forty-two years ago we launched the *Women's Weekly*.
Forty-two years later we relaunched it. I know it is
going to be a great success and you are the person

who is going to make it that. If anybody had asked me what your nickname should be I would have told them 'A Jewel Beyond Price'.

From the bottom of my heart, thank you.

Kerry

Saying thank you was one of Kerry's nicest traits and something he never forgot to do. Whenever he thought praise was merited, he gave it. He also had – and probably still does – a fabulous sense of humour. There was a lot of laughter throughout the company and I loved working there. Running the *Weekly*, which was then the largest-selling magazine in Australia and per capita of population in the world, was one of the most professionally satisfying and happiest times of my career. I quickly settled into my Editorship and began to appreciate even more the *Weekly*'s clout.

The *Weekly* had revolutionised the concept of publishing for women – breaking from the inherited traditions of English journals by treating female interests as news. It had been a great success story, and George Warneke assured me that it was studied abroad as a model of success. Of course, whether the *Weekly* was a champion of women's issues has been debated hotly. It has been criticised by feminists and historians.

Magazines tend to follow behind social change rather than to develop it. Women's Liberation in the sixties called forth many new publications in the seventies. The change in the *Weekly* was merely a revisioning of the seventies woman's needs. It's a matter of record that the magazine didn't take to the streets with the Women's Libbers of that era, but that was because in its early days the extremes and excesses of the movement were of a sort which seemed to be alienating more women than they were converting. And the *Weekly* had a close enough understanding of its readers to know that they would have been alienated if, as I told the Professional Marketing Association in 1978, 'we'd all ripped off our bras and started propping up the bar alongside the boys'. I'm positive that if the *Weekly* had gone in, boots and all, in the early days of Liberation it would only have bewildered the bulk of its readers and probably lost thousands of them. There are times when you can achieve more by hastening slowly. People need time to absorb change, and Women's Liberation was going to change the lives of women forever. We didn't realise just quite how much in the seventies, but we did understand that what was happening was of major significance to women.

There was a rush to label women, something I've always fought against. It was an issue we often tackled in the *Weekly* and that I wrote about in 1976.

Why do people keep giving women tags? We are either housewives, mothers, career women, spinsters, women's libbers or non women's libbers (very popular last year in International Women's Year). Lately I've come across another one: 'The Iron Butterfly'. According to the newspapers I read, Senator Margaret Guilfoyle is one [Guilfoyle was a minister in the Fraser Government]; British Conservative leader Margaret Thatcher is too, and so are Mrs Imelda Marcos of the Philippines and Helen Gurley Brown of America. Even I have been described as one. I protest. I'm me, a woman. No more, no less. Women don't need tags to justify their existence.

In the seventies the majority of the *Weekly*'s readers held the middle ground in Australia's emerging social fabric. This did not mean that the readers were all middle-class, but rather that they represented the silent majority. These women were not bent on taking over the world, nor were they motivated by bitterness. They didn't necessarily see themselves as being better than men, but there was no doubt they were enjoying the opportunities to demonstrate their equality in many areas.

Although we were often criticised for not being supportive enough of the changing woman, this was not correct, but it was fashionable to knock the *Weekly* without reading it. The *Weekly*'s approach may have been softer than the front-line feminists', but there was no mistaking its message. Women were not going to be overlooked any longer. They had become a force to be reckoned with.

A look at several of my editorials illustrates this. We were clearly unhappy about the advertising industry's attitude and criticised it in 1976 for still only looking for the 'Advertising Man of the Year'. Why not an 'Advertising Man or Woman of the Year', we asked, adding 'it seems so old-fashioned in 1976 to ignore women'.

The *Weekly* was critical again of the industry twelve months later when it reported that

the Australian woman in 1977 is quite a different person than she was ten years ago. Like it or not she has undergone an enormous transformation, yet many people refuse to recognise this. Why? Today about 45 per cent of the Australian workforce is made up of women, both married and single. And the number of married women working is increasing all the time.

We warned of a trend in England.

For the first time in that country's history the majority of married women are no longer housewives. Today more than 50 per cent of married women in England also have a job outside the home. Ultimately the same thing will happen here. The changing role of women appears to be unnoticed by a great many people particularly in advertising. So many advertisements in print and on television do not reflect properly a large proportion of women in Australia. We are not shown the way we truly are. We have changed. Many of us are no longer just housewives as portrayed in the advertisements. Nor are any of us as half-witted and gullible as many advertisements make us out to be. The people who make advertisements haven't noticed what women have been doing right under their very noses.

Again in 1977, along with the *Weekly*'s advertising manager Geraldine Paton, I sent a telegram to the organisers of a Supermarketing Seminar with the message that 'perhaps the return to profitability lies in the hand that rocks the cradle and pushes the supermarket trolley'. This was in response to comments made at the seminar about cost problems and a survey which claimed that 'housewives become tense and anxious when they go to supermarkets because they are frightened of being cheated'. My colleagues at the *Weekly* and I thought it was a lot of rot, and even more so when we discovered that women were not represented at the seminar. (A common occurrence – women were unrepresented just about everywhere then.) As the *Weekly* asked: 'How can anyone communicate with their consumer if they deny her a voice?'

The *Weekly* was a tremendous magazine which gave me great joy and satisfaction. I didn't care how many hours I worked. I was doing what I'd been dreaming of doing for years. Being Editor of the *Weekly* was then the top job in Australia for a woman journalist and it was mine. I couldn't have been happier. I inherited the trust of millions of Australians and the task of maintaining that trust and building on it sharpened all of my senses.

It was humbling and exciting to have the responsibility to address the three million or so Australians who regularly read the *Weekly* each week. Humbling because of the loyalty and interest that the readership represented, and exciting because of the opportunities to inform and entertain such a large mass. The *Weekly* went into one in four homes. It was read by almost 45 per cent of all women fourteen and over, and 20 per cent of all men fourteen and over. It was in touch directly, on a weekly basis, with a very substantial and significant proportion of the Australian population. The *Weekly* has always enjoyed a special bond with its readers. It was a relationship that never ceased to amaze me as people all over Australia made me their silent confidante during my time at the magazine's helm.

Australian women read hundreds of thousands of magazines a year and long may they continue to do so! The market has grown considerably since *Cleo* made its debut, to become the first, new mass-market magazine to be published in this country for many years. Now there are specialist titles that cover almost every possible female interest.

I'm often asked what it is that attracts Australian women to magazines. I am sure it is friendship. I believe a woman regards her favourite magazine in very much the same way she regards a special friend. She is willing to listen to it because there is something personal in the way it talks to her. It entertains her, it advises and instructs her. It suggests new things to her, new ideas, new methods and even new values. It keeps her up to date in every area that is of special interest to her as a woman. A magazine addresses a single reader and creates a friendship between her and the magazine that no newspaper or television program can ever hope to compete with.

A good magazine such as the *Weekly*, prepared with one reader in mind, highly attractive and with editorial content designed with a very individual approach to the reader, lives long after it is published – weeks and months in fact. It is passed from friend to friend, from home to hospital, from beauty salons to women's clubs, around the office, literally wherever women get together. A successful women's magazine creates its own powerful network.

No door was ever closed to the *Weekly* when I was Editor. If the *Weekly* requested an interview, it was granted. If the *Weekly* wanted to cover a society wedding (in colour, of course), permission was always given. Everyone, especially its readers, trusted the *Weekly*. We didn't have to offer huge sums of money for our exclusive stories like so many of today's popular magazines do. People were only too happy to have the *Weekly* tell their story for no payment. They were flattered to have been asked in the first place.

The *Weekly* disseminated all sorts of information in a language that its readers could understand. We explained government legislation, such as tax benefits and pensions, often at the request of the relevant government department; we gave information on health and directed our readers as to where to seek professional advice. We prided ourselves on providing clear, factual information on almost any topic that affected the lives of our readers.

We tried to make sure that every fact or comment we published was as accurate as possible. We never bought cheap 'beat-up' interviews with the stars or fiction unless we read it first. We didn't publish knitting or sewing patterns of any kind, without having made them up to make sure they worked. We never published recipes unless we were sure they were good and we had tried them out. Every recipe that we used in the *Weekly*, even if it appeared in the fiction pages, was tested in the *Women's Weekly* test kitchen. Six home economists, under the expert direction of a food editor, ensured our recipes worked.

Our advertising agency, J. Walter Thompson, had researched me – as if I were some kind of product – and advised Kerry that I would be perfect to explain the change in the size of the magazine, as I would be seen as an authoritative figure. So each week I presented national television commercials advertising the *Weekly*'s contents. Like every other advertiser, we had to get the official okay from FACTS (the Federation of Australian Commercial Television Stations) that the contents were suitable for the time slots we had booked. Knowing from my *Cleo* days how much interest there was in women's health, and remembering the man who had asked me for advice on his wife's hysterectomy, I thought the timing was right to do a special health feature on hysterectomies. To my amazement, our account executive at J. Walter Thompson, the advertising agency, rang and said we had been refused permission to show the *Weekly*'s advertisements before 8.30 p.m. because of the hysterectomy feature.

'You're joking,' I said to him.

'No, I'm not. We can't put the ad to air until after 8.30 p.m.'

'Rubbish. I'll ring the guy at FACTS.'

So I did. What, I asked him, was the problem with the *Weekly*'s commercials?

'Well,' he said, 'you can't talk about sex before 8.30 p.m.'

'Sex? What sex?' I demanded.

'That article about hysterectomies . . .'

It took me only a couple of minutes to give him a lesson on women's anatomy and health. The *Weekly*'s advertisements were approved and we went to air in our usual time slots – before and after 8.30 p.m.

There was another big plus that facilitated the planning of our editorial content and that was the hundreds of letters which arrived every week and helped us to keep our fingers on the pulse of Australia's social life. Many of the readers wrote to me addressing me by my first name. They told me about intimate problems in their lives and about the things that worried them about Australia's direction. It was clear in the last years of the seventies that the nation was suffering from a deep and profound sense of confusion. Its values were confused, its sense of morality was confused, and no one seemed able to provide any answers. Our readers were bewildered by the torrents of information washing over them, apparently unable to process the volume of data and deal with it. The tremendous social upheaval of the seventies was already creating something of a cultural malaise.

We were starting to worry about the children and the growth of violence in our community. In my editorial, 'At My Desk', in February 1978, I touched on some of the things that troubled us then. Rereading it today, it seems our concerns are much the same. Once again, we ignored the warning signs that all was not well with what, in the eighties, I described as our 'troubled youth'. I wrote:

Most responsible Australians must be concerned at the increase of violence in our community. It is impossible to ignore it. Stories of violence fill our newspapers. Horrifying stories of brutality and, too often, death. The youth of so many of the victims and their attackers is equally horrifying. Surprisingly, and yet probably predictably, there have been few sensible comments of concern by politicians, community leaders and churchmen. Surely we must ask ourselves why women no longer feel safe walking down a street at night even from the bus stop to the front door; why children are no longer safe when they play in a park or use a public toilet; why some elderly women who live alone are no longer safe from thrill-seeking youths.

Today's young Australians have grown up in different times than, say, my generation. They are children of the electronic era. TV has been, and still is, an important moulder of the way they think. They are children who have experienced the enormous changes and stresses in the Australian family. Many of them are children of working fathers and working mothers. Many of them are children from one-parent homes. Family life has changed but that doesn't mean it is wrong or bad. Working mothers, one-parent families are with us now. They will not disappear.

I think violence is bred from boredom. Young people need stimulation. They need discipline at home and at school as well as love and care. They need safe, supervised places where they can meet and play. They need schools to stay open until 5.30 p.m. so they can study safely until their parents get home. They need our attention and our help in adjusting to the demands of life.

The seventies were a decade when everyone gave women advice. Don't be a women's libber, do be a libber; don't say you're just a housewife; you'll never get on in business if you don't dress the part; don't be aggressive in the office (you'll frighten men); don't go home after work to be with the kids – have a drink with the boys or they won't think you're serious about your career; don't stay to have a drink with the boys as people will get the wrong impression. Everyone dictated to women as if they didn't have minds of their own to work out what they wanted and where they were going.

Women were under-represented in every upper echelon of decision making – government, education, police, public service, the corporate sector, the legal profession – and yet everyone felt they had the right to tell them how they should or shouldn't lead their lives. So much so that occasionally some women even apologised for their choices.

It made me mad and I'd had enough. Women needed a voice. A new decade was dawning and women's views on the current issues affecting our way of life needed to be heard. After all, what was the point of being a liberated woman if it was in name only?

I came up with the idea of running a national survey in the *Weekly*, and to this day I consider 'The Voice of the Australian Woman' one of the most important things I've ever done to get the women's point of view heard in this country. The survey, the first of its kind, included 230 questions covering such topics as marriage, family, education, conservation, child sex abuse and health. The response was astonishing. Some 30 000 women posted back the survey sheets and 10 000 of them wrote letters, too. They shared personal happenings – incest, rape, abortion – and I was touched and moved by their trust. Consensus Research, who evaluated the survey, told me that apart from the census it was the biggest and most successful survey ever conducted in Australia.

People from all walks of life took part; not all of them were regular readers either. For example, at the State Government Insurance office in Perth, 200 copies of the questionnaire were duplicated and handed to female members of staff. What the survey showed opened our eyes. It confirmed that women had changed and that they would no longer be silenced. The conditioned view of the Australian female was blown away.

Sixty-two per cent of respondents believed that national service should be reintroduced to reduce unemployment and, staggering by today's standards, 72 per cent thought that the dole encouraged people not to work. Perhaps this suggested just how radical Gough Whitlam's views had been between 1972 and 1975. It also should send a message to the present Federal Government not to abandon 'work-for-the-dole' schemes.

The way in which the questionnaire was prepared and the scientific way in which the answers were processed made us confident that we had achieved a very accurate reflection of the thinking on many topics of the entire female population of Australia. Women were speaking their minds with a lack of inhibition that was refreshing.

On the subject of incest, which had been a long-kept secret, we discovered that 3 per cent of Australian women had been abused. Of these, 38 per cent were victims before they were nine years old, 25 per cent between nine and eleven, and a further 30 per cent before they were sixteen. We were shocked at this revelation, so much so that before we published I asked the readers for permission to run letters from victims, after first obtaining the latter's consent to publish their stories. As I wrote in my column:

> We believe incest must be discussed and recognised for the illness it is. The consequences are extreme. The women who experienced the trauma will carry it with them for life. Help and counselling is hard to find and often the victims are not believed. Unless we bring incest out into the open it will not go away.

It was clear to us that Australia was a long way from developing agencies to help and protect young children.

Ninety-four per cent of women believed abortion should be available; 60 per cent said it should be freely accessible, demonstrating one of the ways in which women's new-found freedoms were being expressed. Thirty-two per cent believed it should be available if a woman's health was in danger. Coincidentally, the findings on abortion were published at the same time anti-abortion legislation was being introduced in Queensland and the issue of abortion was being debated (mainly by men) not only in the Queensland Parliament but also in the Federal Parliament. The *Weekly* was quoted extensively by opponents to the bill and was said to have been instrumental in its defeat. I'm sure it was. We sent copies of the issue to every politician in Canberra.

Men continually debate the issue of abortion without enough input from women. A woman's right to abortion on demand was raised again in 1997 and debated in Parliament. How many times do women have to say how they feel on this issue? At the beginning of the seventies, the *Patterson Report* said that Australian women thought 'abortion should be legalised but that it should be a personal and not a societal decision'. They also said they felt abortion was distressing. Of course it is. I think the high incidence of abortion means that we need better sex education classes for children and adults. Abortion should be used as a last resort and not as a form of family planning.

The postbag response to 'The Voice of the Australian

Woman' was awesome. The revolution had really taken off. Those 10 000 extra letters filled in missing bits and pieces. Women took the extra time to write to us, expressing their views in greater detail. The vast majority indicated that Australia's education system was failing our youth, at a time when more women than ever were in the workplace and dependent upon the State school system for free childcare. It was the time latchkey children came into existence and women were worried about their kids' safety.

Fifty-seven per cent of respondents to the *Weekly*'s survey indicated that teachers were more interested in higher pay than educational standards. Seventy per cent of women believed that teachers' problems were caused by the lack of interest of government and parents – presumably they meant other parents. Our respondents also indicated that school was too easy for children, that they were allowed to do almost anything they liked and that they were developing rudeness toward their teachers. This rudeness was beginning to be carried home and practised on parents.

Perhaps we were already seeing the emerging trend of our children wanting less of our money and more of our time. The two-working-parent family may have been more economically viable and attractive, but our children were suffering and the educational system was ill equipped to cope with the resulting problems. There was also a concern that the school system might be encouraging children to become misfits rather than well-educated young citizens with a sense of pride and achievement. Women were fearful that the education system was failing. It was, in fact, becoming apparent that ten or fifteen years of social experimentation in schools had been a disaster.

Many expressed concerns about the lack of control in schools, and wondered about just what went on in the classroom between nine and three-thirty. Were our schools instilling a code of communal behaviour in our children which might last a lifetime? Looking back now, though, parents seemed not to ask what their own role was in establishing values. After all, children should be parents' responsibility, not the government's – perhaps it is because Australians have handed over so much 'de facto parental' control to governments that children are so confused.

Eighty-five per cent of our respondents indicated that our country's schools did not give enough attention to teaching basic skills such as reading, spelling and arithmetic. But there was another side to this, too. There was a strong theme in the letters we received which acknowledged that discipline begins at home, and that too many parents were guilty of packing their children off to school as though it were a child-minding centre capable of curing bad behaviour. There had clearly been a move from the educational style of the sixties.

In spite of their anxieties, 52 per cent of women still had an optimistic view of Australia's future, suggesting that we would become a leading nation in the next ten years. In hindsight, how wrong they were, as our living standards have fallen throughout the eighties and nineties; but it is an interesting insight into how women were thinking and feeling as the new decade began. There is little doubt that women are still fairly optimistic about the future, but men appear to be increasingly pessimistic.

In my January New Year column in 1980 I was feeling positive about the future, too, although I couldn't resist pointing out in my editorial that we seemed to be on our way to becoming a nation of unfit slobs.

Australians spend more in retail stores on beer than on fruit, vegetables, bread, milk, cheese, fresh poultry, eggs, butter and fresh fish combined. We spent more on soft drinks than on milk; and confectionery outsold all smallgoods including hams and bacons.

It was a case of the shape of things to come. These days, much to the concern of the medical profession, increasing numbers of Australians are overweight or obese, including thirty per cent of under-18-year-olds, which doesn't bode well for the long-term health of our population. Doctors tell me we're eating much the same as we've always eaten; the problem is, we're exercising less. We need to get up off our bottoms!

But overall I was looking forward to the eighties. I predicted it would be a decade of 'enormous change but challenging and exciting', with technology altering the way we worked and robots replacing humans in many work areas.

'Certainly by the end of the eighties,' I wrote, 'we'll be an ageing population. Immigration Minister Michael MacKellar has asked women to have more children because the birth-rate has fallen so much since 1971 that we are in danger of becoming an old community unable to handle changes and new demands. Mr MacKellar says women should not feel guilty about staying home to raise a family.'

But by now, more than 50 per cent of all married women worked and any thoughts of guilt were far from their minds. Women made up 36.1 per cent of the work-force. The two-income family and the working woman were here to stay. The *Weekly* knew this better than anyone. We knew women were contributing greatly to society and to the workforce, as well as in that most impor-tant area, the family. We treated women as people, and gave them respect, at a time when they needed support and encouragement. As women emerged after many long years in the darkness to stand on their own feet in what had been a male-dominated society – where they were not always treated with equality or respect – I would like to think we helped them to stand tall and walk proudly into that brave new world. I always thought the *Weekly* talked eyeball to eyeball with women in a no-nonsense way. We firmly believed it was the only way to communicate with them properly and to send the signal that they were not alone, regardless of what the person next door or anyone else may have thought of their choices.

I told the *Weekly*'s readers that

our role models in the eighties will be positive women with an optimistic attitude towards their future. They will have high expectations of themselves and those around them and will enjoy controlling their destiny. Their view of the world will be forward thinking, flexible, tolerant and highly involved. Women will still marry and indeed will want to – but it's most likely that we will marry later. Many women will choose not to have children. Those who do have children will have their first babies later and last babies earlier. The family will be very important, of course, but where a generation ago women devoted as much as twenty years to raising a family, it is predicted that this will be squeezed to four to eight years in the future.

Confident as I was about the future of women, my personal future was worrying me. Mac and I had separated in 1976 – we had grown apart. It was a reasonably amicable separation and our divorce came through in 1977. Sometime in 1978, at a World Series Cricket dinner (Kerry changed cricket forever, and for the better, when he introduced World Series Cricket) I met a personable Englishman, Peter Sawyer, who had his own sales promotion and marketing business in Sydney. He swept me off my feet and we married in 1979. But our marriage wasn't turning out the way I'd hoped. I'm sure we both thought we loved each other when we married, but I knew within months that I had made a terrible mistake. As it turned out, Peter must have felt the same way, not that he told me. One year to the day after our marriage, I came home from speaking at a function at Ben's school to find Peter had packed up his belongings and was off to Melbourne. He had found someone else. My second marriage was over.

It was a devastating time for me. One of the afternoon tabloids rehashed an old interview suggesting that my 'work-aholic habits' were behind the break-up of my marriage. This criticism has often been levelled against me and I refute it completely. Sure I work hard and sometimes put in long hours, but I can stop and never have any difficulty putting all thoughts of work out of my mind when I'm in the mood for a spot of relaxation. I always thought Peter was the workaholic partner, but as he was running his own sales promotion business and had a great deal on his plate, I understood the reason why and it was never an issue between us.

I was mortified when my GP suggested that perhaps counselling would help me find out why I couldn't sustain a relationship. When I explained that my husband had walked out on me, the well-meaning doctor backed off. None of my family or my friends had ever thought my marriage to Peter one of my better decisions and while they were concerned about my welfare, their sympathy was in short supply. For awhile I felt dreadfully sorry for myself. I wore black to the office and when I got home in the evening after saying goodnight to the kids, would sit in the lounge room and weep. It took every ounce of courage I possessed to go into ACP each day as though I didn't care at all about what had happened, when in fact I did very much indeed.

As the song says, time heals everything – and it ultimately did. But I've often wondered if the shock and humiliation of my second marriage break-up affected me more than I realised at the time. When you marry again and already have children, their well-being is paramount. At the back of my mind there's always been a little niggle about the effect my turbulent relationship with Peter might have had on Kate and Ben. They had got on well with him and he with them. His departure left a void in their lives and it worried me. Subconsciously – I think – I decided not to expose them to any more romantic danger zones in case I chose wrongly again. Looking at them today and appreciating the well-rounded and interesting adults they've become, I don't regret it either.

At the same time as my marriage was floundering, I began to feel dissatisfied at the way my career was panning out. It surprised me at first. I loved being in charge of the *Weekly* and, even today, I still miss that magazine. It was the professional love affair of my life. I didn't want to leave, but felt the need of another challenge, yet Kerry was so happy with the way the *Weekly* and the other magazines were performing that he wanted me to stay where I was. By now I was Publisher of ACP's Women's Division and also responsible for *Cleo, Mode, Belle, Bride* and the specialist one-shot area that published sections of the *Weekly* as soft-cover, inexpensive but beautifully produced books. I inaugurated this part of ACP's empire and the one-shots have earned millions for the company. Kerry kept saying things like: 'When you're sixty and showing Jamie the ropes . . . ' I used to think to myself, *I'm not sure I want to be doing exactly the same thing when I am sixty*. Capricorn that I am, climbing mountains has always appealed to me!

When, out of the blue, Rupert Murdoch invited me to become Editor-in-Chief of his *Daily* and *Sunday Telegraphs* in Sydney – which would make me the first woman ever to hold such a position on any major newspaper in Australia – I was sorely tempted, as they say. Not long after Peter had left in June 1980, I had lunched with Rupert at a private apartment in Sydney and later at the Savoy while holidaying in London in December of the same year. He is an extraordinary salesman and charming, and when he made me a firm offer to join News Ltd, I accepted. A new challenge was just what I needed and it would take my mind off my marital woes. Perhaps, if I'd still been happily married to Peter, I mightn't have left ACP. Emotions can play havoc with your rational thought process. Looking back, I can see that now.

Rupert tempted me further with another first. He invited me to become a director of News Ltd, a big break in tradition for this previously male-only board. And, as the icing on the cake, offered me my own show on Network TEN, which he then controlled. Unfortunately, he neglected to take TEN's executives into his confidence before he did so, and they weren't happy at having to honour a commitment in which they'd played no part. This did not bode well for any future that I might have contemplated as a TV performer. Still, I had no idea then that Rupert wouldn't be able to deliver on everything he promised.

I agonised before finally deciding to leave ACP because it would mean giving up a great deal. Although Rupert's package was generous, it was nowhere near as munificent as my ACP one, which enabled me to enjoy a fabulous lifestyle. I had every perk you could think of: a substantial salary; a beautiful company home in exclusive Rosemont Avenue in Sydney's Woollahra; a Mercedes complete with chauffeur; a housekeeper; separate allowances for clothes, furniture and alcohol, plus a hire-car account. The company also helped with school bills. I annually travelled overseas with an excellent expense account and frequently holidayed with the children at the company apartment in Surfers Paradise. It was a lot to leave behind and I knew I'd regret giving up some of my entitlements. I would also miss ACP. After all, with the exception of three years in London, I had been with the company since I was fifteen. In a way ACP was like my family – after all, I had grown up in the years I'd worked for it – and I felt very much at home there.

In his book, *The Rise and Rise of Kerry Packer*, Paul Barry wrote: 'When the executives of Consolidated Press gathered in the taproom next to Kerry's office for drinks in the evening, she [Ita] was not spared the male banter in which they almost all engaged. Nor did many go out of their way to make her feel welcome'. That is such rubbish. Male banter has never bothered me and in the taproom, I gave as good as I got. I had become accustomed to being the only woman in the hierarchy at ACP and I was (and still am) totally comfortable in the company of men.

My contemporaries at ACP never made me feel unwelcome – after all, I had been with the company longer than most of them. More often than not, it was more a case of me making my male colleagues welcome, as I did for Mark Day, the former Editor of Rupert Murdoch's Sydney *Daily Mirror*, who for a brief time was Editor of *Playboy*, then part of the ACP stable. The other male executives gave him a difficult time because he wasn't one of 'us' and never really fitted into the culture of ACP. Mark turned up at the taproom one night in shirtsleeves (the others always wore their jackets, even in the hottest summer heatwave) and drank his beer from the can (shock, horror!). But I liked Mark. He was a top journalist with a sense of humour and likeable personality, and although he didn't stay long at Consolidated Press we became good friends. He and Kerry frequently argued – sometimes vehemently – over what qualities a girl needed to make a classy pin-up suitable for publication in *Playboy*. Mark was a bottom man and Kerry was a boobs man. I was often called down to Kerry's office to play the arbiter of taste over pin-ups for *Playboy*. Publishing does land a woman in strange situations at times!

It was this kind of unpredictability that I most loved about working at ACP. There was never a dull moment. There was always plenty of laughter throughout the company, too. Not that Kerry was the perfect boss – far from it. There were times when he was impossible. And he did seem to think he owned us all. It used to annoy the hell out of me to always have to tell my secretary precisely where I was going – even if I was doing something simple like shopping at lunchtime at David Jones – in case Kerry wanted me for something or other. It wasn't good enough for my secretary to inform him I was at lunch and that I'd be back at two. This invasion of my privacy irritated me.

Nonetheless, I was nervous about telling him that I had accepted Rupert's offer. Although Kerry rarely lost his temper with me, I had seen it in action and feared that I might cop a blast on this occasion. I called on him at his mansion in Sydney's eastern suburbs. I am sure he knew why I was there. We made polite conversation for a minute or two and then I told him what I intended to do. He was upset and so was I, but he wished me well and I believed him.

As usual, though, it wasn't long before the Packer temper was up and running. He returned to ACP, called all the Women's Division staff to a meeting and broke the news of my departure to them, suggesting I was a traitor. He cited poor Alice Jackson, a previous Editor of the *Weekly* who'd had the nerve to leave the magazine in 1948 to run *Woman* magazine for Sir Frank's rival, Keith Murdoch, Rupert's father. It is indeed a small world, isn't it?

I'd like to think that when he'd calmed down, Kerry thought about some of the good times and the money I made him and ACP. I also hope he sometimes remembers what he said about me on *This Is Your Life* on Channel 7 in late 1979:

> It has made you a very competent, dedicated and brilliant journalist who has achieved greatness in her industry very early and so quickly. An area, about which people are probably unaware, is just how much you have contributed to women's standing in our community and how much you have achieved for women, without being belligerent, without being angry, but through charm and ability. Thank you for being a friend. You've been a great joy to work with.

Reading his words now, it seems as though Kerry was saying goodbye then, doesn't it? Much to my dismay, he wouldn't allow me back into ACP to say goodbye and to say thank you to my colleagues. It was a pretty mean-spirited thing for him to do and totally uncalled for. After all, I hadn't done anything wrong. As soon as I'd accepted Rupert's offer to become Editor-in-Chief of the two *Telegraphs*, I sought Kerry out to tell him of my decision. I left the *Weekly*, and the other titles under my control in good shape. There were talented and capable people in place to run them. Everything went on smoothly without me. I think I can claim to have run my division well and competently.

But the company folklore had it that hell hath no fury like a Packer when an employee decides to seek fame and fortune elsewhere – as I was about to discover.

I still find it hard to believe what happened to me.
I resigned on 23 December 1980. In between Christmas and
New Year I was ordered to return the Mercedes and get out
of the company house – the sooner, the better. Remember,
my children were young – Kate was eleven, Ben was six.
A $50 000 bonus that had been given to other key execu-
tives and me a few years earlier as a 'loan', with no expectation of it ever being repaid, was recalled and resulted in
me owing ACP money. So they kept all my entitlements
and I had to sell my Channel 9 shares (which I considered
my future nest egg) to make up the shortfall. In retrospect,
I was stupid. I should have stayed put in the house and kept
the car – at least for a couple of months. What would they
have done to me? Thrown me out into the street? I doubt
it. The woman I am today would not have put up with it,
but back in the seventies and early eighties life wasn't easy
for a woman with ambition.

But, to tell the truth, I was a little scared by ACP's reaction. It never occurred to me that the company would keep
my holiday pay, long service leave and superannuation. Nor
did I dream that I would be asked to give back the $50 000.
I had not asked for it. Kerry and ACP Finance Controller,
Harry Chester, made it quite clear at the time that the 'loan'
was a bonus, being paid to four or five of us as a thank you
for our hard work. I had been counting on my severance
package which was worth about $30 000. I had planned to
bank some of the money and then find a new home to rent
before taking up my duties as Editor-in-Chief.

So there I was. Homeless, carless, no money and about to start a new job in a company so unlike ACP that at first I didn't know what hit me. News Ltd was a very macho company then and I was greeted with a hostility that shocked me. But that was yet to come. For the moment, there was nothing to be gained by whining about my lot. It was up to me to sort out my problems. My most pressing need was money. I had one particular ring that held much sentimental value. It was the most valuable thing I owned. I sold it for $10 000. The proceeds enabled me and the children to move home and live comfortably until I was earning money again at News Ltd – and boy, earn it I did!

4

THE EIGHTIES

You would have found your time here much easier if you'd been butch and worn pants.

BRIAN HOGBEN, A FELLOW DIRECTOR AT NEWS LTD

If the seventies had been an eventful decade of change for me, the eighties was to be even more so. I started working for Rupert Murdoch in January 1981 and by 1989 I was running my own company, Capricorn Publishing. In between those two events, I worked for Australia's then other big publishing group, John Fairfax and Sons, as publishing consultant and journalist which included writing for the now defunct afternoon newspaper, the *Sun*, and *Woman's Day*; and I chaired the National Advisory Committee on AIDS (NACAIDS) for the Federal Government. Somehow I managed to write two books and make my debut as a radio broadcaster, first on Sydney's 2UE, then for the New South Wales Labor Council's radio station, 2KY. God knows how I managed to do it all. As I often tell people, it's just as well

I don't need much sleep, but there were times when I did feel in need of a good rest.

Kate and Ben didn't seem to notice my hectic schedule. They were busy with their own lives – doing well at school and sport. Kate had developed into a first-class tennis player, and in spite of my best endeavours to keep him from it, Ben discovered Rugby. I had him happily playing soccer because I felt it was a much safer game than Rugby. But I hadn't counted on Ben growing into such a strapping young man. Coming off the soccer field one day, he was stopped by the Rugby coach who told him he should be playing Rugby. It was a game better suited to a strong boy like Ben, he explained.

Ben came home and at dinner that night announced that he was now playing Rugby. I was horrified. I had thoughts of broken legs, cauliflower ears and all the other things mothers worry about.

I rang my brothers looking for support. I should have known better. They agreed with the Rugby coach – Ben was a natural. To a man, they each asked: 'What position is he playing?' I gave up. Ben threw himself into Rugby and won the award for the most promising player when he was thirteen. When I went to watch him play, I shut my eyes whenever he was tackled.

People often ask me how the kids coped with having a famous mother. Pretty well, I think. They never took my fame seriously. *That* Ita Buttrose was someone else. The Ita Buttrose they knew was Mum – loving, but strict when it was necessary. Ben used to delight in mocking me. He still does. Once when we were doing the weekly shopping at Woolworths he started horsing around, pointing at me and saying: 'Aren't you Ita Buttrose?' over and over again. Finally, I just looked at him and said: 'Son, if they know who I am, they sure as hell know who you are.' It was at such times I remembered the advice my Aunty Billy had given me on rearing sons. 'Boys should be buried at thirteen and dug up at twenty!' That day in Woolworths I knew exactly what she meant.

My life may have been moving at a fast pace but the kids and I still managed to find time to enjoy our family life. One night, I was held up at the office but had warned them in advance that we would be eating later than usual. As I put the key in the front door, Ben opened it, greeting me like a waiter with a napkin folded over his arm. 'Good evening, Madam,' he said. 'We are expecting you.' He and Kate had cooked dinner, put candles on the table, and had even been to the wine cellar and offered me a choice of three chilled whites to go with my meal!

But it was impossible to ignore the fact that in the fast-moving, hang-the-consequences eighties, Australia seemed to be heading out of control. The warning signs that things were not going well were evident. We could have seen them had we wanted to, but we were having such a good time we were blind to it. Children were suffering the curse of neglect. Halfway through the eighties, Archbishop (later

Cardinal) Clancy, head of the Catholic Church in Australia, warned that his priests were telling him that alcohol was the single biggest problem for our youth. 'Once, young people would sometimes have one drink too many,' he said, 'now they drink to get drunk in order to blot out life, at least temporarily.'

We were a nation preoccupied with having a good time. We were also a nation obsessed with greed, but we were not alone in this. Thatcher's children were running amok in Britain popping champagne corks, while Reagan was pushing his own brand of the new dream while fighting the 'evil empire' at the same time. Here in Australia, our obsession with wealth and acquisitiveness knew no bounds.

When I interviewed Archbishop Clancy in 1985 for my 'People' column in the *Sun*, I asked him why so few men were entering the priesthood. He replied:

> The single greatest cause would be the materialism of our age. Society doesn't cause people to think about the priesthood and the religious life. I don't want to bash the media but you could say that materialism is the people's God today, and, in a way, the media is a prophet.

Even the Catholic Church could not resist the power of eighties greed.

It concerned the Archbishop that

people are very much educated and conditioned by the media from before they reach the age of reason. Success is promoted as the one big thing that matters and there is constant pressure on people to attain material success and make a lot of money.

The corporate cowboys flourished in the eighties, but eventually got their comeuppance. Like many others, they borrowed money like there was no tomorrow and with little thought of how it would be paid back. No wonder it was often called 'the crazy eighties'. No one seemed to be fully account-able. The corporate cowboys didn't have to rob a bank to get the funds they wanted either. The banks just about put the money outside their doors for them to take and use as the mood took them. Of course, when the bite hit, when 'the recession we had to have' took over, the people who suffered were not the big guys, but the little people who just needed a loan to buy a house or to hang onto their home. The banks punished everyone for the mistakes of a few. But in the early and mid eighties, few thought about what could happen when and if the boom ended. Get-rich-quick schemes were the order of the day. The motto was 'everything counts in large amounts'. We wanted it all, and we wanted it right now.

In the meantime, there was massive evidence piling up all around us that education was not good enough, that kids were on the streets, that they were neither loved nor wanted, that our nutritional standards were bad and affecting our health. There were warnings galore that something was amiss, but life just zoomed along. It was something I often wrote about as Editor-in- Chief in my column in the *Sunday Telegraph* throughout the four years I was there.

The role of women had changed again. As an editor, I was keenly aware of the fact that the working woman would no longer be taken for granted. She was sensitive and very in touch with her needs in a changing world. If she was not happy with how she was being treated, she didn't hesitate to speak up. Most magazines and newspapers recognised the writing on the wall and made determined efforts to reach 'the new eighties woman'.

So too did Rupert, which was one of the reasons he had cited when he asked me to work for him. He felt the two *Telegraph*s were overly masculine and too heavy in their emphasis on sport. He told me he wanted me to 'feminise' the papers. He didn't tell my colleagues – as a man, I guess he knew how those macho employees of his at News Ltd would react to anything that smacked of femininity, especially if they were told before it was going to happen. It might have been easier for me to implement some of the changes if Rupert had. But he doesn't believe in making life easy, in any way at all, for his editors. As far as Rupert is concerned, editors can sink or swim and even if they do seem to be going under he would never toss them a life jacket.

My first few months at News Ltd were hell. I had never encountered such resistance or resentment. One of the editors who reported to me was openly antagonistic and didn't even bother to introduce me to the other members of the executive team at our first conference. Whenever an opportunity arose he was deliberately rude almost inviting me to complain about his behaviour. Even though I could have happily smacked him across his handsome arrogant face, I had no intention of giving him that pleasure. I hung in there, determined and always polite, hoping my courtesy would drive him mad. When several months later he announced his resignation, it was the best news I'd received in ages. I now had a better understanding of why Mark Day found the culture at Consolidated Press so foreign when he was *Playboy* Editor, after being Editor of Rupert's afternoon *Daily Mirror*. The two companies were like chalk and cheese.

At ACP, women were respected for their ability and encouraged to aim for the top jobs, too. At News Ltd, they were tolerated. Women, especially younger women from other departments, often sought me out to ask me for advice in handling the aggression and discriminatory tactics of their male colleagues. Sometimes this aggression was frightening, and it soon became apparent that it didn't only exist in the editorial areas; it permeated the company, especially in the advertising departments. No wonder fellow director Brian Hogben told me life would have been easier for me at News Ltd if I'd been butch and worn pants, although I'm not sure how my butch friends would feel about such advice!

Some of the male behaviour was out and out sexual harassment, nevertheless the women who came to see me about their problems were insistent that I kept their confidences secret. They were as aware as I was that complaining about such treatment would only lead to their unemployment. It's the price people have to pay for working in a media industry controlled by so few. Blot your copybook with News Ltd, and 65 per cent of the nation's newspapers are no longer available for your possible future employment.

There were times in those early bleak months at News Ltd, when I asked myself what madness had possessed me to give up my comfortable, corporate lifestyle at ACP with all its benefits for this rough, daunting male place? But there was no point in whingeing about my position. No one had forced me to join News Ltd. I'd made my bed all by myself and now it was up to me to find the best way of doing the job Rupert was paying me to do.

One of the favourite games of some my colleagues during this period was to wait until I was approaching the lift and then slam the doors shut in my face. It happened time and time again. If only the perpetrators had known the real effect their childish behaviour was having on me. My determination to succeed increased. I knew they thought running a newspaper was a man's job, but I didn't go along with that kind of old-fashioned thinking. They were wrong and I intended to prove it to them.

There was no thought of family-friendly workplaces at News Ltd, and certainly no consideration at all for a working mother with young children. To be successful at News Ltd, one had to be 'one of the boys' and that meant working the kind of hours men worked, always an easier thing for corporate males to do because they usually have a wife who takes care of all the other things in their lives. Sometimes I used to yearn for someone to do that for me. A 'wife' would have been bliss!

In my job as Editor-in-Chief, I was on call seven days. During the week, I was expected to be in by nine in the morning and I rarely left before eight at night. The page proofs of the first edition would be sent out to my home around 10.30 p.m. for me to check. I would then ring the Editor, talk to him about any changes I wanted done and discuss the second edition of the paper. Because I was also Editor-in-Chief of the *Sunday Telegraph*. I worked on Saturdays as well. I had a morning phone conference with the Editor and was usually in the office by one in the afternoon and left after eight in the evening when I'd been through our paper and the opposition *Sun-Herald* with the Editor and News Editor and we'd shared a bottle of wine together. Sunday was a kind of day of rest. I wasn't expected to actually go into the office, but I was certainly contactable and would always ring the Editor to discuss the page one, three and five leads, as well as the paper's editorial. On Sunday nights, the first edition proofs would be sent out and the ritual would start again.

I had explained to the children that my new job at News Ltd would be demanding but that long-term it would benefit us as a family, because it would enable us to save money and ultimately to buy a house. I employed a live-in house-keeper so that there was always someone at home for them. Yes, it was expensive, but I wanted the children to be happy and comfortable, and it was important that I was able to work without worrying about them.

I told them, too, that I had gone to work for Rupert because he was the best newspaper publisher in Australia and that I wanted to learn from him. I wrote about this more fully in my first book, *First Edition: My First Forty Years*, and was immediately attacked by a Melbourne journalist reviewing my book. He said he was fed up with people like me saying that they regretted the lack of time Rupert had to spend with them on the job. (Rupert's schedule was hectic and not long after I began at News Ltd he started to build his world empire so he wasn't in Australia all that much.) The journalist missed my point, however. I went to News Ltd not just for the challenge, but also to learn from the Sorcerer (i.e. Rupert – I'm spelling it out in case that Melbourne journalist reads this book and misses the point again). I didn't go to learn from the Sorcerer's apprentices. I wanted to work not only for Rupert but with him because, apart from all else, he is a wonderful news-paperman.

This sometimes is lost sight of by people captivated by his fantastic business coups. He is a real pro. He knows about type and layout; he knows a good picture and how it should be handled; he knows how a story should be done. These are the things about our trade that interest me and

I had hoped to learn from him: to do a kind of postgraduate course under a master.

I'm sure most people who have worked on newspapers and major magazines – like me – have never truly wanted to do anything else. The thrill of seeing your story well displayed on page one, or making your paper's poster; of seeing the realisation of an idea emerge on the cover of a magazine; to watch a circulation climb; to ride home in a bus and watch someone read a piece you've written a few hours before – or perhaps caused to be written; the elation of running a story or campaign which has brought about a switch in Government thinking, or the making or unmaking of an appointment. There's nothing like it and I cannot think of any other job which gives such emotional satisfaction.

I don't suppose I had many more than a dozen across-the-table talks with Rupert Murdoch during the years I worked for him and these were spread over London, New York and Sydney. I must say that when I did see him he was always able to wipe all the other million things that concerned him from his mind and give the impression that his major interest in life was his two *Telegraphs*. He is an extraordinary man. In his occasional letters to me, his observations on how to turn a Sunday newspaper into an irresistible read included some of the best advice I've ever been given. His letters give a fascinating insight into the thinking of a man that I regard as without equal in the newspaper business.

My dear Ita,

I have not been reading the *Sunday Telegraph* as dili-
gently as I should. But I feel that the first few pages
are not in a sufficiently settled mold. There should
be comfortable familiarity about a Sunday newspaper.
It is a relatively expensive item and people expect to
spend one or two hours with it. They do not need
big headlines and they certainly don't want to be
either too shocked or depressed. They want a good,
perhaps slightly stimulating read.

I used to admire the old *Sun-Herald*. It never varied
its formula, providing for the middle-class taste and
covering all the major subjects of the week. Now it
is just boring and over written. The old Packer *Sunday
Telegraph* sometimes used to scintillate, but it could
never dent the *Sun-Herald*'s leadership with its seemingly magic formula.

Now that the *Sun-Herald* has been taken over by
new hands [there had been executive changes at the
paper] surely we could capture some of its old chem-
istry. All this, and, of course, be best by far in sport!
And, maybe this last element is most important of
all – a majority of the department store and food
advertisements!!!

I'm sorry to go on like this, but I'm prompted by
the feeling that you and Alan [Farrelly] may be trying
too hard to wake up and worry the good people of
Sydney every Sunday morning.

While I was Editor-in-Chief, much to Rupert's delight –
and everyone else's at News Ltd – in 1982 and for the first
time in its history, the *Sunday Telegraph* outsold its rival the
Sydney *Sun-Herald*. Today, it is the largest selling newspaper
in Australia. I put our success in the eighties down to a
couple of things – determination and hard work on my part
and that of then Editor, Alan Farrelly, as well as the rest of
the *Sunday Telegraph* team; and having the good sense to take
Rupert's advice on what people look for in a Sunday paper.

We also introduced our readers to Bingo, an expensive
exercise but one on which Rupert was prepared to gamble.
Australia's biggest gambler Kerry Packer would have
approved, I'm sure, even though there have been times when
Rupert has been critical of Kerry's gambling activities and
involvement in Melbourne's Crown Casino.

The *Sunday Telegraph's* success wasn't due only to Bingo
though. At the time, the advertising trade magazine *B&T* ran
an article on the battle of the Sunday papers.

In early 1981 the *Sun-Herald* held a clear lead of 50 000
over the *Sunday Telegraph*. The introduction of Ita
Buttrose in late January [1981] began a steady decline
on the *Sun-Herald's* last audit period, the margin fluc-
tuating between 20 000–30 000. The introduction of
Bingo in September 1981 brought the *Sunday Telegraph*
line ball with the *Sun-Herald* before the end of February
1982. Bingo continued into March and the current
audit period and it was not until early June that the

Sun-Herald introduced Super Bingo with prizes more than $200 000 and began to regain its former margin.

But the *Sun-Herald* had left its run too late. The *Sunday Telegraph* was selling 669 812 each week, the *Sun-Herald* 661 523. There was some criticism about Bingo but it was – and is – hardly new for any newspaper to engage in promotion. 'If you're not doing Bingo you're doing something else', I told *B&T*.

Alan Farrelly and I had done something else, too. Following Rupert's letter about comfort and familiarity, we had studied the *Sun-Herald* thoroughly. We then introduced all of its best qualities into the *Sunday Telegraph*. Bingo provided the finishing touches to our takeover plan. The readers loved Bingo. It took off – so much so that in New South Wales the government began to worry that Bingo could affect the success of Lotto, in which it had an interest. Why buy a Lotto ticket when you could play Bingo for the cost of your favourite newspaper and win great prizes, too. Restrictions were placed on the types of Bingo games we could offer in our newspapers. But given the growth of gambling activities in Australia, the success of Bingo was hardly surprising.

The eighties was a time when the working woman began to have a bigger say in Australia's way of living, from how we shopped to how we did business, holidayed and played. It was a time, too, when women began to raise their voices a little louder. Many men were blissfully unaware of how offensive they sometimes could be. I recollect a lunch with a group of male executives where I reacted to a story that one of the men told. 'Our company has just appointed a woman to an executive position,' he said. 'She is highly qualified and better still, when she prepared some reports for me last week, they were so good you couldn't tell a woman had done them. They could have been done by a man!' When I objected to his condescending attitude, I was told not to get aggressive and feminist.

That was the kind of corporate culture with which businesswomen had to contend. But if women's business advancement had its hiccups, at least there was the realisation that the working woman was here to stay and reaching her had become crucial to the market-driven society. In the eighties, the people who stayed in business were those routinely offering the products, services and shopping conveniences that women were clamouring for. They were also taking more and more responsibility for major purchasing decisions such as cars and holidays. Australian life was being transformed.

There were at least two major changes to shopping habits, both directly related to the then changing role of women. First of all, the fashion industry of the eighties experienced difficult times, because it still assumed it could dictate terms to women on the kind of clothes they would wear. But they were to discover that if women wanted low, casual heels, only to be told that high heels were the look and all that was available, then women would not buy new shoes at all, preferring to make do with what they had.

Women were also fed up with buying their autumn/winter fashions in February with the thermometer doing handstands and somersaults. They also did not want to think about spring/summer fashions in June's winter weather. Australian women were waiting for a resourceful and brave retailer to start marketing when the demand was right, but that would have required a management miracle.

In the eighties, women were far too busy to even think of winter overcoats in February. They just didn't bother because they did not have the time or the inclination. Designers agreed that their goods were in the stores too early, but the retailers just didn't get the message that few women wanted to buy a winter suit in February, only to put it away until the cooler weather came along in May, just to see it selling for half price in June! Not much has changed these days – retailers still offer women winter clothes in February, our hottest month, and then complain that fashion isn't selling well. It never seems to occur to them to ask women what they want and then take the advice they're given. In the eighties, it wasn't something they even considered. There were no women on the boards of the major Australian retailers and very few in anything like top management either.

At an eighties lunch of women chief executives at which he was a special guest, the then managing director of David Jones, Rod Mewing, told us that he hadn't met a woman with the right qualifications to be on the David Jones Board.

This from a man who ran a company where women provided 70 per cent of the buying power! No wonder in the nineties David Jones briefly lost its way and in 1997 posted a 40 per cent drop in profitability. Rod Mewing never knew how close he came to getting my lunch in his lap! These days, with a new management team and a period of cost-cutting and reconstruction, David Jones is working hard to regain market share. Its flagship Elizabeth Street store in Sydney is considered to be Australia's most beautiful store and the retailer's current CEO, Peter Wilkinson, is conscious of the importance of meeting the fashion needs of his stores' customers.

Back in the eighties retailers consistently failed to do this. For instance, they ignored women's changing taste in fabrics. Busy women wanted easy-care, easy-wear fabrics that were of good quality and would take them from the office and then out to dinner if necessary. They stopped buying clothes that needed constant ironing or care because they didn't have the time to waste on such chores. Yet fashion houses continued to offer women clothes they no longer wanted to wear, and they still are. Women dress far more casually these days, even for the office, but there are still rows of boring 'little suits' being offered to them. Power dressing is no longer fashionable, or necessary, for the successful businesswoman.

The second major casualty of women's changing role was retail trading hours. Women were asking for extended hours (but the retailers were resisting, of course, with the same 'heads in the sand' mentality that has always plagued their progress). It is a sad but undisputed fact of life that most men hate to shop and, in my experience, most of them aren't much good at it either! They are far too impatient for one thing, and are reared on the old 'shoot it, bag it, take it home' mentality, which would drive a discerning woman shopper mad. Women did not stop shopping once they entered the workplace. But having become full-time workers, they simply couldn't shop during the day with regular opening and closing hours. They needed, indeed demanded, a new sensitivity on the part of retailers toward their plight. Clever retailers would have realised they were on to a jackpot if they could corner the market of accessibility. I fancy women would have paid just about anything for that in the eighties.

In reality, trading hours were a major deterrent for most shoppers, not just working women. Convenience, surely the most important element of retail trading, was something retailers chose to overlook. It was too much bother because – and I'm sure this was a crucial factor – they would have to change the ways they were doing things. No one ever wants to do that, do they? Many retailers with their boards of male directors (most of whom had stay-at-home wives) simply could not accept that the working woman was here to stay and that, ultimately, it was this woman who would dictate the way their businesses would operate in the years ahead. In the seventies, Australia's population grew by 17.7 per cent; the workforce grew by 24.9 per cent, while the percentage of women in the workforce grew by 37.6 per cent. By 1980, 50 per cent of married women under the age of 54 were working. How could retailers have been so blind as to what was going on?

Reaching the working woman with their advertisements and getting her to spend was a major headache, but still they didn't think of opening at the right times for her. Time-savers in products and services became the working woman's lifesavers. When buying food, for example, she no longer shopped around as intuitively as she once might have done. She settled for the corner store or any shop that suited her needs and, when she began to include pantyhose and cos-metics on her weekly shopping list, forced supermarkets to expand their offerings, a move that cut into the traditional markets and department-store territory.

Convenience killed many small businesses, like delis and butchers, as did the development of the large, one-stop supermarket. Labour-saving devices such as the microwave and TV dinners also began to emerge. Families began to eat out more, because women didn't have the time, or the energy, to cook dinner at night. Women's changing role brought about many adjustments in our shopping habits, yet there was continued resistance from retailers and unions to their demand for an extension and liberalisation of shopping hours. It had worked elsewhere such as the USA and Britain and those countries hadn't fallen apart, so why couldn't we do the same thing here?

Saturday morning was the most horrible day of the week

for many working mothers in those dark ages. We not only had to get all our shopping done on a Saturday morning before closing time at noon, but also get the kids to their sports commitments. It was always a sickening rush, and I'm sure I wasn't the only woman who staggered home with a terrible headache after buying the meat, groceries, fruit and vegetables, picking up the dry-cleaning and whatever else had to be done between nine and noon. It was dreadful and the last pressure women needed in their already stressful lives.

The change in shopping hours finally began in Sydney in the eighties, with late-night shopping on one night of the week. This was followed by shops staying open beyond noon on a Saturday. Then consumers began to call for Sunday trading as well as Saturday. Nowadays, supermarkets like Woolworths and Coles, for instance, trade seven days a week from early in the morning until late at night. Customers can shop till they drop whenever it suits them. The change in trading hours might have happened sooner if retailers had had the sense to move women into the upper echelons of management, so they could keep their fingers on the pulse of shopping trends. After all, who better to understand the needs of women shoppers than women executives? Alas, some things never change.

Australian retail management, with one or two exceptions, like much of Australian management, has never enjoyed a good reputation. The Karpin Report (1995) reinforced this. In its report to the Federal Government it said that Australia

Ita Buttrose

lacked managers with vision and know-how. Most women
who have ever strived for top management know that only
too well. The great torrent of women who had flooded into
the workforce in the sixties and seventies had settled for fairly
low-paid jobs because they were happy just to have an income.
Of course, the push came for equal pay and job conditions,
but even today there is still room for improvement. In the
eighties, however, there were not many women in the upper
levels of management in Australian industry. I was one of very
few to have a leading role in any organisation and I often felt
isolated and wished for the company of other women.

In 1983, I spoke at a Leader's Lunch in Perth, an initiative of the then Premier Brian Burke. I listed Australia's
top ten companies, all of whom had no women at the
helm or on the board and hadn't really given the situation
much thought either. Things were going well enough, why
rock the boat?

In fact, mine was a very solitary role as a leading corporate figure and a woman. The eighties were a difficult time
for aspiring women. Men had put up more roadblocks.
I think they were somewhat in awe of the momentum that
had begun in the seventies and they were marking time in
the eighties. It must have dawned on some of them that
women had plenty of patience – after all we'd been waiting
for quite some time and we'd been able to see first-hand the
many mistakes that men had made. What's more, some men
even confessed to such things in the bedroom, never realising that women were happy to learn from their mistakes,

wherever they heard about them. In my view, the whole feminist movement ground to a halt in the eighties, unsure what to do next to advance its position.

Even though a great deal of lip service was paid to women's advancement in the eighties, it didn't amount to much. There was very little change, as a close examination of company structure, parliament and even the union movement shows – in spite of women like Jennie George, the first woman president of the Australian Council of Trade Unions (ACTU), who was succeeded in March 2000 by Sharan Burrows. Jennie joined the ACTU executive in 1983 and like many an ambitious woman before her has had a traumatic time, and partly because she has a deep – some say almost masculine – voice. So many personal things come into play when businesswomen's performances are judged, none of which has anything to do with how she is doing her job. I'd be a rich woman if I'd been given a dollar for every time someone has said to me that were 'turned off' by Jennie's voice.

My old magazine adversary Dulcie Boling, who used to edit *New Idea* before it went down-market and suffered a serious circulation drop, spoke for many women when in an interview with the Melbourne *Herald* in August 1985, she said:

> I think women are very resented in business, very much so. In a lot of businesses, women are there as tokens; people watch them very carefully. If you put

a man into a senior position, his colleagues are probably very supportive, give a lot of advice and help, and he can make mistakes. But if a woman makes mistakes, it's highlighted, people are waiting for you to fall flat on your face.

Women get confusing advice from a wide range of sources. I'm forever reading articles on how women should conduct themselves, what they should do, what they should wear. You never see articles which say 'Forget about all of that garbage, get on with the job, put your head down and your tail up, learn your business very thoroughly, forget yourself and get on with the job'.

Dulcie's advice was spot on! In the eighties there were simply too many token women. Something significant was happening however, but because it was something to do with women, it more or less went unnoticed. Women were becoming better educated but there was still room for improvement as the National Policy for the Education of Girls, released by the Commonwealth Schools Commission in 1987, reminded us. It found that 'girls were less likely to do maths and science courses and that compared with similar boys schools, many single-sex girls schools lacked the facilities and staff for physical education as well as many aspects of science and technical education'.

The report told of girls at a coeducational school who claimed the only place they could meet to escape the harassment of the boys was the toilets. At another school in an industrial suburb with high levels of unemployment, teachers reported that girls fell asleep during the day, having worked through the night helping their mothers who worked from home as low-paid outworkers. But even worse, I thought, was the number of girls who told the Commission that they would rather be boys than girls, because they thought boys had a better deal from day one.

Never in my bleakest moments have I wished I was a boy and I doubt we'd find many girls now who feel that way. Things have changed. It's not girls who have low self-esteem and enthusiasm these days – it's boys. Girls are forging ahead, and I am delighted. But as the mother of a son, I worry for our boys.

The eighties were good to me and challenging. I was voted Australia's most popular woman for the second time and Bob Hawke, by then Prime Minister, was voted the most popular man, also both times in 1979 and 1984. I was also voted as the best-known woman in Australia. In another poll, people were asked who they would most like to be if not themselves. More women said me than anyone else, but I'm sure they'd change their mind if they knew how hard I worked. For instance, as I correct this book it is 6.30 a.m. on a Sunday and I expect to still be hard at work doing this until midnight!

Towards the end of 1983, John Laws rang and invited me to lunch. Over a particularly good bottle of white (John has such style!) he asked if I'd consider filling in for him while he took some time off. John had throat trouble and was planning a long break. He told me he thought I was a natural and would have a bright future in radio if I ever gave up print. My adrenalin was bubbling. John had offered me a new challenge – something I thrive on.

Radio was every bit as enjoyable as he had told me it would be. It is a wonderful medium – powerful, instant, demanding, but great fun. I loved it. Radio is competitive and incomparable in dealing with basic news. It is able to get off the mark quicker than print and television and I venture to say it is, as a rule, more accurate. When 'Lawsie' returned from holidays, 2UE confirmed his opinion of my potential and offered me the afternoon show. I took it.

I relinquished my job as Editor-in-Chief of the *Daily Telegraph* and continued on with my *Sunday Telegraph* responsibilities. My days were controlled by the clock. My father called it a 'timetable life'. I rose early to exercise, make the children's lunches, and read the papers before driving the kids to their respective schools in time to be at News Ltd by nine, and by eleven I was on my way to 2UE to do the twelve-thirty to three shift. By three-twenty I was driving back to News Ltd. I also made the weekly radio and TV commercials for the *Sunday Telegraph* and wrote my weekly column which was syndicated to other Sunday newspapers in the News group around Australia, giving me a weekly readership of over four million. As with the *Weekly*, I regularly received a great many letters from readers, which kept me well and truly in touch with the everyday concerns of Australians.

I also learned to drive, something I'd never bothered about before. Not long after I'd become Editor of the *Weekly* Kerry had given me a Mercedes and a driver as a birthday gift. I had been happy enough to get a bus to work, something that horrified Kerry and ACP Finance Controller Harry Chester when they found out. They just couldn't believe the Editor of *The Australian Women's Weekly* travelled by public transport. It didn't worry me at all because I found the bus journey relaxing. I'd touch up my nails (quite a skill on a bumpy, double-decker bus) and then read the papers.

News Ltd was happy to include a car in my package but alas no driver, so there was nothing for it but to learn to drive. I asked my brothers to give me some driving lessons, took a week off work for an intensive course with a driving school teacher, and got my licence when I was forty-one. Afterwards, when I would drop Kate off to school with P plates on my car, she would tell me she was proud of me and that her school friends considered me a role model.

The eighties taught me a very valuable lesson, summed up by a couple of experiences. The first is best illustrated by a comment made by Denise Everingham, wife of the then Chief Minister of the Northern Territory, in 1979. She said that the community would have to come to terms with what she described as employment emancipation. She argued that although women were becoming more prevalent in the workforce in general, it was still unusual to find women occupying top positions in business, commerce, the public service and politics. She said, 'Unfortunately, we have often uncomfortable evidence that what society believes, and what society does, can be two different things.'

This was in spite of the fact that by now more than two million Australian women were in the Australian workforce, making up more than a third of the total national workforce. Yet the rules which governed work, and which were originally and quite reasonably set up to apply to a virtually all-male workforce, still predominantly applied. There was no thought given to modifying them to account for the large proportion of women who went out to work each day. Women choosing professional careers were expected to organise their careers the same way as men.

It wasn't easy. Perhaps this was part of the reason for the lack of women in top positions. Wherever you looked at the beginning of the eighties, the picture was bleak. For instance, there were no women in the top of banking, although the Bank of New South Wales (now Westpac) 'bragged' about their one female assistant manager in Rockhampton, Queensland, assuring everyone that it was a very large branch! This, of course, was the very able Helen Lynch who worked her way up through the ranks to become Westpac's Chief General Manager of Corporate Affairs before leaving the bank in 1994.

Political leaders may have admitted that the working woman was here to stay, but a look at the political scene of those times was hardly encouraging for any woman with political ambition. There were only six women in the Federal Senate, no women in the Federal House of Representatives, and the six State parliaments had only 22 women members out of a total of 553.

Denise Everingham's quote is also well illustrated by the treatment given to Lindy Chamberlain. In 1985, I had the fantastic (for a journalist) opportunity of speaking to Lindy and her husband, Michael, for a series of articles I wrote for the *Sun*. Their lives were caught up by a public drama far greater than themselves. Their fellow Australians had judged them long before they went on trial. Lindy became a martyr, not for the public good, but because we simply could not accept her non-emotional image. She was just too strong for her own good, an incredible example of superwoman, that we as a society could not understand. Perhaps she was living proof that what we believe and what we do are often contradictory.

On 30 October 1982, after two inquests and a trial Lindy Chamberlain had been sentenced to life imprisonment for the death of her daughter, Azaria, in 1980 at the Ayers Rock campsite in the Northern Territory. She and Michael were there holidaying with Azaria, and their sons, Aidan and Regan. The baby disappeared and Lindy said that a dingo had taken it. The prosecutor didn't believe her. Neither did the jury. She was sent to Berrimah Jail, a bleak prison in Darwin, with no parole period. Michael, was given a suspended sentence as an accessory after the fact, and placed on a good behaviour bond.

His thoughts about Lindy were revealing. He said, 'I'm sure she sheds many tears but she is not the kind of woman who puts her heart on her sleeve'. All of Australia knew that. Her stiff upper lip had lost her valuable public sympathy and support. Intriguingly, at her trials it seemed half the men in Australia were in love with her – if not her, then her strong image – while most women disapproved of her. Because she appeared as a strong, determined woman and most women hated her for it.

After I talked to her in jail in Darwin, I wrote:

Lindy Chamberlain sat across the table from me, looking small and frail. During her trial she had been 42 kilograms heavier. She is now thirty-two and a shadow of that silent, stony-faced woman. She is a woman with hope still, but a woman hurt by the constant rumours circulating about her. The one that stung her most was the rumour that Azaria had died as a ritual sacrifice in some way. It was claimed that Azaria meant 'sacrifice in the wilderness'. Lindy told me sternly that the name Azaria meant 'blessed of God'. When I asked her if she had murdered her baby, she looked at me and said no she hadn't.

I believed her, but many did not. If only she'd broken down in court, I'm sure the public perception would have been different. Quite possibly she might not have been sent to prison either. But Lindy told me she believed her jury's inability to understand the complexities of the forensic evidence in her case, led to her being jailed.

After my interview with her was published, her mother, Avis, wrote to me, and gave a completely different picture of Lindy.

Oh, if people could only know how she loved tiny Azaria, how wonderfully happy she was to have a little girl of her very own. Not for anything would she have harmed a single hair of her head. If people had witnessed and listened to the heartrending sobbing that we have on so many occasions, they would understand the depth of grief and the heart-brokenness that Lindy experienced. She has never been one to let the world see how she feels . . .

Did the world in their hunger for sensational gossip forget that this little lass had had a precious baby snatched away by death and later another baby twice cruelly taken from her? As the North American Indians say, 'We should not criticise another until we have walked two weeks in their moccasins'. We have not the slightest question that the truth will come out. Lindy's name will be completely cleared, allowing her to come back home to all of us and be with her little ones again where it is her right to be.

Almost three and a half years later, after further evidence was found at the alleged murder scene at Ayer's Rock, the Northern Territory Government unconditionally released her. Simultaneously, a report by South Australia's chief forensic scientist, Dr Andrew Scott, challenged the assessment of forensic evidence used against her. Lindy's conviction was quashed in 1998. She and Michael later divorced. Lindy remarried and lived in the United States for some years before returning to make her home in the Hunter Valley in New South Wales.

'Affirmative action' were buzzwords for women in the eighties. Dr Anne Summers took over as head of the Office for the Status of Women in the Prime Minister's Department in 1983, and later claimed the affirmative action policy was her greatest achievement because it argued for real jobs based upon real 'merit'. People were suspicious of it nonetheless. Many asked why equal opportunity wasn't enough.

Anne argued that equal opportunity needed affirmative action to become a reality. EO was the objective and the goal; affirmative action was the way to get there. The legislation required that companies report to the Federal Government once a year about what they had done to advance women. The goal of the affirmative action policy was a series of techniques to ensure that women had equal opportunity.

It was a natural enough step to take at the time. After all, by 1986 women comprised 39 per cent of the entire workforce. Anne Summers was an example of the new working woman of the eighties. She was strong and outspoken; highly educated, with a PhD. Her book *Damned Whores and God's Police*, which told the story of the history of women in Australian society, was successfully submitted for her Doctorate of

Philosophy. It sold more than 30 000 copies and was used as a textbook by universities and schools.

Anne was concerned about the hostility of women towards other women, particularly those climbing into the seats of power in a man's world. Their reaction was similar to that public antipathy shown toward Lindy Chamberlain. We created superwoman, but it seemed we did not want to live with her.

Jim McClelland, the former Labor politician, lawyer, Whitlam Government minister, judge and Royal Commissioner, said in 1986:

> Women should work. Total domesticity is fatal to the development of personality. Women are better than men are. I mean it. They have more guts, less vanity. There are very few men who in their bones accept women as their equal.

That was very true in the eighties. Bronwyn Bishop, a minister in the Howard Government, was an up-and-comer during the eighties. She failed to gain a Senate seat in 1984, but in September 1985 she became the first woman to head the Liberal Party in New South Wales. As president, she said she had two ambitions: 'I want to see Nick Greiner elected as Premier of New Wales and John Howard, Prime Minister of Australia'. She must have had a better crystal ball than most – both men made it.

I once asked her if she found it tough to hold down a

job traditionally reserved for men. She replied, 'Not really. I hadn't really plotted out or predicted exactly how I thought it would be. I knew it would be challenging. I am enjoying it. I'm a tough old bird'. After the political shock of 1993, when John Hewson led the Liberals and lost the unlosable Federal election, Bronwyn was even touted in some circles as a possible contender for the Lodge, but in 1985 she was just another token woman who was said to have got the New South Wales job because she was a woman. She would have none of that, though. 'No way, I won that election on merit,' she said. But she earlier admitted, 'A woman's fight against men in politics is a lifetime's work'.

Even women who were not in politics could appreciate the sentiment. We may have had affirmative action, but there wasn't much to show for it. Women striving for advancement in the corporate sector were continually hitting their head on that wretched glass ceiling.

At an Australian Institute of Management function in Melbourne in November 1987 I repeated something I often said in those times:

Intelligent corporations should or must link their future with the advancement of women executives. If business and industry are to make full use of all the human talent in Australia, there must be profound changes in both the structure and attitudes of our corporate thinking.

Any company wishing to increase its activities

should welcome and encourage the supply of talent provided by women seeking executive positions. The working woman/wife household is the dominant segment in the Australian market. It has particularly important implications for consumer products, companies and organisations that provide them with marketing and communications support services.

Having female executives involved in the development, evaluation, marketing, distribution and sale of produce will provide management with daily direct access to the ultimate consumer. Intelligent corporations should or must link their future with the advancement of women executives.

It's simple really. Ask a woman what she wants, listen and then deliver. In other words, companies that want to market successfully to women would be advised to seek their input on how best to do this. But not in Australia, and certainly not in the eighties. Australian management was comfortable doing things the way they had always done them. There was very little real change in attitude, although there was plenty of talk about advancing women.

Enterprising women with ambition were only too aware of the barriers and there were times when the glass ceiling seemed too impenetrable. Women began to talk among themselves about opting out of corporate life and setting up their own businesses. They were weary of fighting the fragile male ego.

Other things were happening, too. For the first time we heard about something called 'women's burnout'. I identified with this immediately. I was working hard and trying to cope with the myriad demands made on me, as well as caring for Kate and Ben. I knew my body was sending me warning signals. Like most working mothers I was always close to exhaustion. Not that I told anyone. At this point in the eighties women still weren't ready to admit that they perhaps were overloaded. I was no different from my sisters. I was still in superwoman mode.

I interviewed a Melbourne psychologist, Dr Francis McNab, for *Woman's Day* in 1985 and he said women were committed to performing at work, to working in the home, to being a good wife, or a friend or a lover, and to being a mother. Men on the other hand usually had only two areas of required performance – they had to be a husband and they had to perform well at work.

McNab warned that women suffering burnout often were too tired to perform their mothering duties in the best interests of their children. 'Although many mothers who are working do give a great deal of attention to their children,' McNab said, 'our society hasn't given parents, and particularly women, the kind of support and back-up they require.'

At the same time, when Californian businesswoman Carole Orsborn set up an organisation called Superwomen Anonymous in America with the motto 'Enough is Enough', she had two thousand members in two weeks. She wasn't happy. She didn't like the life she was leading. Her children were a success, so were her marriage and her career, but she was a mess. Tired and tense most of the time, she knew she wasn't leading a quality lifestyle. It probably marked the beginning of the end of superwoman.

But not here. Not yet. Australian businesswomen were still preoccupied with that never-ending task of finding ways to make their voices effectively heard. When my good friend, Sydney publisher Barbara Cail asked me to be a foundation member of Women Chiefs of Enterprise (later a group of us broke away and established Chief Executive Women), I didn't hesitate to say yes. The organisation fulfilled a long overdue need for women who had made it to the top to meet and to network with others of a similar ilk. It was wonderful to have each other's support, because most of us did feel isolated in the rarified atmosphere in which we worked. Our aim was to break down barriers that hindered women's progress and to come up with solutions to problems we encountered in and out of the boardroom.

Many of Australia's best-known businesswomen joined Women Chiefs, among them fashion designer Carla Zampatti; the clever Imelda Roche from Nutri-Metics; family planning pioneer and then deputy chair of the ABC, Wendy McCarthy; the banking executive, now multiple company director, Helen Lynch. Some great friendships that still endure today, began.

During the eighties, I received many tempting offers of employment. The headhunting firm Spencer Stuart and

Associates invited me to submit my name to the board for the ABC as a candidate for the post of Managing Director of the Corporation. I am a great believer in and supporter of the ABC, but I knew I wouldn't be happy working with the then board – well-meaning people I am sure, but without much, if any, practical experience in administering a national organisation, and who were light-on in media knowledge and experience.

Robert Holmes à Court sent his General Manager, John Reynolds, to talk to me about a job in Perth on his *Western Mail* and to anchor a current affairs program on his TV Station Channel 7. This was a tempting offer, but I thought it best that the children stay in Sydney close to their father. I wanted them to have a good relationship with him and he with them.

While I was enjoying radio, I wasn't sure if I wanted to stay on at the *Sunday Telegraph* and I was uncertain about which direction to take. My dilemma resolved itself quite unexpectedly when I got a late-night phone call in November 1984 from the then Federal Health Minister, Neal Blewett. When I said yes to his offer of chairing the National Advisory Committee on AIDS (NACAIDS), I took on an extraordinary assignment that would test me in ways that I would never have thought possible.

5

AIDS and the Eighties

By the time AIDS regresses, as no doubt it will, society will be different. We will have learnt a great deal about the problems of human behaviour, how difficult it is for people to change. There will be a great many deaths, a great deal of suffering and a huge cost to the public purse.

Professor David Penington, Chairman of the AIDS Task Force, June 1985

David Penington was correct. On a personal level, AIDS did teach me a great deal about human behaviour. AIDS is the kind of thing that brings out either the very worst or very best in people. When Neal Blewett told me that the Federal Government thought I had a role to play in helping to stop the spread of AIDS in Australia, I felt it was my duty to do so.

Blewett told me the Government was looking for 'a major public communicator in whom the public had great confidence, someone who would tell them the truth about a virus called AIDS, someone who could give Australia's most serious and expensive public health problem the high profile it needed'.

But when I agreed in 1984 to chair the National Advisory Committee on AIDS (NACAIDS) I had no idea of the extent of the project I was about to undertake. I'm pretty sure David Penington didn't realise how onerous his job would be either. I didn't know much about AIDS but then no one did, not even the medical profession.

Blewett later told me that when he took over the health portfolio in 1983, he came across a file note that said something like: 'Oh yes, there is a virus called AIDS. It seems to affect gay men'. We were soon to find out that AIDS represented one of the biggest threats to mankind that we could imagine. Even the World Health Organisation (WHO) confessed that it had underestimated the magnitude of the disease.

NACAIDS' role was to coordinate advice from State governments and community groups to the Federal Government on legal, social and preventative issues and to come up with and implement a national AIDS education strategy. The AIDS Task Force dealt with medical and scientific issues relating to transmission and treatment of the virus.

It didn't take me long to discover just how perplexing the HIV/AIDS virus is. I studied everything I could find on it. I listened to tapes of AIDS conferences and experts when driving in my car. I went to Sydney's St Vincent's Hospital to talk with people with AIDS and also with the many doctors involved in AIDS care and research, particularly

Professor Ron Penny, the Director of Immunology at St Vincent's, who became a good friend.

Ron was generous with his knowledge and an excellent teacher who made sure I understood the medical and scientific consequences of the virus. There's no way I would have been able to talk to the people of Australia as confidently as I did without his early lessons. Ron ultimately became Deputy Chairman of NACAIDS and was also on the AIDS Task Force, which was important, as there needed to be good communication between the two committees.

Unlike many others who accepted government roles, I was one of the few without a hidden agenda. I wasn't seeking another appointment in the health area or any other area for that matter. I wasn't after research or compensation money nor did I want to win the Nobel Prize for finding an AIDS cure. I only ever had one aim – to stop the spread of HIV/AIDS in Australia.

After my appointment was announced, advertising man, John Singleton, rang and told me that AIDS would be bad for my image. He was so convinced of this that in May 1988, when I was Editor-in-Chief of the Sydney *Sun-Herald* and his agency had the paper's advertising account, he had me researched – without my knowledge – before he would 'allow' me to be used as the *Sun-Herald* presenter on TV.

Jeanne Strachan from Inview Market Research Analysis reported back.

There has been little change in Ita's credibility or

recognition in five years. I was surprised by your question regarding Ita Buttrose's association with NACAIDS. Her AIDS work has if anything improved her status in the community by extending her authority, particularly with male viewers, beyond the magazine and newspaper sphere. There is no doubt she is a most authoritative and recognisable national presenter.

AIDS not only made Australians think about their sexual activity, it changed their perception about the medical profession. When AIDS came along and doctors had to admit they didn't know how to stop its spread, people were shocked. How could they not have some instant cure up their sleeves? The medical profession found it as hard to believe as the rest of us. What's more, a great many of them were frightened of getting AIDS, not only because of their own sexual behaviour and drug-taking habits – doctors are no different from the rest of the human race – but also because they were at the coalface and had to treat people with the virus. People were not routinely tested for AIDS when they went to hospital; therefore it wasn't possible to know if they carried the virus. Doctors felt they were being asked to play a kind of Russian roulette.

Strange as it may seem, I sometimes get the impression some people are upset – even resentful – that Australia was successful in slowing down the spread of HIV/AIDS. This is particularly so with the second wave of the epidemic into the drug-using community which has occurred in many other countries, including the United States. Australians were told in the early days of AIDS awareness that hundreds of thousands of people might die from AIDS – why didn't that happen?

It didn't happen because Australia was quick off the mark with its education programs, which were thorough and effective; and because Neal Blewett managed to persuade his political colleagues in all parties that prompt action and funding was needed to educate Australians about the threat that the virus represented. The World Health Organisation has consistently praised Australia for its approach and hailed us as a model for other countries to emulate.

The first case of AIDS in Australia was diagnosed in 1982. In April 1987, Blewett told the Parliament that there were 442 cases of full-blown AIDS of whom 238 had died. There were no accurate figures on how many people were actually infected with the virus. But in 1985, Penington announced that the Task Force estimated that there were at least 50 000 people with the virus in Australia. Blewett later repeated this estimate when he spoke to Parliament in 1987.

Australia was one of the first countries to get a national AIDS education program up and running, which I am sure is one of the reasons we have been so successful in slowing down the transmission of the virus. We were also the first country in 1985 to introduce screening in all the nation's Red Cross blood banks. We could have been quicker with the latter, as people with haemophilia know only too well.

But blood bank screening was a controversial issue. When it became apparent in the early eighties that AIDS was a disease spread by blood, and in Australia seemed to be confined (as far as anyone then knew) to the homosexual community, some public health officials said that all gay men should be stopped from donating blood. The gay community found this unacceptable and discriminatory, arguing that there was no proof that all gay men were infected or in danger.

Not surprisingly, in the early days of the virus when community fear was at its highest, gays distrusted everyone. Later, they saw AIDS as an opportunity to build a power base and edge out everyone else who wasn't homosexual. But in the beginning they were frightened, which was understandable. Many gay men had friends with the virus. They knew the prognosis. How many gay men would die before a cure was found? Before AIDS, many gay men had come out of the closet. The general community had become more tolerant of their choice of lifestyle. Would AIDS force gays back into the closet? Would they be persecuted because of AIDS? Would they be blamed for its spread? Would AIDS put the cause of gay rights back to what they considered the dark ages? Any decision that seemed to deny them their rights was challenged by the gay community, including their right to donate blood. They argued that only promiscuous gay men got AIDS.

It was in this kind of environment that a medical

committee, the forerunner to the AIDS Task Force and chaired by Penington, had to determine who could give blood and came up with the recommendation that 'promiscuous gay men would be asked not to give blood'. The early, pre-1985 days were difficult ones for the medical profession. In an interview he gave to journalist Michael Gawenda, (now Editor and Associate Publisher of the paper) in the Melbourne *Age* on 2 May 1987, Dr Ian Gust, one of Australia's foremost virologists and head of the virus unit at Melbourne's Fairfield Hospital, gave an insight into some of the pressures he and his colleagues experienced.

> For those of us who have been deeply involved, it has been tremendously confronting and an enormous learning experience. We have had to confront issues we had never previously considered and deal with aspects of human behaviour we had not known about. It had confronted us with our own prejudices and forced us to examine our own sexuality.
>
> Sometimes in our desire to show we lack prejudice, some of us have been excessively tolerant. Sometimes we have made recommendations, which were more moderate than they should have been in order not to offend groups, which were under enormous pressure anyway, groups threatened with annihilation.

Gust told Gawenda that the watered-down blood bank recommendation was a mistake. We as public health workers should have acted according to the worst case scenario rather than the best. What was a promiscuous gay man, anyway? As a consequence we had infected blood donated.

People with haemophilia were badly affected by the virus. By 1985/86, some 30 per cent of them had acquired HIV through infected blood products. NACAIDS member Jenny Ross, who later became Executive Director of the Haemophilia Foundation, had heard information from the United States about fears regarding the safety of America's blood supply early in 1983. She began to agitate for better screening of blood here, but her warnings seem to have fallen on deaf ears. Australia's blood supply was made partially 'safe' when donor-screening forms were intro- duced in 1984, and 'safer' when HIV testing began in April 1985.

In 1984 NACAIDS wasn't convinced that the Red Cross blood bank was being run as well as it should be. But getting our concerns across was difficult, because the blood bank was a kind of sacred cow and it wasn't the done thing to criticise this essential voluntary organisation, run by well-meaning retired medical practitioners and haematologists. We were particularly worried about the delays of some Commonwealth and State committees in setting up adequate screening programs.

Finally, I wrote to Blewett with NACAIDS' view that much

better management practices needed to be put in place at the blood bank. Blewett rang me in somewhat of a panic. What if 'others' got their hands on my letter? Under the *Freedom of Information Act*, it was possible. NACAIDS' concerns could cause people to panic, Blewett said. As I told him, we weren't left with any other option but to write – unable to get any action any other way, we felt it was the only means left to us to ensure necessary steps were taken to improve the way the blood bank was being run. It was something that could wait no longer.

We were greatly relieved when the Government took our advice and acted on it. Better management practices were put into place at the blood bank. Later in 1989, people with medically acquired AIDS were given $13.2 million by the Federal Government, to start a Trust Fund. Financial settlements in all States followed over the next three years, in total over $100 million. Some argue that this represents an acceptance of some responsibility. Others dispute this, saying you can't accept responsibility for something you don't know!

NACAIDS' first meeting in 1984 was incredible. There we were – a diverse bunch of people, most of whom had never met before. There were Penington and Penny, Dr Tony Adams (the New South Wales Chief Medical Officer), Cath Healy (a nurse representing the ACTU), Jenny Ross, Phil Carswell and Lex Watson representing the gay community, Dr Jenny Lind from the AMA, Red Cross representative Noreen Minogue and a couple of people from the Commonwealth Health Department. None of us was properly introduced, including David Penington and myself. Nor did anyone from the Commonwealth Health Department talk to us together about what they hoped our respective committees would achieve. We were more or less sat at a table and told to get on with it. So we did.

But it wasn't all smooth sailing, which wasn't surprising, because almost everything to do with AIDS took us into uncharted territories. I am sure no one on NACAIDS, or the AIDS Task Force, ever imagined that one day we'd be talking to the nation about its sexual habits in our effort to stop the spread of AIDS. It appeared to be difficult for some members of the medical profession to accept that there was a need for all kinds of skills apart from medical and scientific ones. As almost anyone who has ever been to a doctor knows, as communicators many of them leave much to be desired, yet if AIDS educational strategies were to succeed, then effective and honest communication was vital.

It was apparent right from the beginning that David Penington didn't feel happy about NACAIDS, although it was never clear why. Although a member of the committee he publicly challenged NACAIDS on a series of issues, one of the first being the appropriate role of antibody testing in AIDS education. Blewett had to call a special summit to obtain a consensus – something Penington didn't like. It was agreed that while testing should not be undertaken lightly or indiscriminately, all individuals at risk of AIDS should be encouraged to seek confidential counselling; that the decision to have the test performed should be made voluntarily by the individual being tested, with informed consent, with every endeavour to guarantee confidentiality and with the full knowledge of the medical, social and legal implications. It was agreed, too, that testing did not represent a solution to the AIDS crisis.

Penington often challenged Blewett's authority and once accused Neal of plans to cut funding. Penington frequently preferred to do things his way. For instance, when NACAIDS set up a working party to advise on the development of prevention strategies for both urban and rural Aborigines, I wrote to him three times asking for the AIDS Task Force participation and for someone from the Task Force to be on the committee.

On 19 November 1986, Penington finally replied, but not to me. He wrote to Blewett:

> The question of representation of the Task Force on the Working Party established by NACAIDS to advise on AIDS in Aborigines was discussed. It was the unanimous view of the Task Force that it would not be appropriate for us to be represented on that Working Party. Rather we would be happy to provide whatever advice is of value to the Aboriginal community directly and would be available to assist the Department of Aboriginal Affairs in the development of their own strategies.

He later bypassed the Federal Government in advising

the northern States on the screening of Aboriginal communities. Penington knew of HIV-positive Aborigines in the Northern Territory and recommended sending a Senior Health Department official to investigate and report back. But only that – to report back.

No one on NACAIDS could understand why the Task Force members thought it would be 'inappropriate' for them to be represented on the Working Party. The threat of AIDS to Aborigines was all too real for there not to be a united approach to AIDS education in their communities. Being left to deal with it ourselves, NACAIDS invited submissions from Aborigines so they could develop their own AIDS prevention strategies. I visited several remote Aboriginal communities in the Kimberley and Pilbara regions of Western Australia in 1987, some of which could be reached only in a single-engine aircraft. Conditions were primitive, some as bad as I've seen in Africa. Some worse.

The Aboriginal elders knew all too well the threat AIDS represented to Aborigines. They knew the need for education programs. One of their most successful initiatives was Condoman – who was a dead ringer for the Phantom, a hero among young Aboriginal men. When he had sex with a new partner whose sexual activity was unknown to him, Condoman was smart – he used condoms. It was a simple, effective message. The only people who didn't like it were the American owners of the Phantom copyright!

A great many people had a view on how education programs should be conducted and who should be in charge of them. Some people didn't want them run at all. Some of the States (especially Queensland) simply wanted to trace infected people. In New South Wales, there was talk of quarantining people with the virus.

The media was sometimes hysterical about AIDS and all too frequently went overboard and ran stories with headlines that caused people to worry unnecessarily, too – like 'Mosquitoes cause AIDS', 'Swimming pools – AIDS danger', 'AIDS virus could be passed on in teacups', 'Public toilets: risk of AIDS'. At a press conference in the early eighties, Neal Blewett urged a commonsense approach, adding: 'One of our great worries is the amount of alarmist reporting, some of it quite irresponsible.'

The Government made some errors but then why wouldn't it? We elect men and women to Parliament because we assume they think like we do. There was no rulebook on AIDS that could be consulted. No government had ever had to cope with a deadly virus with no cure and at the same time discuss sexual practices, condoms, homosexuality, blood transfusions and death with its electorate. Parents have trouble telling their children the facts of life – even doctors find it hard to talk to their patients about sex. Not surprisingly, politicians found it equally difficult to confront the men and women of Australia about such things. AIDS took a great many of us into unknown realms.

In September 1985 I interviewed Ron Penny for my column in the *Sun*. 'We're seeing the loss of reason against emotion,' he said. 'The large bulk of the community, the heterosexual members, will not get AIDS but they're the ones making all the fuss and they're influencing decisions that really should be made by people primarily at risk – that is homosexual men, bisexual men, intravenous drug users and prostitutes.'

But in 1986, Penington returned from the June AIDS conference in Paris with the news that the risk of AIDS spreading to the heterosexual community had been firmly placed on the international agenda. He told Blewett that the world medical and scientific opinion was that there was a very real risk of the AIDS virus spreading into the heterosexual community and that there was a need for a campaign to shock the Australian public. They had to be alerted to the dangers of AIDS.

NACAIDS, which had the responsibility for national education strategy, appointed a steering committee under the guidance of Bill Taylor, head of the Federal Health Department's Communicable Diseases Branch. Research was commissioned to look at the needs of Australia and come up with an appropriate approach. NACAIDS agreed with Penington's call for shock tactics. Too many Australians were apathetic about AIDS, and they didn't want to change their ways either. The consensus – to use the favourite word of Prime Minister, Bob Hawke – was that we needed something that would make Australians sit up and take notice. The research told us that 98 per cent of Australians believed there was a need for an education campaign to warn people of the risks, but that most

Australians considered AIDS irrelevant – they saw it as somebody else's problem.

Ten agencies pitched for the right to design NACAIDS' educational campaign and some excellent ideas were submitted. After a great deal of deliberation, Grey Advertising was appointed. They knew what we wanted – a campaign that would well and truly alert people to the fact that AIDS represented a potential threat to all sexually active Australians. The Grim Reaper hit the TV screens in April 1987, with a powerful impact. When I first saw the TV commercial, I felt sick in the stomach – the effect of the Grim Reaper was so forceful.

Some people were offended by the advertising campaign. Some were horrified. Some no doubt experienced the same reaction as I had. The campaign showed the Grim Reaper taking his victims, representing different groups within the community, in a sixty-second commercial. The commercial began with a tenpin bowling machine lowering ten people onto the alley. The Grim Reaper bowled a ball down and struck the people down one by one, including a mother and baby.

There were some complaints, particularly from parents who said their children had been frightened by the advertisement. That was positive, since we wanted people to take the disease seriously. On the first day, callers expressing their horror jammed switchboards at television stations throughout Australia. AIDS telephone counselling and information services around Australia, their funding topped up with money from the Federal Government, received 40 000 calls.

Neal Blewett reminded the nation:

> We hoped that parents would discuss the advertisement with their children because it is important in our educational strategy that families talk about AIDS. You have to remember that this commercial is competing with a whole lot of other advertisements, a whole lot of other static there in the community. Unless we can make an impact, then it will get lost among all the other advertising.

Some mothers said that their children were having nightmares. NACAIDS received hundreds of letters, some critical, some full of praise and most wanting more information. My assistant Graeme Head and I worked late into the night for some months answering them all.

Some people criticised the campaign for not being explicit enough. Phillip Adams wrote in the *Australian* that he didn't think the advertisement got to the explicit heart of the matter, and that we should have been willing to 'shun metaphor and euphemism and to mention the unmentionable fact that might save a lot of lives. Namely, that receptive anal intercourse, among homosexuals and heterosexuals, is overwhelmingly the main method by which AIDS is being spread'. Adams believed that the threat of transmission within the heterosexual community by normal vaginal sex had been exaggerated.

David Penington wrote to the Editor of the *Australian* a
few days after Adams' column had appeared.

> Phillip Adams put the view that the sexual trans-
> mission of the virus which causes AIDS is virtually
> restricted to anal intercourse. Your readers should
> know that this is scientifically incorrect . . . although
> I am personally of the view that the transmission of
> infection occurs much more readily with anal inter-
> course than with normal vaginal intercourse.

Although NACAIDS members warned of the dangers of anal
sex when they talked to groups throughout Australia, we had
great difficulty in getting the Federal Government to approve
use of the word 'anal' in our education brochures. On one
occasion, NACAIDS was meeting in Sydney approving the final
text for a number of booklets. We believed Australians would
understand the need to be as frank as possible about the virus
and that the time was now right for the words 'anal intercourse'
to be mentioned in our brochures. We were sure there would
be no major community outcry or harm done to the Government. Research told us that people accepted that AIDS
information had to be explicit.

It was agreed that I should leave the meeting and call
Neal Blewett in Canberra to ask him to okay our
recommendation. I spoke to him three or four times that
afternoon, trying to get him to approve what we wanted to
do. He kept saying he'd get back to me – he had to confer

with his colleagues. Our decision making – or rather the Government's – wasn't helped by the fact that the year was 1987, and Australia soon would be going to the polls. The Government didn't want to do anything that might upset the electorate. On his last call to me, Blewett said he and his colleagues were adamant. No mention was to be made of anal sex in the brochures. The Minister called the shots. There was nothing we could do to change his mind.

NACAIDS could have leaked its disapproval about this decision to the media – some AIDS experts seemed to have a hotline to several journalists and were continually stirring up a hornet's nest. NACAIDS felt there was nothing to be gained by this approach. The Government may not have been brave enough to allow the word 'anal' in print, but there was nothing to stop any of us mentioning it when we talked about AIDS education to community groups and concerned citizens around the country. So that's what we did. We were grateful, though, to Phillip Adams for writing about anal sex. It was a great help to our education strategy. We didn't mind how we got the message across!

In his book, *Australia's Response to* AIDS, Professor John Ballard from the Australian National University commented that some of the informational brochures put out by NACAIDS bore 'the fingerprints of interference by politically timid ministerial offices. There is politics here, but it is the politics of difficult choices'.

That 1987 election campaign came at a bad time for NACAIDS. Our funds were frozen and the release of our education booklets held up. There was to be no spending on anything until after the election. We wasted valuable time on following up with detailed education to maximise the impact the Grim Reaper television commercial had made on the community. The media briefly forgot about AIDS and concentrated on the promises being made to the electorate by Prime Minister Hawke and Opposition Leader, Andrew Peacock. Bob Hawke and Labor were returned to office. Neal Blewett kept the Health portfolio.

The media, however, never forgot – and still hasn't – something I said in an interview with reporter Glenda Banks for the Melbourne *Herald-Sun* in 1987. In a throwaway remark, I told her that along with some other well-known Australians I had decided to become a radical celibate. It didn't seem like an earth-shattering statement to me at the time. Celibacy made sense, given the many uncertainties about the virus. I was somewhat overwhelmed when I saw the newspaper posters 'ITA TELLS: MY LIFE WITHOUT SEX'.

This ultimately led to an incredible encounter with reporter Mike Munro for Channel 9's *Sixty Minutes* in 1989. Mike didn't beat around the bush. 'When did you last have it?' he demanded. I told him to mind his own business. But can you imagine this question being put to a woman anywhere else in the world, or ever being asked of a man? Even now, journalists feel compelled to check on whether or not I'm having 'it', so much so that I worry that if I should ever contemplate another serious relationship I will have to ask the media's permission for true love to take its course.

When I gave the interview to Glenda Banks, I was trying to impress on Australians the need for safe sex and the dangers of multiple sexual partners. If you didn't know where the person you were planning to sleep with had slept the night before, don't do it – that kind of thing. The media may not have got the message, but I'm pretty sure the rest of Australia did.

The Grim Reaper put AIDS on the social and political agenda in Australia to an extent that would have been inconceivable twelve months earlier. By August 1987 AIDS education had been introduced in many schools; the law on the sale of needles and syringes had been liberalised in several States; and for the first time ever condoms were being advertised and sold in supermarkets.

As for the Australian people, 97 per cent of them had seen the Grim Reaper advertisement and 95 per cent of them thought the campaign had increased awareness. There was no doubt that it had. People everywhere were talking about the virus. Australians could never claim that they were not warned about the potential threat of AIDS. Sixty-one per cent of young people aged between sixteen and twenty-four, surveyed after the Grim Reaper advertising, said they were acting or thinking differently as a result.

So much time was wasted on the debate about whether NACAIDS overestimated the threat to the heterosexual community. I was as concerned as everyone else that we should give out the right messages. When I went to the Third World AIDS Conference in Washington in 1987, in an effort to find out the truth, I asked US Surgeon General Everett Koop whether he thought AIDS posed a threat to heterosexuals and he said: 'Yes, because doctors and scientists don't fully understand what the AIDS virus in Africa means to the rest of the world yet. We simply can't rule out that many heterosexuals ultimately could be affected by the virus'.

At Australia's Second National AIDS Conference in Sydney in 1986, the late Dr Jonathan Mann, then WHO's AIDS coordinator, put a forceful case for caution in the heterosexual community and the need for education campaigns. If those of us charged with putting together a national education strategy did not take the advice of the doctors and scientists about AIDS, whose advice were we to take?

Some newspapers suggested that NACAIDS was following 'a gay agenda' which was nonsense and untrue. At the time of the Grim Reaper campaign, of the fourteen members of NACAIDS, only two could have been regarded as representing the interests of homosexuals. I used to wonder who fed journalists such untruths and why they didn't bother to check their facts with me or some other member of NACAIDS.

It seemed difficult, if not impossible, for some journalists to grasp the complexities of AIDS and the issues we had to work through. They were more intent on trivialising issues. It annoys me intensely, even now, to look back over some of the stuff that was written. On 2 May 1987, Michael Gawenda wrote in the *Age*: 'The committee Ita Buttrose chairs is dominated by the gay community, and what the advertisement [Grim Reaper] is designed to do is take the pressure off and say AIDS is everyone else's problem. They don't want it identified as a gay problem.'

Gawenda's source for this incredible accusation was, according to him, 'a leading researcher with the AIDS Task Force'. This was so insulting. NACAIDS had Task Force members on it – David Penington, who had resigned from NACAIDS several months earlier, but had advised Blewett he intended to remain a corresponding member so he would get all NACAIDS' papers, had received and approved all the material relating to the Grim Reaper campaign. Alterations Penington had asked for had been made. Before the Grim Reaper went to air, he saw the complete campaign.

There were other allegations that NACAIDS had 'made up' the threat to heterosexuals, but this is not true. We obtained our medical information and statistics from the doctors on NACAIDS and the Task Force. No one doubted Penington's knowledge about the virus – he was, after all, the expert and everyone on NACAIDS respected that. Prior to the Grim Reaper going to air, in a special supplement in the Melbourne *Age* on 7 April 1987, Penington advised:

There has been clear evidence for over a year that while the infection is predominantly in the male homosexual community, rising numbers have been identified among persons of both sexes who use illicit drugs by intravenous injection. There is also, slow but definite spread among heterosexual individuals, particularly young people with many sex partners.

There were other statements in the Gawenda article that I felt deserved a response. I wrote to the *Age* but was told my letter was too long to print. I couldn't believe it! Here we were in the middle of the most important public health campaign in Australia's history. The *Age* had made allegations about my committee, our strategies and me, and yet they had decided my letter was too long to print. We were the people that the Federal Government had entrusted to tell the Australian people the facts about AIDS, but the *Age* didn't think my letter worthy of publication. My own journalistic experience told me otherwise.

It is not my aim in writing about these things now to stir up old controversies; but I do want to set the record straight. AIDS was the most difficult health issue we, as a nation, had confronted. NACAIDS' aim was to contain the epidemic, not create a situation where – in later years – we would have to preface all our comments on the way we dealt with AIDS with the words 'if only'. If only we'd told everyone how to protect himself or herself; if only we had acknowledged the extent of drug use in our community; if only we had planned for our health services to cope with the magnitude of the problem.

In Federal Parliament, Neal Blewett described AIDS as 'the most serious public health problem to face Australians since Federation'. President Reagan called AIDS Public Enemy Number One. By 1987 more than 20 000 Americans had full-blown AIDS; and the virus had spread rapidly outside of America's homosexual population into the prison population, among drug users, and especially among the poor and under-privileged, such as black and Hispanic Americans.

By 1987, 80 per cent of New York's drug-using community were HIV-positive – some 200 000 people. Unlike Australia – where NACAIDS supported the AIDS Task Force's initiative of the introduction of needle exchange programs so drug users could get a clean needle in exchange for a dirty one – public health officials in New York, as their response to AIDS, actually made needles and syringes harder to obtain. It didn't stop drug taking; it simply made people share needles.

By 1988 AIDS was the biggest killer of women between twenty-five and thirty-four in New York. This was the way it was most feared AIDS would spread to the heterosexual population: through women – women who had sex with men who were either bisexual, or used intravenous drugs. Many infected women are drug users themselves.

Surgeon General Koop told me there might never be a cure for AIDS. 'It could become a disease the world has to learn to live with.' He said he thought that ultimately AIDS would become a disease of the underprivileged and poor. 'Sex is often the only thing they can enjoy without having to spend any money,' he explained.

Looking at the spread of the virus in Africa, India, Thailand, the Philippines, New Guinea, and all countries with a great many people living in poverty, it seems as if Koop's predictions for the virus's future were correct.

AIDS has devastated Africa. I've been there twice – once while I was chair of NACAIDS in 1987, and again in 1995 for

World Vision Australia whom I advised on communication strategies. By 2001 infection rates in sub-Saharan Africa had reached twenty per cent or more of the adult population. South Africa, Namibia and Botswana are likely to lose more than one-fifth of their population by 2010. When I went to Africa in 1995, I heard of a village in Tanzania that had 90 000 orphans.

WHO says that AIDS has wiped out all the health initiatives that have been made in Africa in the last twenty years and predicts that AIDS will have an even greater impact on India, where it estimates 3.6 million people have the virus. Many researchers believe the figure to be much higher since many of the infected have not been tested. Present indications are that by 2010 more than 30 million people in India could be infected with the virus.

Excellent and expensive drug treatments and education programs have allowed Australia to control the epidemic, but that doesn't mean we can ignore what's going on in many of the world's developing countries. By the beginning of 2001, nearly 20 million people globally had died from HIV/AIDS and 35 million people were infected with the virus. If transmission rates continue at their present level, the pandemic will surpass all of the world's previous great plagues, which is a sobering thought. Many countries close to Australia are battling the epidemic, but seem to lack the know-how, means and initiative to do so effectively. I believe we have a role to play here and that it's in our interests to see that the region in which we live and trade prospers. Australian expertise should be available to assist countries like China (estimated to have 10 million HIV-positive cases by the end of 2010), New Guinea, Vietnam, Cambodia, Thailand, Burma, Malaysia and Indonesia to develop massive, long-term AIDS education and care strategies.

Combining NACAIDS with my other commitments left me little time for much else. Sometimes I lamented not having time for a few simple pleasures like a walk in the park. Most days I rose at 5.15 a.m. and went flat out all day before collapsing into bed around 11.30 p.m. Private pursuits became a thing of the past. I needed all of my energy for my jobs.

By 1985, I had joined John Fairfax and Sons writing for the *Sun* newspaper and *Woman's Day*. I had left 2UE and gone to 2KY, the New South Wales Labor Council-controlled radio station in Parramatta in Sydney's west, where I hosted the prime-time morning slot of nine to twelve. But NACAIDS was a full-time job and then some – although it wasn't meant to be. I wasn't paid for NACAIDS work – I simply received sitting fees for chairing committee meetings, like any other Government chairperson. By 1987 I was working a sixteen-hour day Monday to Friday and, to put it mildly, I sometimes felt a little tense. My only relaxation was a late Friday afternoon massage, and on a few occasions I had to cancel even that.

When a crisis occurred, I was expected to drop everything and handle it. Blewett particularly wanted me to talk to the State Health Ministers at their annual conference in Fremantle in 1987. It was important that they knew what NACAIDS' agenda was, and what we considered would be the priorities in the next twelve months, so they could brief their respective governments and get funding for appropriate State AIDS programs. 2KY agreed that I could go to Fremantle and do my show from a radio station in Perth on the landline back to Sydney.

With the time difference, this meant flying to Western Australia the day before, getting up at 4.30 a.m. so I could be at the Perth studio to prepare my show and go to air at 6 a.m. (9 a.m. in Sydney) and then, as soon as I had finished, driving speedily to Fremantle to address the health ministers, before dashing back to Perth to get the noon return flight to Sydney!

Every day was demanding. Sometimes, before I went on air at nine, I would have given five or six press interviews over the phone about AIDS issues, while preparing for my show in between times. When I got home in the evenings, I would put on my answering machine. I was in no mood to talk to anyone.

One morning I got in my car before 6 a.m. to drive to Parramatta and found myself yelling. I can't remember what about now, but probably something like 'I hate my life'. When I got home that night Ben told me he had heard me as he lay in his bed, dozing before getting up. 'What were you screaming about in your car?' he asked. I knew then that I needed to do something about my life. I went to the doctor. He asked me how many hours I worked. I told him that if I counted them I'd probably frighten myself. 'Are you enjoying your life?' he asked. 'No, I hate it,' I told him. 'All I do is work.'

He told me I had to change the way I was living. I knew he was right. One thing I was sure of was that if I had only six months to live, I wouldn't have been leading the kind of life I was. The choice was between 2KY and NACAIDS. But really, there was no choice. Stopping the spread of AIDS was far more important to me. As it turned out, 2KY helped me. At about the same time I was consulting the doctor, 2KY had decided to give me the flick. Not that they told me – I found out by chance from the media when they rang to tell me that broadcaster Gary O'Gallaghan was joining the station to take over the breakfast show from Ron Casey, who was being moved to my 9 a.m. to noon slot, making me redundant.

Blewett later apologised to me for not talking to the New South Wales Labor Council about the importance of the work I was doing for the Federal Labor Government and Australia. 'I think you lost your job because of AIDS,' he said. 'I'm sure of it,' I told him. I didn't miss 2KY. It's important to me to be able to respect the people I work with. Any organisation that is too gutless to tell me to my face that I'm no longer wanted for whatever reason is not a place I want to be employed.

With 2KY out of the way I was able to concentrate more fully on my AIDS work. I enjoyed the challenge it represented but this baffling disease, which had united people around the world in the common fight to stop it, challenged us in ways we never imagined. The Commonwealth Health Department decided to make better use of my knowledge and offered me a consultancy, which I accepted. I travelled to many parts of Australia talking and meeting with an enormous cross-section of Australians, discussing public health prevention strategies and trying to allay community concerns. I represented the Australian Government in AIDS discussions with the governments and medical professions of England, the United States, Africa and New Zealand.

I don't think there was any section of the community in Australia that I didn't speak to about AIDS while chair of NACAIDS – politicians, church leaders, the gay community, women, the media, school students, university students, the unemployed, doctors, health-care workers, prisoners, prison officers, taxicab drivers, school principals and parents.

Ron Penny and I called on the Catholic Archbishop (now Cardinal) Clancy in 1985 and over a cup of tea asked him if he had a spare monastery that we could use as a hospice for people with AIDS, as the AIDS caseload was putting a strain on Sydney's hospitals, particularly St Vincent's. The Archbishop was very sympathetic, but explained that spare monasteries were snapped up within the Catholic community as soon as they became vacant and, although he didn't have one available at the moment, he would certainly keep NACAIDS in mind.

Not everyone was as polite as the Archbishop, however. Sometimes I was abused in the streets. 'Hey Ita,' yelled a man as I crossed the road to 2KY one morning, 'why do you care about those bloody poofters? Let them die.' On another occasion, while I was walking my dog in Sydney's Centennial Park, a jogger recognised me and asked: 'You're Ita Buttrose, aren't you? What right do you have to go round spoiling our sex lives?' He was so aggressive I was scared for my safety. I got a great many vile, anonymous letters, too, from people who signed themselves 'Concerned Christians', with suggestions that were anything but Christian, on what to do with people with AIDS. Such letters simply made me more determined to do the job the Government had asked me to do.

There's no doubt AIDS threw into disarray our long-held conceptions of what matters are for open discussion, and the terms in which those discussions could be conducted. AIDS taught us all that we must be frank when we talked about the virus.

Whatever we may know about AIDS now, though, we weren't quite sure back in the eighties. There were enough cases, not only in Australia but also around the world, that showed AIDS could be spread by heterosexual intercourse. What wasn't known was whether the virus would explode among heterosexuals as it had done among homosexuals. It doesn't appear to have done so in Australia.

Is that just our good fortune, or did our education campaigns have something to do with it? There's no doubt in my mind that it was the latter. Our education programs were thorough and effective and as a result we were able to slow the spread of the virus. Would Australians have wanted us to wait and see, or would they rather we warned them – given what doctors currently knew about AIDS – regarding any 'at risk' behaviour that could jeopardise them? Was NACAIDS' advice all that hard to take? Don't sleep around. If you don't know where the person you're sleeping with slept the night before, make sure he uses a condom.

Even though some people attacked me in print for encouraging condom use as the means to safe sex, I regularly pushed the point to people that abstinence, celibacy, monogamy or whatever other term they wanted to throw into the ring would be the only truly safe way. A Tasmanian woman accused me of 'being irresponsible with other people's children' and that my comments would 'only assist the spread of AIDS'. Actually, I was telling people that 'abstinence is the best way to beat AIDS' and 'faithfulness to one partner' is the other option.

No one kidded themselves that condoms were the perfect way to stop the spread of the virus. They were substantially protective but not absolute, however they were certainly better than nothing. NACAIDS urged sexually active Australians to put a condom in their wallet or handbag – and many young people took our advice.

Whatever else AIDS taught us, it signalled that whether we liked it or not, the sexual revolution was over for the time being. It was declining before the world became aware

of AIDS, but AIDS dealt it a decisive blow. It was disinte-
grating because people were forced to become more aware
that we had pushed unacceptable boundaries. That was what
the eighties were all about. We had the chance to tell kids
that abstinence is the right way to go, and at the very least
to teach them the responsibilities of sex.

AIDS forced us to review our 'crazy eighties' behaviour
and to address some very important issues. The emergence
of a new morality was one of the most important consequences of AIDS. Interestingly, it was not the result of either
a moral or religious revolution – it was purely the result of
self-survival based on fear. A great many Australians turned
away from the casual sex and promiscuity which flourished
and were encouraged in the sixties and seventies.

Woodstock could never happen again after the arrival of
AIDS. 'Free love' was now a dirty word, because everyone
knew it was not necessarily love or free. Indeed, it could
come at a great cost. Free love had meant sex with anyone
you chose, with no complications and no strings attached.
The problem was, free love could not take account of
someone's sexual past – his or her history.

In recounting some of the events of those sometimes
turbulent years, it might seem that there was only time to
disagree. That was not the case – most of us were far too
preoccupied doing the job the Government had asked us
to – but with something as devious as the AIDS virus, there
were always bound to be differences of opinion. My work
with NACAIDS led me to places and experiences that I will

never forget, like sitting in St Vincent's holding the hand of a dying man, trying to comfort him. His parents didn't know he had AIDS or that he was homosexual: 'I was the fourth son,' he told me. 'My father wanted a daughter. He was always disappointed with me.'

I wrote for some months to a young Greek man in his early twenties whom I had met at an AIDS fundraising function in Melbourne. His parents didn't know he was gay either, or that he had AIDS. He didn't know how to begin to tell them. Telling their parents they're homosexual is still a problem for a great many ethnic men.

Then there was the young mother with two kids, whose husband had contracted the virus in a bisexual encounter. She'd had no idea that from time to time he made love to other men and when he was first diagnosed he blamed her for giving him the virus. When the truth came out, she agreed to nurse him at home – he was, after all, the father of her children – but she wasn't finding it an easy thing to do. I doubt many other women would have either.

The number of bisexual men in Australia is not known as there are no accurate figures. Because such men live with a lie it is difficult to find out the truth. But in 1987 Penington admitted that bisexuality was a major concern, and revealed research which showed that in the past year one married Australian man in twenty had had sex with another man.

I'll always see the sparkling eyes of young Troy Lovegrove, whose mother Susie died from AIDS and unknowingly passed on the virus to her son. He was a dear little boy and it was hard not to think of my own son when I shared a croissant and lots of jam with Troy one morning at an AIDS fundraiser at Sydney's Taronga Zoo.

I spent an afternoon with three teenagers with haemophilia who had the virus. They told me that keeping their infection a secret was almost harder to handle than having the virus. Their parents worried that if people knew, they'd be asked to leave their schools. They felt like outcasts.

There were the street kids, already outcasts, who had shared needles and contracted the virus because of their drug habits. They were tough kids and put on a brave front, but they didn't fool me. The mother in me wanted to weep for them. There were many times AIDS made me feel like crying and not only in Australia.

When I was in Africa in 1995, I sat in on a World Vision support group for women with HIV in Nairobi, Kenya. The chairwoman of the group began to tell her story. She was fifty-six. She had progressed from HIV-positive to full-blown AIDS. Her husband had died the year before. No, she didn't know he was sick. He hadn't told her. The time came when she began to feel constantly unwell. She went to hospital, was tested, and told she had HIV. There was no counselling. She thought of committing suicide. What could she do? Who would help her? By chance, she ran into someone who told her about the World Vision support group. I sat there wondering how I would cope in a similar situation. She continued with her story: 'My only child is infected, too.' The husband of her thirty-three-year-old daughter Celia had infected her. Like her mother, Celia didn't know her husband had the virus. Stories like this one are common in Africa.

By 1988, though, my NACAIDS' job was done. I rang Neal Blewett and told him I would be resigning and, at the same time, would give up my consultancy with the Commonwealth Health Department. He thanked me for the work I'd done and invited me to become a member of a new AIDS committee he was setting up, which would incorporate some of the NACAIDS team as well as the AIDS Task Force to steer Australia into the next phase of its response to the epidemic. I agreed to become a member of ANCA – the Australian National Council on AIDS. In 2001, I agreed to become a patron to the Sixth International Congress on AIDS in Asia and the Pacific, which will be held in Melbourne. Given the explosion of AIDS infection rates in the region, there will be much to talk about.

During its four-year existence, NACAIDS achieved a great deal. The national education program had been run and other educational programs developed. Educational booklets for everyone in the community had been developed and distributed. NACAIDS had established working groups in a number of important areas such as discrimination, legal issues, HIV drug users, the media, Aborigines, the ethnic community, churches – we particularly needed the churches' support for educational programs in our schools and we knew there was also a growing need among people with AIDS for pastoral care and counselling.

We looked at issues affecting adolescents – employed, unemployed and with low literacy. There were other workshops that brought us in contact with prisoners, who told me their biggest fear was being jabbed with an infected needle. The prison warders at Long Bay in Sydney told me the same thing.

We also considered the issue of medical practitioners' education – something that was needed in the early years of the epidemic. For instance, when it became apparent that the blood supply had been contaminated before 1985, the blood bank and hospitals instigated searches for patients who might have been infected by transfusions prior to the blood supply being made safe. Ten people, who had received contaminated blood and were traced by the blood bank, had been to their doctors when the virus was quite advanced and they were very ill – and none of their GPs had diagnosed AIDS. Subsequently some 172 people were identified as being infected by transfusion.

NACAIDS developed ideas, policies and recommendations on a wide range of non-medical issues. Like other countries, Australia might have been stumped medically, but we had no difficulties progressing with all the non-medical issues. It's a matter of some pride to me, and I'm sure to the other dedicated men and women who served on NACAIDS, that our approach has been recognised worldwide. We were consistently asked to share it with the United States, Europe, our Pacific/Asia neighbours and Africa. The work NACAIDS did is now the blueprint for the Commonwealth Health

Department for policies on non-medical issues relating to AIDS, and the casebook for any future health epidemics.

The people I met and the work I did on NACAIDS had a profound effect on me. I might have started with little knowledge about the virus, but there was very little I didn't know by the end of my term as chairwoman.

The twentieth century was remarkable for advances in public health and in medical science and technology. It was ironic that in its closing years we were faced with AIDS, one of the most frightening and potentially socially disruptive pandemics of all time. We have seen, and will continue to see, enormous social change directly attributable to HIV/AIDS.

AIDS forced a massive rethink. More traditional moral values attained a new honour and sanity. Many did not agree with this. George Negus wrote (*Bulletin*, 21 April 1987): 'It's to be hoped that the basically commendable Ita Buttrose-led national zeal to contend with AIDS does not spawn some obscure form of obsessive post-sexual revolution prudishness.'

It doesn't seem likely, if American evidence is anything to go by. Now that 'drug cocktails' seem to be successful in halting the progress of AIDS in people who are HIV-positive, the signs are that people are once again forgetting that perhaps the human race wasn't meant to have multiple sexual partners.

Recent statistics released by the US Centers for Disease Control and Prevention reveal 65 million Americans have an incurable sexually transmitted disease. Fifteen million new STD cases are reported annually – with chlamydia, a disease that often has no symptoms, topping the list at three million cases a year. The figures show an annual infection rate of one million cases of genital herpes, 650 000 of gonorrhoea, 120 000 of Hepatitis B, and 70 000 of syphilis. While these particular STDs are being diagnosed in such large numbers (gonorrhea increased by nine per cent between 1997 and 1999), the HIV/AIDS infection rate in that country has dropped to 40 000 new cases per annum.

Do these figures perhaps suggest that in the twenty-first century, some other kind of fearful sexually transmitted disease awaits us? It is my hope that the warnings of NACAIDS will not be forgotten as the new century gets under way. Sometimes I am a little afraid that they will be.

6

GOING OUT ON MY OWN

ITA *is far better than anything we have in Europe, possibly*
because it feels so personal. As if talking to your best friend
at a dinner party. This best friend is thoughtful, positive,
provocative, enthusiastic, imaginative, well informed and
can give you her reasoned opinion about almost anything.
ITA *would seem to be required reading before going out*
in the evening.

BRITISH AUTHOR SHIRLEY CONRAN, 1990

It was inevitable I suppose that one day I would set up
my own business, but when I accepted Max Suich's offer
to join John Fairfax and Sons in 1984, it was the further-
most thought from my mind. Suich was Fairfax's Chief
Editorial Executive and he painted an exciting picture of
my future with the company, which I held in high regard.
It was prestigious, well managed and seemingly secure in
the Fairfax family hands. James Fairfax had succeeded his
father, Sir Warwick, as chairman and I liked and respected

him. I was thrilled to have been asked to work at Fairfax and looked forward to the opportunities that awaited me. I remember thinking I was set for life. I should have known better!

My first few years with the company were as exciting as Suich had promised they would be, but in August 1987 foolish Warwick Fairfax junior – James's half-brother – launched his ill-fated takeover bid for the great media empire, only to succeed in destroying it. What a debacle it was. His misguided attempt to privatise John Fairfax and Sons, which the Fairfax family had controlled for 150 years, saw the company stripped of its television, radio and magazine interests. It was the kind of stupidity that took your breath away. If only he could have exercised patience. He would have ultimately succeeded James as Chairman and would have been far better placed to bring his plans to fruition. Instead, Warwick threw the place into turmoil from which it still hasn't recovered.

For a while it looked as if the Canadian newspaper proprietor, Conrad Black, might give Fairfax the stability and management expertise it needed when his company Tourang bought Fairfax in 1991. However, unable to get Federal Government approval to increase his stake in the company and fed up with delays in decision making and constant changes to our media rules, he walked away from Fairfax and Australia in 1996 selling his shares to Brierley Investments.

The company lurched on. In ten years it went through eight chief executives. Then in 1998 Brian Powers, the

former Managing Director of Kerry Packer's Australian Consolidated Press Holdings, became Chairman, prompting all
kinds of speculation. The commentators had a field day.
Was Power a Packer plant? No evidence to support that
hypothesis has been uncovered. That same year management guru, Fred Hilmer, former Dean of the Australian
Graduate School of Management at the University of New
South Wales become CEO. Not long after his appointment,
Hilmer told journalists he wasn't 'an avid newspaper reader',
hardly the kind of remark to inspire confidence in staff or,
for that matter, shareholders.

Kerry, who owns fifteen per cent of Fairfax, has never
made any secret of his desire to control the media group,
but is stymied by Australia's cross-media regulations which
prevent television or radio owners gaining control of any
major newspaper in the same market. Most pundits believe
he is just biding his time, a view I support, but we shall have
to wait and see. Young Warwick's folly allowed Kerry to
snap up Fairfax's magazine group, making him Australia's
biggest magazine publisher. This was late 1987. I hardly
needed to be told that my prospects of any continuing
involvement with *Woman's Day* to ACP were not good.
Richard Walsh, the then Managing Director of ACP, had
never made any secret of his dislike for me – although I'm
not sure why this was. On one occasion, when we'd both
been asked to lunch at the home of fashion designer Carla
Zampatti, she had sat us together thinking we'd have much
in common. However, on discovering his fate, Richard

(within my hearing) asked her to sit him elsewhere. She was shocked. So was I!

I had been writing a weekly column for *Woman's Day* that the readers seemed to like and I also made the magazine's TV commercials. Its circulation was on the increase and everything was going well. In spite of this, as soon as ACP began to publish *Woman's Day* any future I might have had with the magazine vanished. For a magazine junkie like me, in need of a regular fix, it was a bleak event.

I was still writing features for the *Sun*, the Fairfax afternoon daily, but even that assignment was looking more and more doubtful. There were strong rumours that Warwick was going to close the *Sun* down because it wasn't making money and, like afternoon newspapers worldwide, it had a declining circulation. Everyone at Fairfax was on edge and uncertain about the future – me included. Although my contract still had more than a year to run, I needed more job security than the prospect of only twelve months' income. By now Kate was nineteen, studying Architecture at Sydney University and Ben, fourteen, was still at school.

Former Sydney journalist, Marty (Martin) Dougherty, whom I'd got to know during my time at News Ltd where he was formerly Editor of the *Daily Mirror*, was one of Warwick's trusted advisors. Along with Laurie Connell, the Western Australian buccaneer, who set up Rothwells Merchant Bank (it had collapsed by the end of 1988), Warwick had appointed Marty to the Fairfax board.

Warwick hired Connell for a fee of $100 million to

advise him on the $2 billion-plus takeover bid, even though the latter's reputation as the banker you approached after all other traditional lenders knocked you back was well known. As well as becoming a director Marty was appointed Chief Editorial Executive, which turned out to be another of Warwick's errors of judgement.

I phoned Marty and asked if there was a job I could do in what was going to be left of the Fairfax carve-up – the *Sydney Morning Herald*, the *Sun-Herald*, the *Age*, and the *Financial Review*. There was! Marty was looking for someone to 'fix up' the *Sun-Herald*. Would I like to become Editor-in-Chief? It was the answer to my prayers and the thought of competing against my old paper, the *Sunday Telegraph*, had a certain spice to it. Editors thrive on circulation battles. My adrenalin was already firing in anticipation. Not long after this conversation, Marty introduced me to Connell, a short, flashy and pudgy man, who at the time was living it up in an expensive penthouse suite complete with piano – which he told me he couldn't play – at Sydney's Intercontinental Hotel. The day I met him Connell was looking pretty pleased with himself and gave the impression that he was enjoying being associated with a distinguished family such as the Fairfaxes.

Marty might never have got a foot in the door of Fairfax had it not been for Warwick's mother, Mary, Lady Fairfax. Marty always claimed to have won her confidence and I know he worked hard to do that. In the years before the abortive takeover, he and his wife Ros, were frequent visitors to her magnificent mansion, Fairwater, at Double Bay and Mary often dined at the Doughertys' rented waterfront apartment at nearby Point Piper. On one occasion, I sat next to her at such a dinner and it was obvious that she and the Doughertys had a warm friendship. According to Marty, Mary placed so much credence on his advice that she had recommended him to Warwick as a man to have on his takeover team. I've always found Mary Fairfax a shrewd woman, even though, to some, appearances might suggest otherwise. She must have kicked herself afterwards for allowing herself to fall for Marty's blarney.

When *ITA* interviewed James Fairfax in December 1991, following the publication of his book *My Regards to Broadway*, he indicated that his stepmother's role in the failed takeover bid was important at various stages of the whole process. She certainly had a difficult time explaining her actions in the takeover. He wrote about her interference in the running of the newspapers and the embarrassment she caused by phoning Fairfax journalists – against company policy – and asking them to cover social fundraising events of which she was a part.

As far as James was concerned, Mary was the force behind Warwick's move. 'From the mid-1980s when she began to concentrate on her son's succession, she influenced him with her views about the management and this, com- bined with the already instilled belief in his own ability, sent him on his way.'

James told *ITA* that: 'Warwick was brought up to believe

he was a boy genius, the answer to everything.' However, James always had had 'grave doubts about Warwick's ability, even before the takeover'.

Much to my dismay and embarrassment, before the *Sun-Herald*'s Editor, Ray Odlum, was formally told of my appointment, Marty (for some reason known only to him) leaked my appointment to *Bulletin* columnist, Dorian Wild. Later, when Dorian came to work for me on *ITA* Magazine, I asked him who'd tipped him off about my *Sun-Herald* appointment. 'Marty told me,' Dorian said. Why Marty did it, I do not know. It was totally inappropriate, hardly good management. When I tackled him many years later, he couldn't remember why he'd been so thoughtless.

It didn't bode well for my time at the *Sun-Herald* and it certainly didn't get me off to a good start. Understandably, Odlum wasn't pleased. Neither was I. It was a disastrous way to start a new job, particularly at such an uncertain time in Fairfax's history. The company was in havoc. Before I officially started, I asked Odlum to lunch to try to sort things out, telling him I hoped we'd be able to work well together. He gave me the impression he wanted that, too, and we shared the same aim – to make the *Sun-Herald* the best Sunday newspaper in Australia.

I didn't realise what a mess Fairfax was in. Warwick's manoeuvrings had destabilised the place. Journalists are insecure people at the best of times and Marty Dougherty had angered the Fairfax journalists by appointing Andrew Clarke as Editor-in-Chief of the *Sydney Morning Herald* in place of

Chris Anderson, one of the company's (under the old regime) favoured sons. God knows why the journalists objected to Clarke – he was a respected journalist with plenty of runs on the board. His problem was that like me, he was a Dougherty appointment. All was later forgotten and forgiven however, and in 1993 he became Editor-in-Chief of the *Sun-Herald*. But no one could have predicted that in 1988!

As well, Marty had installed computer terminals in his office on the fourteenth floor, giving him access to the computers used by the journalists. To them, it smacked of management interference in editorial and it was unacceptable. They were disgruntled and unhappy. Then he appointed his brother Paul, also a journalist, as a buffer between himself and the company's editors and senior staff. Everyone, including Editors-in-Chief, was expected to talk to Paul about issues they wished to discuss with Marty, and Paul would pass the information on.

I'd known Paul longer than I'd known Marty. He was a nice enough bloke but not the right man for this sensitive role. He lacked the know-how to advise senior editorial people on how to run newspapers, having never run a major newspaper himself. It was insulting to all of us. Marty told his brother he could approve our editorial requests and ideas as well. I managed to see Marty without Paul being present and I reminded him of his assurance that I would report only to him. I had no intention of now reporting to Paul. Marty said he'd think it over. I also suggested that he should remove the 'offensive' terminals. I felt I knew him well enough to give him this piece of advice. You don't need them, I told him. But he would have none of it. He told me to mind my own business.

But Marty's time at Fairfax was almost up. Ten senior journalists on the *Sydney Morning Herald* had resigned. Without them the paper was in serious trouble. Warwick couldn't afford anything to harm the *Sydney Morning Herald*, his principal cash cow with its lucrative classified advertisements – he needed the money. Marty was informed he would be reporting to a new Chief Executive Officer, Peter King, and not, as previously agreed, to Warwick. Marty resigned. Chris Anderson became Group Editorial Director and moved the offensive terminals off the executive floor. Ron Cotton, an accountant by training, who had worked for Fairfax before in a senior management position, was appointed Group Managing Director Operations in February 1988. We all hoped – well, I know I did – that the place would settle down so that we could get on with our professional lives.

But in March, Peter King notified the staff that the *Sun* was closing; so was the up-market and not high circulating *Times on Sunday*. Staff cuts were to be made throughout the company. People had been offered and had taken redundancy payments. The journalists, artists and photographers were nervous and upset. There were new rumours every day about what next was to happen to the company. No one knew what to believe.

The executives had their own battles too – they were jockeying for positions of power and knifing each other whenever they got the chance. Peter King, a friend of Warwick's, had been Managing Director of Royal Packaging Van Leer Holland in Johannesburg, South Africa, and appeared to know very little about the practical realities of running a newspaper. A couple of times he called in to the *Sun-Herald* offices on a Saturday afternoon around 3.30, a Sunday paper's busiest time – not even Rupert annoys his editors on a Saturday afternoon. No one has time for a chat, but chatter Peter King did. Odlum and I would be trying to write posters, or discuss story placement for pages one, three and five – the pages that always go to press last – and there was King, trying to be friendly and asking us the most basic questions about newspapers. It drove us nuts, and neither of us could work out how to politely tell the boss to get lost.

I was in an awkward position. I was seen as a 'Dougherty appointment'. He was gone. Some of the journalists resented my presence. There were all kinds of untruths and rumours being spread about me; even the fact that an office had to be built for me seemed to be a worry for some. Why, I don't know. I had to have an office and there were no spare ones in the *Sun-Herald* area. I presume it was something Marty discussed with Warwick and the order to get it done was given before I took up my Editor-in-Chief role.

The office was pretty basic and built with glass walls from ceiling to floor, giving me no privacy at all. I felt like a goldfish in a bowl. No other Editor or Editor-in-Chief was expected to work in such 'open' surroundings. It was agreed that blinds would be put in. Criticism followed that I was elite, and wanted to isolate myself from the 'workers', which was crap. Then there was a great deal of fuss about my furnishings. I'd never encountered anything like it. A desk was bought. Rumours abounded that it cost $20 000. I would have had to have rocks in my head to spend a sum that large on a desk. I knew how sensitive the issue of money was, especially with all the jobs that had been lost. There were other extraordinary rumours, too, about my lavish private bathroom.

If my critics had thought through the issue, it would have dawned on them that the money had nothing to do with me anyway. It wasn't my decision to build an office. I wasn't in charge of building budgets. Why would I be? As far as I knew, $20 000 was the total sum allocated to build a new office and that included the furnishings. Stories about my $20 000 desk appeared in Fairfax newspapers including the staff newspaper. I couldn't believe it. Here we all were, players in a company whose very existence was threatened by Warwick Fairfax's flawed ambition, and intelligent people who should have known better were preoccupied with a desk.

People whose professional reputation depended on them getting the facts right were distorting the truth, for reasons that were not clear to me. All sorts of people used to visit my office – they would have known there was no bathroom and certainly no lavish expenditure on decor. But the stories still persisted. Management was too weak to get them stopped, or maybe they didn't want to. Maybe they wanted to make me unhappy so that I wouldn't stay. Who knows?

This was the kind of company Fairfax was during Warwick Fairfax's bungled time there. It was, to put it mildly, not a happy place. There was no effective management of the company and there appeared to be no long-term plans for the papers, certainly not the *Sun-Herald*. We were left mainly to our own devices. Everyone felt unsettled and anxious. People had seen their workmates lose their jobs. They were worried about their own futures. I understood this. It never seemed to occur to my colleagues that I felt the same way.

I occasionally passed Warwick in the car park. I'd go to say hello and he would sidle past me with his eyes down. The message was clear – do not talk to me. I didn't particularly want to, but it's customary to say good morning to the man you work for even if you don't respect him. I remembered the first time I'd met him. He was just a small boy of three or so. The *Women's Weekly* photographer Keith Barlow and I were at the Fairfax home to take pictures at some function Mary Fairfax was hosting. She wanted to show Keith and me something upstairs and insisted we come with her. As we got to the top of the stairs, a sweet-looking child with long blond curly hair rushed up to us. Keith was enchanted. 'What a lovely little girl!' he said. Mary looked at him, a little frostily I thought at the time, before replying: 'This is my son, Warwick.' Perhaps it's hardly surprising that

Warwick Fairfax was not like any other media proprietor I had encountered.

He later said that Marty's appointment of me as Editor-in-Chief was something he had objected to – that he had asked Marty if the timing were right to make senior appointments. I wish he'd had the guts to tell me of his misgivings when I met him before accepting the appointment. He simply told me he was looking forward to me coming to Fairfax and that he had no problems working with or for a woman.

In spite of all that had happened, I was looking forward to working with Marty's replacement, Chris Anderson. He had a great reputation and had written to me in December 1987, when he was Editor-in-Chief of the *Sydney Morning Herald* and my appointment was officially announced. It could be said he was one of the few people at Fairfax who gave me a warm welcome: 'Every best wish for your new job at the *Sun-Herald*. As you know, I edited the paper nearly ten years or so ago. If I can give you any help, support or assistance, please give me a call.'

On 19 March 1988 there was a State election in New South Wales. Nick Greiner led the Liberals to victory. Newspapers usually sell well at election times and all of us on the *Sun-Herald* team worked our guts out to produce a good report of the elections. We were pretty sure Greiner had won, even before the poll was declared, as we had done exit polls on all the marginal seats and knew that the swing to Greiner was big enough to give him victory. We took a gamble (well, I took a gamble – the team might have agreed with me, but I know whose neck would have been for the chop if we'd been wrong!) and put the paper out with a massive page one heading declaring the Liberals had won, before the poll was officially declared.

The *Sunday Telegraph* was still playing it safe, saying it wasn't clear which party would govern. By morning it was, of course – but there are plenty of sales to be made with the early editions of a Sunday paper on a Saturday night as people head home after a night out. We had a terrific sale that weekend – around the 700 000 mark and were justifiably pleased with ourselves.

Even management was stirred into action. Ron Cotton sent us three bottles of champagne for what he called our 'champagne effort'. Chris Anderson sent me a handwritten note: 'I thought the coverage was fine – a lot better than the *Sunday Telegraph*. However, I'd like to see more reporting, more open pages up front'.

We drank the champagne and got on with producing the paper. On 11 April, I received another handwritten note from Anderson: 'Thought Sunday's paper was a vast improvement. It's great to see it on its way again'. And on 1 May, he sent a very positive note: 'Again I thought the *Sun-Herald* showed today that it is getting on top of the opposition.'

No one could blame me if I assumed that Chris Anderson was pleased with the job I was doing. By now, Ray Odlum had moved on. David Hickie, who had been Assistant Editor, had become Acting Editor. There was less friction on the paper, although the company was still a melancholic place. It reeked of unhappiness. Unexpectedly, Anderson asked me to come and see him. 'Look,' he said, 'I don't think you're ever going to be able to create the paper I want. I want you to leave.'

It was Thursday, 23 June 1988. I had just returned from making the paper's radio commercials at a recording studio around the corner. The *Sun-Herald* for the following Sunday was half completed. There wasn't much point me arguing with Anderson; nothing to be gained by asking what had gone wrong when everything, according to his notes, was going right. I wasn't about to do a Harold Evans, the former Editor of the London *Times* who locked himself in his office, so legend has it, when Rupert wanted him to quit.

Anderson and I agreed on the termination payment. Then I said to him that as it was Thursday evening and much of the paper was planned and some of it completed, if he'd like me to finish producing the paper, I would do so and finish up with Fairfax on Saturday night. He just looked at me and said: 'I don't know why I like you.' Well, I don't know why he didn't. He hardly knew me and hadn't bothered to get to know me. We never talked newspapers and he knew that I had not been given a decent chance to show what I could do with the *Sun-Herald* in only four months. But I wasn't going to lose much sleep about it – then or now. I presume what Anderson meant by his peculiar remark was that I was behaving in a professional manner. I don't know how else he would have expected me to behave.

What no one knew, including Anderson, was that I had already made up my mind to leave Fairfax. It was such a miserable place in which to work that I didn't want to stay. I have never seen any point in not enjoying work. Life is too short to waste it doing something that doesn't make you happy. But I had intended to complete the term of my contract and to give the company reasonable notice while doing the best I could to liven up the *Sun-Herald*. I certainly hadn't expected to be 'turfed out' by Anderson for no apparent reason, certainly none that he was able to explain to me.

It was a kick in the guts and I was somewhat stunned, but I returned to my office, finished off whatever had to be done and went home without saying a word to a soul about what had happened. Anderson didn't tell anyone about it either, I don't think. I was in the office by eight on the Saturday morning. In the afternoon, not long before the first edition of the paper was due to be finished, I wrote a couple of paragraphs saying I was resigning. I felt as if I'd written my own death notice, and before placing it in the paper called the staff together to tell them I would be leaving.

It was one of the hardest things I've ever had to do. The whole day had been tough. Most of my colleagues were sensitive enough to realise what I must have been going through. Some of them went out and bought some champagne. After the paper had gone to press we had a drink together. I thanked them. People went home. The second edition changes were discussed and put through. The staff who worked late on Saturday doing the late changes to the paper went to the pub for a drink. I'd said I'd mind the fort until nine. Then I went home. So ended four and half years with Fairfax, including my brief time on the *Sun-Herald* – very short, and not so sweet.

The following week Barbara, my secretary, was tidying up. 'A journalist came in from the *Sydney Morning Herald*,' she later told me, 'and asked me to show him your "lavish bathroom". I opened the door to your office and told him if he could find it to let me know.'

Several weeks earlier, on 30 May – my day off; I didn't want to be accused of not being a good employee by doing this in Fairfax time on one of my working days – I had called on a man who had once said to me: 'If you ever have an idea that you think might appeal to me, come and see me.' When I went to see him that day at 3 p.m., what I had in mind appealed to him enormously – a magazine called *ITA*, for women over forty, like me. Within twenty minutes he had agreed to back me, and asked me to put together a cashflow plan for him to look at. I could scarcely believe my good fortune. I drove home singing. On the way, I passed St Joseph's Church at Edgecliff where the funeral of my best friend, Marjorie McGowen, had been held six weeks earlier. I thought I'd pop in, thank God for my good fortune and light a candle for Marj. But the church doors were locked, one of the casualties of the unsafe society in which we live. I sat in my car outside St Joseph's and said a silent grateful prayer instead, and wished Marj were still alive so that we could have celebrated together.

My early departure from Fairfax speeded up the time-table for *ITA* but there was a lot to do before I could put the new magazine on sale. By July the backer, who to this day prefers to remain anonymous, had approved the cash-flow plan and advanced me starting-up money. I had no idea what to call my new company. 'What star sign are you?' asked my backer. 'Capricorn,' I said. And so Capricorn Publishing Pty Ltd was born.

I was certain there was a market that would welcome a magazine like the one I had in mind. *ITA* would be for women who believed there was a life beyond the goings-on of the then overexposed role models like Fergie and Di and the gaggle of half-starved film stars who featured so often in the popular women's magazines. I felt the timing was right for a magazine that recognised women's intelligence and their interest in environmental and political matters as well as the good life of course – like eating, going to the theatre, opera and ballet and shopping! Fashion, health and fitness would be an important part of the editorial mix, as would features on men and women who were making a difference to our way of life. Above all, *ITA* would be unashamedly Australian and would promote the very best our nation and its people had to offer.

Writing in the advertising trade journal *B&T*, Fred Brenchley referred to my market as 'post-feminist or just educated, affluent and middle-aged'. At about the same time,

BRW magazine identified my target market as a powerful consumer group, profiling them as 'empty nests, full pockets'. They sounded good to me. I hoped they had $5 to spare in their pockets for my new magazine.

It made sense to me to call it *ITA*, although not everyone agreed. The Ita Buttrose knockers immediately proclaimed I had some kind of ego problem. I didn't. I've never had that personality hitch and I could never understand the fuss in some quarters of the media about my decision. I wasn't the first person to use her name for a business enterprise and I won't be the last. John Singleton called his agency Single-ton, Len Evans named a vintage after himself, Beppi gave his name to his restaurant in Sydney, Prue Acton, Trent Nathan and Peter Weiss put their names on their fashion labels. Hairdressers like John Adams, Lloyd Lomas and Joh Bailey named their hairdressing salons after themselves. Alan Bond even named a university after himself. A few years later, Poppy King called her lipstick range Poppy and no one uttered a derisive word.

As far as I was concerned, it was the commonsense thing to do. I knew my name was well known throughout Australia and that 'Ita' would have instant recognition for most people. As Tess Lawrence wrote in her column in Melbourne's *Sunday Press*: 'Ms Buttrose would have been a drongo to have risked calling the magazine anything but *ITA*, such is the power of her public profile.'

The women I hoped would buy my magazine knew the kind of person I was and could expect my magazine to reflect the standards I believe in. I didn't have a cent to waste on expensive marketing campaigns and nothing like the kind of promotional budget I had, for instance, when I relaunched *The Australian Women's Weekly* for Kerry Packer in 1975 and we spent $1 million to get our message across.

It didn't take me long to discover there was nothing easy about running my own business, but I did savour the freedom it gave me to make my own decisions. I was conscious however of the responsibility that came with my new-found liberation. I was now accountable for the livelihood of men and women who trusted me to do the right thing as far as their ongoing employment was concerned. I didn't want to let them – or my backer – down.

In the beginning our major challenge was to come up with a compelling description of our target market. Someone suggested we say *ITA* was for the 'mature market', but to me that suggested a slab of Brie ripening on a plate and I doubted our readers would like such a comparison! Not long before *ITA* was launched, an American, Frances Lear, started her own magazine *Lear's* in New York, also aimed at older women. Frances was a woman of independent means, financing her venture with $25 million from a $112 million divorce settlement won from her television producer husband, Norman. Because she disliked the word 'older', she declared that her magazine was 'For the Woman Who Wasn't Born Yesterday'. I loved the description and decided it would be the perfect way to explain what *ITA* was all about. So I used the slogan too. I've never had any worries knocking off good ideas. What's more, there's no rule that says we can't. If I've seen something working for a competitor, I've been quick to latch on to it. No one should ever hesitate to do that – initiative doesn't come with copyright restrictions.

We encountered yet another stumbling block with the advertising industry, which wasn't the slightest bit convinced about the viability of our potential market. When I sought Dennis Merchant's advice on what to charge for a page of advertising in *ITA*, and told him the magazine was for women over forty, he was horrified. He insisted that I couldn't possibly mention the word 'forty' and expect to be successful. Women couldn't bear to be reminded they were THAT old, he insisted.

As the boss of Merchant and Partners, the biggest independent seller of media advertisements, Dennis knew the marketplace. We debated the matter for hours. In the end commonsense prevailed. It would have been foolish of me not to heed his counsel. I changed the target market to women thirty-five plus. Dennis was happy. I do wish, though, that he'd argued as vehemently with me on what to charge for a page of advertising in *ITA*. It was soon apparent that advertising agencies thought our price too high – over $6800 for a casual page of colour. Yet when my Advertising Manager, Bina Gupta, and I had asked Dennis's opinion on what to charge, he told us that he thought $6000+ was a reasonable price for a full page. Of course, like most Australians, he had no idea that our economy was about to nosedive in the dramatic way it did.

I'm not blaming Dennis for our lack of advertising support. I was always grateful that his company often recommended *ITA* to its many clients, but I can see now that it would have been smarter to charge far less for a page of advertising in the magazine's early years. Lack of advertising support was always a problem for *ITA*. Still, that's the way the cookie crumbles. I didn't have to listen to Dennis and no one made me take his recommendation. But I did.

Going out on my own was a gamble, but taking risks excites me and leading a life that didn't include an occasional rocking of the boat would be boring. I had my fair share of sleepless nights and self-doubts though. Was I right about the woman who wasn't born yesterday? Was she out there waiting for something like *ITA* to come along? Was the editorial mix I had in mind the right one?

I began seeking out people to join me in my new enterprise. Ainslie Cahill, who had followed me from the *Weekly* to News Ltd, and had worked for author Morris West, agreed to become General Manager. I confided in her the name of my financial backer and his desire to remain anonymous. We agreed it would be safer if he had a nickname, so we dubbed our benefactor 'Charlie.' Later, everyone at Capricorn Publishing was aware of 'Charlie', but only a few knew who he actually was.

We set up office at my home in Sydney's Bellevue Hill with the dining-room table as our communal desk. At one stage there were five of us there, sharing two phones and conducting our business with three curious cats and Brutus, my friendly black labrador, keeping an eye on us. Kate and Ben thought it was tremendous to have me working from home and didn't seem to notice the disruption to our domestic routine.

In between times Ainslie and I went office hunting. Conscious of the need to watch our budget, we were occasionally disheartened by what was on offer at the price we could afford to rent. Finally, we found pleasant professional premises in a tree-lined street in the inner-city suburb of Surry Hills and once we'd painted the place inside and out and in feminine colours of peach and soft grey and replaced the carpet, were pleased with our choice. More people joined us; some, like Bunty Turner, Patsy Hollis and Alan Mackenzie, had worked with me at Consolidated Press. It was like old times. The vibes were good and we were eager to get started.

As had happened with *Cleo*, the advertising industry did not support *ITA*'s first issue, although with its sixteen pages of advertising, it fared better than *Cleo*, which had managed only seven. But it still wasn't much for a 132-page magazine. When I spoke at an advertising industry lunch in Sydney a few days after *ITA* had gone on sale, I asked them why a group that constantly asks consumers to support and buy new products is so reluctant to do so itself?

'If the consumers were as negative as the industry is, I think you would contemplate cutting your wrists,' I said. 'Surely it would be logical to assume that the first issue of a magazine like *ITA* would sell extremely well, if for nothing else but its curiosity value, and that therefore it would be an excellent place in which to advertise?'

Those advertisers who were smart enough to understand such things got value for their money. When they booked their ads *ITA*'s print run was going to be only 100,000. Then I increased it to 110,000 to cope with the demands from supermarkets and finally to 160,000 to cover the newsagents' requirements.

Prime Minster Bob Hawke had agreed to officially launch *ITA*, which we deemed a great coup. How did this come about? Towards the end of 1988 businessman Rod Muir had asked me to have a coffee with him at his Sydney apartment. Often described as the father of FM radio in Australia the one-time disc jockey had made a fortune through buying and selling radio stations and in his 'retirement' had turned his hand to a variety of projects, including corporate videos. He was particularly taken with the spectacular new Parliament House in Canberra, designed by Italian architect Aldo Giurgola and opened by Queen Elizabeth in May 1988 and wanted to make a tourist video to capitalise on the 6000 people who daily visit our nation's seat of power. Muir asked if I'd 'host' the video, offering to advertise and also to help organise an exclusive photo shoot for *ITA* as part of the deal. When I accepted, I found that my role included interviewing all of Australia's living Prime Ministers.

I talked to Mr Hawke in his office with its stunning Tasmanian huon pine furniture and afterwards, as he showed me aspects of the new building that he particularly liked, the PM politely inquired what else I was doing. I brought him up to date with my plans for *ITA* and, as we shook hands goodbye, he wished me well and to let him know if he could help in any way. On the way back to Sydney, I mulled over our conversation, wondering if he'd really meant what he said. A few weeks later I rang Mr Hawke's office inviting him to launch *ITA* – the rest, as they say, is history!

Because Parliament was sitting, the launch had to be held in Canberra. This suited me because I knew the press there would treat us more kindly than Sydney's media, which is so blasé and quick to find fault. Canberra also had the country's highest proportion of women aged 35 to 54, the very group we wanted to reach. There were other pluses. Media representatives from every State and Territory work at Parliament House, which has landlines to all of the nation's TV and radio stations, making it easy for me to give interviews. As it turned out *ITA* attracted so much publicity both prior to and at the launch that I cancelled all paid advertising for the first issue. We simply didn't need it. I used the unanticipated windfall to promote our second and third issues.

Bob Hawke's backing for me and *ITA* was invaluable and something for which I'll always be grateful. Not only did he launch the magazine, he also wrote a signed message of support for the first issue. His office had arranged for the launch ceremony to take place at Parliament House at 10 a.m. The date – February 15, 1989. We had an excellent turn-out of press, politicians and notable women like Wendy

McCarthy, Annita Keating and Carla Zampatti, but as I waited near the elevators for the Prime Minister to arrive I felt on edge.

'Not nervous are you?' was the first thing the PM asked when he saw me. I nodded. 'Don't be,' he said, patting me reassuringly on the shoulder. 'This is going to be a great day.' His confidence boost was just what I needed. We walked briskly towards the waiting group. Mr Hawke was in good form and said many flattering things. When he told guests that the best way to earn a women's respect was to take her seriously, the applause was spontaneous. He also said: 'The imagination, the foresight and the determination of women like Ita Buttrose are, in my opinion, changing the face and the culture of this country.' It was nice of the PM to say such things but I was just one of many women making a difference.

When it was my turn to speak, after thanking Mr Hawke, I acknowledged his Government's unwavering allegiance to equal opportunity and affirmative action. But it also seemed opportune to remind him that many Australian companies still had a token commitment to the advancement of women – not only was the number of females in corporate boardrooms dismally low, but a recent study of our top companies had revealed almost no women in the upper echelons of decision making. I also drew his attention – respectfully of course – to the fact that there was no woman in Cabinet either.

There was much talk in the eighties about women's

progress, but in reality we hadn't advanced all that much. In 1988 the International Labor Organisation (ILO) released a survey that showed women, wherever they lived in the world, faced more obstacles than men when setting up their own businesses. It also confirmed what many of us already knew: women continually ran up against a mass of prejudices, mainly from financial institutions, preventing them from getting capital and credit to start a business.

The 1988 Australian Business Woman of the Year was a classic example. Perth-based Nancy Reid owned and managed a multi-million-dollar seafood exporting business. Four Australian banks turned her down simply because of her sex. Consequently, she went offshore for finance and found support from an international bank in Japan. When she won her award she warned: 'Australia is behind the rest of the world when it comes to financing women in business.' Once aware of her success Australian banks approached her and asked Reid to change her financial structure.

My bank wasn't much use to me either. On those occasions when cash-flow hiccups meant I needed bridging finance for a week or ten days in order to pay bills and wages, it would advance what was needed providing I signed over the rights to my house for the same short period. But the only time in six years that I requested an overdraft in order to secure some new business that would have helped us greatly, the bank said no. (The balance sheet of a small business is rarely encouraging reading for a bank, even one that had lent millions to irresponsible company bosses, directors and corporate cowboys in the greedy eighties.) When that evening I shared a bottle of wine with Ken Saville, my faithful and hard-working company accountant, we both muttered unprintable things about banks.

After *ITA*'s auspicious debut I immediately set off on a whirlwind tour of Australia, beginning in Melbourne where Lord Mayor Winsome McCaughey officially welcomed the magazine to Victoria. In Queensland, Brisbane's Lord Mayor Sally-Anne Atkinson did the honours. Similar events were organised in Sydney, Hobart, Adelaide and Perth, along with as many public relations activities as we could dream up. Even though we were a national magazine, parochial Australia likes to be made to feel important, therefore it was essential that we were seen to have a presence outside of our home base in Sydney, as well as an interest in interstate local affairs.

Six months after the launch, I knew I'd made a serious mistake in putting such a high price on a page of advertising. There was too much resistance and the feedback was always the same: for a new magazine, *ITA* was too costly. We reduced the casual rate to $5600 and offered a $4400 page rate for a twelve-month schedule and Bina and I crossed our fingers and prayed that our new cost structure would be favourably received.

In August 1989, in an article published in the Melbourne *Herald*, Ian Oshalck wrote, '*ITA* seems to be in trouble mainly due to the fact that it has been virtually ignored by the advertising industry'. He quoted media guru Harold Mitchell whose advice I'd sought in the early days of planning. 'I warned her that she would have to be prepared to be in it for the long haul and have deep pockets,' Mitchell said. '*The Australian* went twenty years before it went into the black.' I never thought *ITA* would be an overnight success, but neither did I ever contemplate that I might have to wait that long before it became profitable and I can't seriously believe that Mitchell did either!

The following month, 1989 *Ad News* reported on a Roy Morgan survey that revealed *ITA* had a readership of 372 000, putting it ahead of other magazines in its price range (such as *Vogue, Belle, Mode, Follow Me* and *Portfolio*). Advertising increased marginally, but we still didn't crack enough of the twelve times schedules that allows a publisher to plan ahead with confidence.

A couple of weeks later I gave an interview to *New Idea* explaining the reason behind our lower rates and said I was optimistic about advertisers' reactions. The reporter asked me if I was worried about failing. 'I've had plenty of failures. Most people have. You give every project your best shot, that's all you can do in life,' I replied.

But by now we were feeling the impact of Australia's domestic airline dispute. Planes had been grounded in August that year as pilots took industrial action for pay rises outside of the accepted wage-fixation guidelines. They resigned en masse and hotels, restaurants, holiday operators, business travellers and any other kind of company that relied on airline travellers for its livelihood lost valuable dollars. Some went out of business altogether. Advertising that we'd counted on (from resort hotels in Queensland, for instance) was immediately cancelled. This was a disaster and one that we couldn't have predicted. We had needed this business and there was no way of replacing it.

We were worried as to the final outcome of the dispute, but encouraged by our circulation which by the end of the year had had settled to about 60 000 a month. This was an excellent circulation for a niche title by anyone's standards, but our ongoing struggle for advertising continued. My brother, Will, rang to tell me how he'd given short shrift to someone who had rung to laughingly tell him about the office sweep taken by a Sydney advertising firm. They had punted on what month ITA would close in the first year. This was the kind of smart-ass attitude I was up against.

There was one other piece of ill fortune that was yet to confront us and that was the 1990 recession which Paul Keating had said 'Australia had to have'. In 1991 Keating replaced Bob Hawke as Prime Minister. By 1992 unemployment had reached eleven per cent, the highest level since 1932, the worse year of the Great Depression. If I known how severe the recession was going to be, I probably never would have started *ITA*!

Economists had predicted a downturn in the economy – it was inevitable after the stockmarket crash of 1987 – but few could have envisaged the severity of what was to come. Capricorn Publishing lurched on. In the first issue of the

magazine we had announced the setting up of the *ITA* Club
for readers who took out an annual subscription to the magazine. We were keen to build up this important segment
because the up-front money would be useful for our expansion. The enthusiastic response took us by surprise and we
quickly had to appoint a special manager to look after our
subscribers' needs. We organised lunches for them with
guest speakers who spoke on the environment, investment
and health; we arranged film and theatre previews as well as
fashion parades that included styles for women who were
more than a size 10. We offered product-sampling, usually
skin-care and other beauty items that we enjoyed checking
out too! By the third issue we had started the *ITA* Travel
Club, which was warmly received by subscribers who travelled on our tours to Alaska, the Caribbean, New York,
England and Europe. I managed to take a few weeks off to
go with one group to Alaska, which I thought magnificent,
and a few years later accompanied Club travellers to the
Caribbean. I had a fabulous time, even though I had to write
articles for *ITA* and host cocktail parties and dinners while
travelling – but, on the whole, *ITA* Club members were a
convivial lot and I didn't find my responsibilities too
onerous.

The *ITA* Club provided a valuable meeting place for our
readers, some of whom, like many other Australian women
lived on their own. In a society that placed – and I think
still does – much importance on couples, many women led
a lonely existence and didn't feel comfortable going out by

themselves. I wanted the *ITA* Club to give such women a friendly, safe environment in which to meet others with whom they'd have interests in common. Not all our Club members lived on their own, of course. Many were married and raising families, while others combined professional careers with their home duties. They led busy lives, but were more than happy to go out and have a good time, if someone did all the organising for them.

One enterprising bloke shared this view. He came along to a Club lunch in Sydney at which our guest speaker's topic was the environment. I had asked for questions and when our sole male guest put up his hand, laughingly said how terrific it was that one of our members had brought along a token man. Not at all, the chap protested, and then confessed to being a bona fide *ITA* Club member, having joined because he was sure it would be a wonderful way to meet members of the opposite sex. There were cheers all round.

Most of our readers were confident, strong-minded women, but even so the thought of the menopause was unsettling for many of them, but only because it was then difficult to get reliable information. *ITA* was one of the first women's magazines to write about this issue in a major way. Even today, with our population rapidly ageing, very little appears in women's magazines about this inescapable female condition. We used the *ITA* Club to run 'Big M' health forums with enlightening sessions hosted by doctors who dispelled the prevailing myths and talked about the benefits and drawbacks of hormone replacement therapy as well as alternative treatments. Question-and-answer time was incredible – we all learned so much. We also campaigned for a national breast cancer screening program for all women, a cause dear to the hearts of our readers. On one occasion, I gave an interview to ABC radio in which I was very critical of the Government's tardiness and suggested that if men got breast cancer that screening would have been readily available.

This led to a lunch invitation from my old friend Neal Blewett, who was still Health Minister. Over coffee, he reached into his briefcase and pulled out a marked transcript of the radio interview and some copies of *ITA*, and began to debate some of the points with me, before assuring me that Government was moving as fast as possible and would I please stop hassling it. But the screening programs had been an election promise and the situation was too serious to stop now. After all, 2000 women were dying of breast cancer annually; another 3000 were having mastectomies. I like to think that *ITA* played a part in making sure the Government honoured its undertaking to try to stop this particular cancer – sooner, rather than later.

On the magazine's first anniversary I conceded that it might have been wiser to have started *ITA* as a bi-monthly. Perhaps if I'd given advertisers more time to get used to the magazine's philosophy and its somewhat lone voice, extolling the virtues of the spending power of the older woman, they would have had more confidence in what I was trying to do. Even though in 1988 37 per cent of Australians were over forty few companies had grasped the potential of the over-forty-five market. It wasn't until the baby boomers began turning fifty in the mid nineties that attitudes began to change significantly. Nowadays, I often hear the facts and figures that I talked about in *ITA*'s early years used by agencies and advertisers who simply didn't want to know when I quoted them.

ITA's first birthday gave me the chance to do some fine-tuning to the magazine's design. It also had become imperative to find ways to cut costs. I began by reducing the size of the magazine from A4 to what is called the 'standard' size, common to most magazines. I did this reluctantly because I thought *ITA*'s larger, distinctive format worked well, but we were operating with a substantial debt – producing a national magazine in a country the size of Australia doesn't come cheaply. Our change in size saved a considerable sum on paper costs and production. I'd taken the staff into my confidence as to why this cosmetic cut was necessary and they appreciated my honesty. Nobody, wherever they worked, took their jobs for granted in the Australia of those times, but I reassured my team that even though money was tight I had no intention of giving up.

In spite of its slimmer look, *ITA* still gave the appearance (I think) that all was well. I impressed upon the staff that the magazine not only had to look confident but so did we because, if for one moment anyone suspected otherwise, the media would attack us like a pack of dingoes.

Our cash flow was abysmal and meant that Capricorn Publishing was slow in paying its bills, something that embarrassed me. Every three or four months, Ken Saville and I would visit 'Charlie' to request extra funds, so that we could pay outstanding accounts. 'Charlie' always came to our rescue, but not before he gave us lessons in how to handle difficult creditors. 'Tell them you will pay half this month, a quarter next month and a quarter the month after. They will be happy to know they are being paid and will accept it.' His advice was always spot on.

It was apparent that *ITA* would not be enough to allow Capricorn Publishing to flourish; we would need to find other work if we wanted to prosper. In February 1990 a Canberra contact informed me that the Federal Government had invited tenders from publishers to produce something called *TaxPack* – an easy-to-use guide to paying tax. Our bid just made the closing date. There was much jubilation when we heard that our tender was successful.

TaxPack seemed like an excellent initiative to us, but simplifying something as complex as income tax didn't turn out to be as straightforward as we'd hoped. We not only had to design *TaxPack*, but also edit copy supplied by the tax office bureaucrats into 'people talk'. Easier said than done, believe me: public servants, rather like lawyers, have a strange language all of their own. We also had to cope with the 'nerves' of the tax office staff who'd been given the responsibility of bringing *TaxPack* to fruition. Understandably they were under pressure. *TaxPack* was a completely new approach –

their career prospects could be harmed if it weren't well received by the public and the Government.

Shortly before *TaxPack* was due to go to the printer's a couple of Australian Tax Office (ATO) executives commandeered one of our offices to speed up the approval process. This made everyone at Capricorn Publishing edgy because none of us had ever before worked in such close proximity to Big Brother! But it was necessary because we were up against the clock and the checking of page proofs had been taking too long. After we'd made our corrections, the pages would go to Canberra where a consortium of people took days to turn them around. Time had run out. If *TaxPack* didn't get to the printer on schedule it would delay its delivery to eight million homes around Australia. That would have been unthinkable.

We often worked back until midnight and, as the pages were completed, Alan Mackenzie came up with the idea of putting them up on the walls of my office. By the time we'd finished the job I was literally surrounded by *TaxPack*, not an interior decorating look I'd recommend. *TaxPack* won universal praise and has been produced annually by the ATO ever since. But wouldn't you know it – having shown the ATO how to produce a user-friendly product, our assistance was no longer needed to handle future editions.

Much to my regret, Ainslie announced her resignation in July 1990. Her departure was a blow because she was more than a work colleague and efficient general manager – she was also a friend and my confidante on many matters.

But I understood her decision. As she said in her note to me 'it is time to start a new life outside of Sydney where we can improve our lifestyle and Woody [her husband] can pursue his career. Despite the distance, I'll always be on hand if needed.'

A few months after she and Woody had set up home in Orange in the Central West of New South Wales it occurred to me that in this whizzbang age of computers and fax machines Ainslie could still work for me. Orange was only a three-and-a-half-hour drive from Sydney and an hour by plane. When I suggested that she could take charge of our special promotions by telecommuting, Ainslie agreed almost immediately. She was enjoying Orange's pleasant lifestyle, but missed the stimulation of a job. It was an ideal arrangement for us both.

Life went on as usual. I studied readership figures and had brainstorming sessions with our advertising team trying to come up with clever ways to get us that essential advertising revenue we were still seeking. Sometimes we surprised even ourselves with our creativity. Circulation sales weren't neglected at this crucial time though. I made frequent promotional appearances at newsagents to sign copies of the magazine and regularly took part in shopping-mall events where our supermarket outlets were. Whenever any opening came along to talk about *ITA*, I took it.

The recession was affecting the company badly when we celebrated the magazine's second birthday in February 1991. Subscribers from the country had begun to write letters saying they could no longer afford to buy *ITA* even though the annual subscription was only $50, because they needed the money for their families. I doubt Prime Minister Keating living comfortably with his family at The Lodge in Canberra had any idea of just how devastating the recession was for many Australians. Canberra's isolation often cushions politicians from the realities of community concerns. People were so strapped for cash that even refunds of $10 were sought.

Nonetheless, we decided to celebrate turning two by publishing the results of a survey, 'Speaking for Ourselves'. We had published the questions in *ITA* a few months' earlier. We wanted to know more about our readers for two reasons – firstly, it would provide us with useful information that might attract advertisers and, secondly, their answers would provide an instructive insight into older women's attitudes.

Six thousand women responded to the survey, which was weighted to reflect the views of the general population. Encouragingly, I thought, one in three (38 per cent) said they intended to enjoy sex until they died or reached the age of 100! Perhaps this had something to do with changing contraception and it came as a surprise to learn from sixty-five per cent of respondents that either they or their partner had been sterilised; 81 per cent of women in their forties admitted this. Ninety per cent thought contraception should be taught to children in secondary school and that women's health checks (such as pap smears and mammograms) should be free.

Six of the top ten concerns of our respondents however related to the environment. They believed the world was experiencing a major environmental crisis; that industry should be heavily fined for polluting soil, air and water and that present penalties for polluters and illegal waste dumpers were inadequate; that killing endangered species for clothing for accessories was unacceptable and so too was killing whales and turtles to obtain ingredients for cosmetics

I wonder how these women feel about Prime Minister Howard's often-stated argument that Australia is 'a special case' and should be exempted from world moves to stop the use of fossil fuels because it would be damaging to our economy. Such thinking suggests that big business has 'got' to him, because it's common knowledge that fossil-fuel emissions are a direct cause of global warming. Perhaps the same kind of blinkered attitude affects the current members of Cabinet. Graham Richardson once told me that, when he was Minister for the Environment in Bob Hawke's Government, his biggest problem was convincing his Cabinet colleagues to take conservation seriously.

The revelations of 'Speaking for Ourselves' prompted me to introduce a 'Green Section' to *ITA*. As far as I was aware, no other women's magazine had yet used recycled paper and the timing seemed perfect for such a development. The readers enthusiastically praised the decision. Although the recycled paper was not the same quality as the glossy stock we used for the rest of the magazine, I was more than pleased with the printing results and, because I believe that each of us does have a role to play in protecting the environment, contemplated printing the entire magazine on recycled stock. There was another plus: the recycled paper was thick and made the magazine look bigger and therefore better value for money.

But once again advertisers let us down, even the ones with products they claimed were environmentally friendly ones. Some companies did support us – we by-passed advertising agencies and dealt with them direct – but it soon became clear that many Australian businesses espoused a 'commitment' for the environment which was nothing more than rhetorical. They didn't want their advertisements printed on recycled paper, only environmentally unfriendly glossy stock would do for them.

If we were finding the going tough, at least we weren't alone, though that wasn't much comfort. At the beginning of 1991, the *Financial Review* reported: 'The fall-out in the magazine industry continues as declining advertising revenues force the closure of several magazines and mergers and restructuring among others.' In the previous six months *Now, Savvy, Follow Me, Follow Me Gentlemen, Australian Investment, Investment Planning* and *Big Beautiful Woman* had closed.

I was approached to buy *Big Beautiful Woman* and briefly considered it. I knew that Australian women's body shapes were becoming larger and that their fashion needs were not being catered for seriously by manufacturers. Unlike *ITA*, other women's magazines rarely included fashions for ample-sized women. Even though the average female size

Just sixteen, and a first-year cadet on the *Daily* and *Sunday Telegraph*s in Sydney.
This snap was taken at the Composing Room's Christmas party.
My mother had given me permission to have one beer!

At twenty-one I married Alasdair (Mac) Macdonald in Sydney. The year was 1963. Mac was still studying Architecture at Sydney University. I was Social Editor of *The Australian Women's Weekly*.

While I was Women's Editor of the *Daily* and *Sunday Telegraphs* I won the *Sydney Morning Herald*'s fashion contest at the AJC Spring Racing Carnival at Randwick in 1967. I was astonished at my good fortune. Sir Frank Packer was absolutely delighted!

I returned to Consolidated Press in 1970 after three years overseas. Soon after, I became Editor of the *Sunday Telegraph* Magazine. It was a black and white newsprint magazine, the forerunner of the colour magazines that appear in our weekend papers in the nineties.

Members of the team at our weekly conference included (from left) Mike Gibson, Elisabeth Wynhausen, Jock Veitch and Samantha McKay. Mike now hosts the morning show on Sydney's 2GB. Elisabeth is a special features writer at the *Australian*.

In 1975 I was appointed Editor of *The Australian Women's Weekly*. By now Mac and I had two children – Kate was seven and Ben was three. Combining career, motherhood and marriage was no mean feat. I often felt utterly exhausted!

Packer power players circa 1976 – with Dawn Swain, Sam Chisholm and Ian Kennon when we were all senior executives in the Packer empire. Dawn is still an executive at ACP. Sam went on to head up Rupert Murdoch's British Sky Broadcasting and Ian and I met again at 2GB in 1996 when we both worked briefly for John Singleton.

Consolidated Press has always known how to give a good party. In the seventies they were often black tie. Nan Musgrove looked particularly elegant at this retirement party, held in 1977 for long-time employee Miss (Fairy) Faircloth, Sir Frank's long-suffering but devoted secretary. Chain-smoker Kerry is in the background.

Kerry not only paid for staff parties, he enjoyed going to them, too. He was a good host and made sure there was always plenty of French champagne! At Fairy's farewell, someone obviously had made us laugh at something. Kerry has a great sense of humour and always appreciates a good joke.

Petticoat penetration at the Conpress group

Kerry Packer's memo to Consolidated Press executives and associated TV station managements had made it quite plain.

It was there in three matter-of-fact paragraphs; a women (undeniably chic, attractive and competent) had finally proved she was worth more to the company than merely being editor of that most sacred of all Consolidated Press cows; the Australian Women's Weekly.

Ita Buttrose (daughter of a former journalist), has made it in the aggressively masculine Packer publishing world.

Cast your eyes over the management names of the Fairfax press, the Murdoch companies, the Herald and Weekly Times and all the other large publishing 'empires.

You will not yet find a woman among these with the same degree of responsibility given to her by the Packer group.

"Miss Ita Buttrose," said the Kerry Packer memo, "has been appointed editor in chief for women's magazines, Australian Consolidated Press Ltd. This is effective now, but she will remain editor of the Women's Weekly during a short transitional period.

"Mrs. Dawn Swain has been appointed editor and will assume that responsibility as quickly as possible.

"Miss Buttrose's appointment as editor in chief will allow her more time to supervise projects which we have in mind.

"This has not been possible in the last 18 months, as the successful changeover of the Women's Weekly was our number one priority. This we feel has been achieved."

Naturally, had the company's gamble with the Women's Weekly format and content changes under her editorship not been adjudged the success Kerry

Buttrose

Packer is satisfied they are, the memo might never have been written.

Still involved with the Weekly in overall control but freed of detail and day to day editorial responsibilities, she is looking at two new Consolidated Press

I was in seventh heaven running the *Weekly* – the job was as exciting and fulfilling as I knew it would be. By 1976 I was Editor-in-Chief, and by 1977 I was Publisher of all Kerry Packer's women's magazines. He gave instructions for the press to be notified.

In 1978 John Singleton gave his official retirement lunch party at Len Evans' Bulletin Place restaurant in Sydney. As his 'best bird mate' I was invited to join in the fun. John didn't stay retired long, and in the nineties he rarely drinks at lunchtime as he's seriously into fitness and keeping thin.

In 1979 I was awarded an OBE for services to journalism in the Queen's Birthday Honours List. Dad and my second husband, Peter Sawyer, came to the presentation at Government House, Sydney. Afterwards we celebrated with a glass or two of champagne.

was (and still is) 14, advertisers didn't want to have anything to do with the 'big' women and like *ITA, Big Beautiful Women,* was short on advertising pages. I sympathised with the plight of the magazine's owner, but I had enough problems to occupy me for the time being.

Even up-market *Vogue* was in a quandary – its circulation had dropped alarmingly and in an attempt to win back readers it cut its cover price by a dollar. I thought this was a clever move and believed *ITA* might increase its circulation, which like *Vogue's* was being affected by the recession, if it followed suit by reducing the cover price from $5 to $3.95. There was no guarantee though that increased sales would follow such a decision and when we did our sums, we realised it was too big a risk to take. We needed every cent we could make.

A few months later I temporarily mused whether a centrefold – shades of *Cleo* – might be a good gimmick. We couldn't afford regular paid promotion on television and radio so I was always on alert for publicity-generating ideas. I was a guest on the Steve Vizard's late-night TV show on the Seven Network and somehow the subject came up. Steve bragged that he would have been a suitable candidate for the *Cleo* centrefold. It was the opportunity I'd been waiting for. Would he like to be *ITA's* first nude centrefold? It was an irresistible challenge. The audience went wild when he said yes. Next morning it was the talk of the town. But alas, a couple of days later, a Vizard spokesman rang to tell me Steve didn't think he was in good enough shape to pose, could the centrefold shoot be put on hold for six weeks. A further excuse followed, and then another. I knew exactly what had happened. Vizard was a typical Aussie male – all talk and no action! Men can be so disappointing sometimes.

At the end of 1991 we had outgrown our Surry Hills office and moved offices to larger premises in nearby Redfern. We were planning our Third Birthday Issue when an old friend, Greg Jones, rang to say he intended to produce the musical *Gypsy*, with his then partner Geraldine Turner in the role of Rose. Opening night would be in Sydney at the end of May 1992. Would I like to do the program? I had never edited a theatre program before, but I had loved musicals since I was a girl and once even thought of becoming an opera singer. It was the kind of job I knew I'd enjoy. I accepted Greg's proposal and agreed to give the show publicity in *ITA*. We did a cover story on Geraldine and offered readers a free sample cassette of her singing the show-stopping 'Everything's Coming up Roses.' It was specially glued to the bottom left-hand side of the cover and easy to remove. We'd done a similar promotion the previous year featuring Luciano Pavarotti to coincide with the great tenor's Australia-wide concert tour. Pavarotti's cassette featured two beautiful operatic arias and his popularity had added several thousand sales to that month's magazine. Geraldine's cassette, while not quite as successful as Pavarotti's still resulted in a healthy lift in circulation. We were delighted – but then everything came to an abrupt halt.

Greg Jones couldn't raise the necessary finance and had to cancel the show. The damn recession had struck again!

However, our unsuccessful endeavour received publicity that caught the eye of promoter Harry Miller, who was part of a syndicate planning to stage a concert version of *Jesus Christ Superstar*. Harry had once acted as my agent and although we had parted ways for reasons that are no longer important, I'd always admired his entrepreneurial spirit. He and his partners wanted an exciting and different program for *Superstar* and he thought perhaps I could give it to them. He needed our concept in a hurry because he and his partners wanted to have the program locked away by the end of the week. We had two days to come up with a suitable design. Once again we burned the midnight oil, but were confident that Harry and his colleagues would like our concept. They did. Our success was quite an achievement because it broke the stranglehold that the Playbill Organisation had enjoyed for years on the production of programs and also souvenirs for major theatrical events in this country. We gave Playbill boss Brian Nebenzahl a colossal fright for which the theatre-going public should be forever thankful since it brought about a long overdue improvement in the design and content of theatre programs.

Jesus Christ Superstar was a fabulous success for everyone connected with it. We sold a record number of programs and made a healthy profit, not enough to wipe out our debt, but enough to make us think that perhaps we were at last turning the corner. Other theatrical promoters sought us out. We designed the program for Andrew Lloyd Webber's *Aspects of Love*. John Frost, the talented producer behind the Gordon Frost Organisation, approached us and we worked very closely with him on a number of his hit productions. Feeling confident, we bid and won the rights to produce programs and merchandise for the Sydney Festival for three years. By now we had set up a merchandising division that designed and produced T-shirts, key rings, mugs and other memorabilia.

Our show business expansion complemented *ITA*. A 1993 Roy Morgan readership survey revealed that the magazine's readers liked theatre, ballet, opera, music and art and that *ITA* enjoyed the highest women's magazine readership profile in this area. We were able to offer readers preferential booking opportunities for some shows, as well as previews and free tickets and snared interviews with sought-after stars.

Unfortunately, the success of the 1993 Sydney Festival was marred by a dreadful summer during which it rained constantly and heavily. The usual big crowds did not turn up for the free performances in Sydney's Domain. Those hardy souls prepared to brave the weather were preoccupied with keeping dry and were not in the mood to buy programs or merchandise. As if that weren't enough, the Festival's box office appeal was not up to the standard of previous years. We'd had to guarantee a sum of money to the organisers to get the business in the first place – but, after costs, didn't have enough to cover the initial payment. We heaved a sigh of relief when we successfully negotiated an instalment payment plan, and optimistically told ourselves that we'd soon have another theatrical success.

But we had woken the sleeping tiger. When he realised how serious we were about getting a decent slice of his business, Brian Nebenzahl began to fight back, offering huge sums of money up-front against profits from program sales to producers who appreciated getting sometimes as much as $200 000 when their shows were in rehearsals. There was no way a cash-strapped company such as ours could match Nebenzahl's inducements.

By now Australia's economic recovery was under way, albeit slowly. As the year progressed, big business began to perform better, but medium and small businesses were not seeing much change in their fortune. Most small firms were saddled with debt, just like Capricorn Publishing. Many went broke and closed.

Fortunately for us, a new door opened. In March 1993 I heard on the grapevine that Telecom was searching for a company with our kind of experience to undertake an urgent commission. We prepared a company profile that made impressive reading and sent it off to the name I'd been given. Two days later Telecom representatives came to our offices to check us out. Shortly afterwards we were appointed 'preferred supplier' for the organisation's corporate identity change from Telecom to Telstra. We had to design a special 'secret identity' program, plus a wide variety of merchandise for Telecom to present to its staff at launch evenings that were to be held around Australia the following month.

Telecom wanted to keep its new logo 'hidden' in the program, which would be handed out at each venue. We did this by incorporating a serrated-edged square, which looked like part of the cover design, into the front of the program. At the crucial moment the audience was told to pull off the square – and there underneath was the new Telstra logo. It worked perfectly and the Telstra people were full of praise. Not only had we done a difficult job in an almost impossible time frame, we'd also kept total security on the project. This was a major concern for Telecom/Telstra who had warned of terrible penalties if any safety breach occurred.

In relating all of these activities, I find myself wondering why on earth we didn't succeed. It certainly wasn't for the want of trying, but without its proper quota of advertisements *ITA* never operated profitably. The debt we carried from our early start-up years increased during the airline dispute and the recession and, although the money we made from diversifying enabled us to pay our most pressing and necessary creditors, we were never able to wipe the slate clean.

7

Closing *ITA*

Congratulations on a great magazine and commiserations on its
demise. You, and it, deserved better. But we all know that when
it's about women and/or ageing, it's one step forward then pause
until everyone else gets it. It was gutsy of you to take that
step – so thank you.

Hazel Hawke

I never worked so hard or made so many sacrifices as during
the six years I ran Capricorn Publishing. I tightened my belt.
I often didn't pay myself. I moved house to something less
expensive. I cut back on the things I most enjoyed. I gave
up some of my memberships to clubs that I'd belonged to
for years. I never put any of my expenses like lunches or my
car lease through the company. To put it mildly, this was
not the most successful financial period of my life. I'm not
moaning about my lot – far from it. I'd made the decision
to run my own business and I was prepared to do whatever
was necessary to make it a success.

I know that life is what you make it. Few people really want to know your trials and tribulations and, as I've never been one to weep on others' shoulders, now didn't seem the time to start. It was my life and I was the one who had got myself into this particular situation. I thought I looked pretty crook but it's only now, writing this book and looking back at old photographs, that I can see how stress and the constant worry of debt was taking its toll. There was a time when I lost my sparkle. In 1996, when I was lunching with 'Charlie', he told me how well I looked and how he now realised just how much running *ITA* against so many odds had taken out of me.

I tried once, unsuccessfully, to tell my gynaecologist how I felt when I went to see him for my annual check-up. 'How's business?' he asked me. 'Terrible,' I replied.

It was all I could do not to shed a tear. I was so dog-tired. I'm sure it's exhaustion that stops a great many small business operators in the end. Lack of sleep makes coping with never-ending problems onerous. Even optimists like me get worn out sometimes.

'I have such a rage in me,' I told the doctor. 'I've never felt anything like this before and I'm having enormous difficulty sleeping. I wake up in the night and can't get back to sleep. I try not to worry about it,' I assured him. 'I figure if I'm meant to sleep I will.'

'What you need is Serepax,' he said. 'It will help you sleep.'

'No. I don't want to take Serepax,' I replied. 'A doctor

prescribed it for my mother years ago and it had a terrible effect on her. She couldn't stop taking it. She became allergic and was quite sick. She developed an awful rash.'

'It won't be the same for you. It would be worse if your immune system didn't function as well as it should because of lack of sleep.' He was determined that I take the rotten stuff.

'I really don't want Serepax,' I said again. My gynaecologist got cranky. 'I suppose you're the type of woman who wouldn't take Hormone Replacement Therapy!'

'Not if I didn't want to,' I replied. He was annoyed with me and it showed.

He wrote out the prescription for Serepax and gave it to me. As I left his suite of offices, I went to the Ladies and threw the bloody thing in the bin.

Who did he think he was? If he'd seen the effect Serepax had had on my mother he would have understood my reaction. I am a sensible woman. He should have understood that and respected my reasons for not taking Serepax.

Trying to share my predicament with a doctor was hopeless and I didn't think I'd do much better anywhere else, so I got on with trying to make the best of things. Thank heavens I hadn't completely lost my sense of humour. I had great fun delighting my friends with my gynaecologist's Serepax solution to sleeping problems, although I didn't tell them the true cause of my insomnia.

One thing I learned early in my career – when you're Ita Buttrose, people seem to think your life is a breeze.

There's an expectation about how you should live and how you should behave. You have to keep up appearances even when it's the last thing on your mind. Some days I could hardly get myself out of bed. I felt so tired, so depressed. My body was stiff with tension. Sometimes it took me a couple of seconds to stand up straight. But I kept going, because somewhere deep inside me was a little voice telling me that today might be the magical day when I would see a light at the end of the tunnel. Occasionally, I'd talk to myself in the bathroom mirror. 'You can do it. You will do it. Get on with it.'

I confessed this once to a journalist interviewing me for an article and he was quite taken aback. 'You talk to yourself in the mirror? Isn't that rather American?' Who knows and who cares? All I know is that when you're the boss of a small business you have to talk to someone and the beauty of talking to yourself in the mirror is that no one answers you back! It does help to give yourself a pep talk.

Although the people who worked for me knew me well, I doubt they had any idea just how difficult I was finding it to keep on going. They were hard workers and as far as I knew were committed to the success of the magazine. I know we all thought we were producing a quality product, sometimes running stories that would not have been run elsewhere in Australia. We were proud of that.

It was *ITA* in October 1993 that broke the story about the abandoned Chinese orphans, mainly girls, that no one wanted – neither their parents nor the Chinese Government.

We published photographs of the 'dying room' of an orphanage in China where baby girls were left, with little nourishment and no loving. One photograph showed four little babies lying in the same cot. Three were very weak, one was dead. Poor little babies who deserved to live and whose only crime was to be born female. In China, as is the case in many Third World countries, boys are preferred to girls. If we think women still have a long way to go to achieve true equality in Australia, just imagine how far women in China have to go.

Our story was syndicated around the world and particularly captured the hearts and minds of many people in Britain who sent us money and letters wanting to know what they could do to help China's girl babies. We set up a fund with the Law Society of New South Wales to help the children. *ITA*'s commitment to such issues had earlier won us a commendation from the Human Rights Commission.

We campaigned for women who needed compensation for the damage caused to them by silicone implants; we looked at the law, and in particular the insensitive remarks about rape made by some judges. We ran articles on women's and men's health – the latter is in a perilous condition. Men need to be encouraged to look after themselves better than they do, particularly those over 50 (my preferred personal age group nowadays!) who continue to treat prostate cancer as a taboo subject even though it affects as many as one in twelve men. Two thousand men die each year in Australia from this particular cancer. It is a dreadful and unnecessary waste of life and mainly due to the fact that men are too embarrassed to discuss their prostate problems with their doctors.

Our interest in women's health was wide-ranging and included female-eating habits and dissatisfaction with body shape. Eating disorders affect too many women and, in order to raise awareness, we organised the Women's Nutrition Forum in Sydney in June 1994. At that time one in ten Australian women was clinically iron-deficient usually due to poor eating habits; two-thirds of young women (aged 18 to 30) were dieting to lose weight because they disliked the look of their bodies and – heaven help us – were only satisfied with the shape of their ears!

ITA examined many of the issues that Australia will have to face in the twenty-first century as its population grows older: such as caring for elderly parents; the frightening growth in elder abuse; and the changes that will need to be made to our houses and apartments when older Australians won't want to walk up too many stairs, for example. Health care, retirement planning – finance generally – all of these subjects were included in our editorial. We reminded our readers time and time again that the only truly independent woman is the one who has financial independence.

We applauded the contribution women from other countries were making to Australia. We were one of the first magazines to write about Muslim women and how they were adjusting to life in our country. Later we talked with Vietnamese women and on our cover ran two pretty young

Vietnamese girls in their national dress. Sales dropped by 7000 that month as racist Australia exercised its choice not to buy. We also received phone calls, many from people with what seemed to us European accents, saying how much they disliked Asians on our cover. I was somewhat taken aback to hear people – who possibly once were 'New Australians' – espousing such hate about a couple of little Vietnamese children. But there were also plenty of people with dinky-di Australian accents who rang to complain about our cover girls. No wonder that during 1996 and 1997 the One Nation founder Pauline Hanson was able to garner such support for her anti-Asian immigration policies.

ITA's editorial also included travel and culture. Our readers loved books, films, theatre, opera, ballet, symphony music and the ABC. As a result, I was always trying to find ways to talk about *ITA* on ABC radio or TV. Our readers also liked knitting and sewing. At first I couldn't work this out – not in such modern times. Then I realised that *ITA*'s generation of women were pioneers. They were brought up knowing how to cook, sew, knit and clean, with no expectation of having a career. Things changed. They kept working, paving the way for women to enjoy the careers they take for granted today, but their old pastimes like knitting and sewing still give them pleasure.

Fashion was always popular with our readers, who frequently complained about the difficulty they experienced in finding clothes that were appropriate for their age group and were available in their size. What a continual battle this is.

Buttrose*

Towards the end of 1993 Harry Czeiger, the CEO of Forbat Styles Pty Ltd, a long-established and respected manufacturing company in Sydney, approached me about starting a mail-order fashion label, 'Exclusively ITA', to try to fulfill this need. He suggested we form a partnership and offer a select number of classically styled garments to our readers which could be bought by mail order. *ITA* always achieved good results for advertisers with direct market products. We put this down to the fact that our readers trusted us. If we promoted something this way, they knew it was okay. This concept worked beautifully for the fashion range. Women adored our styles.

Harry then suggested we design a retail range for boutiques. 'Ita's Collection' was developed and publicised in the magazine and was also well received. We presented the clothes at *ITA* Club fashion parades and were able to show the versatility and practicality of the range. Nothing was too expensive. We used easy-care fabrics and flattering styles. Our readers couldn't get enough of them. The profits from these ventures went back into the company.

ITA encouraged women to 'live' their lives, a philosophy I always advocated in previous publications that I've edited. 'Never apologise for your choices,' we insisted. We talked to professional women with hugely successful careers, and picked their brains for advice for others who wanted to follow in their footsteps. But we were also conscious of the escalating numbers of women starting their own small businesses and encouraged our readers to support them, to use their services and their products. Anything that could help women achieve success in business was high on *ITA*'s agenda.

Naturally we explored relationships and romantic topics. Despite what some fuddy-duddies might think, older women don't lose their sensuality or interest in the opposite sex. Our article 'Would You Take a Younger Lover?' caused much debate among ourselves as well as our readers. Like them, not all of us were in relationships – although we would have liked to have been, but Australia's chronic shortage of men is a common problem for women aged forty-plus. Maybe younger men were worth considering. Women with sons in their late teens and early twenties weren't convinced! However, Linda who was quoted in *ITA*'s article gave us much food for thought.

> Older men tend to be the 'did you come' type, like they somehow equate sex with giving you the housekeeping money. Younger men mightn't give a damn about your orgasm but they are creative, they're more into touch and feel, than older men. Older men, once lovemaking is over, don't have a lot of interest … younger men tend to talk. They're more spontaneous, too. Like they might just jump up in the middle of everything and say, let's go away for the weekend.

Our preoccupation with men wasn't confined only to the benefits of having a man – we also looked at their rights.

I believe many men do not get a fair deal in custody battles in divorce cases and that children suffer as a result. Children need both parents. It's not in their best interests that so many of them are being raised in fatherless households. In some instances, the Family Court has let men down – but that's not to say that some men don't treat their families badly.

ITA was critical of men who dumped their first wives for younger females and, when we wrote about Australia's growing phenomenon in 'The Discarded First Wife Syndrome', discovered that we'd opened a can of worms. More women than we'd anticipated responded angrily about being given the heave-ho by their husbands without any warning after years of marriage and almost always for a younger woman turned on by his power. The unsuspecting first wife – having coped with the children, ironed shirts, cooked, cleaned and handled all the crises as he forged ahead in his career – was as mad as hell about her lot. 'I gave him the best years of my life,' one said. 'Now he tells me I no longer suit his lifestyle!' So much for being a loyal wife, another woman wrote bitterly, still in shock from her 50-something husband's announcement that he was ditching her for a 28-year-old who worked in his company. Another reader said her husband had discarded her for an Asian teenager after 30 years of marriage. 'He says she makes him feel young.' The physical aspect was also signifi-cant. As Noeline Hogan, whose film-star husband Paul gave her the boot for his *Crocodile Dundee* co-star, Linda Kozlowski, told us: 'How can a 50-year-old female body compare with a 29-year-old female?'

Most first wives, by the way, get to keep the kids, but lose the financially secure future they had with their husbands. This was a common grievance. Family homes are often sold. The first wife moves into something smaller, while the second spouse enjoys the trappings of his success. It's commonplace to see older men with their younger wives – often young enough to be their daughters – and a second family. Many of them enthuse about the joys of fatherhood the second time around, explaining that they never had time for their first family due to career pressures, as their first wives know only too well! As *ITA* challenged its readers: How can there ever be solidarity among women as long as our younger career sisters believe it is okay to bundle out first wives and walk off with their husbands?

I knew all about the anger and misery of unwanted first wives. When I was 20 my father had married his secretary, Margot, who was more than 30 years his junior. My mother never remarried. She and Dad had been married for twenty-five years and as far as she was concerned, Dad was the only man in the world for her. Mum's life was never the same after the break-up. I often heard her crying at night about her loneliness. She died after a short illness in January 1994. When the doctors told us there was nothing they could do, my brothers and I sat by her bedside, sometimes together and at other times taking it in turns, at Sydney's Royal Prince Alfred Hospital – there was no way we were going to allow Mum to be alone when she died.

As I kept watch, I reminisced: coming home after school

when we lived in the States, opening the front door to hear Mum's beautiful piano playing. I can see her now across the room sitting at the baby grand. It gave me such joy to find her there and I loved her accomplished playing. She gave me my first piano lessons and, when we were young, would play the piano after dinner for family singalongs.

When I was in my early teens we regularly went to the movies at the ancient picture show at nearby Watsons Bay. It was about a twenty-minute walk from our home in Parsley Bay. We used to call these evenings our 'girls' night out', a custom I continued with Kate. There was one film night, however, when I cheerfully could have strangled Mum. We'd gone to the opening night of *Cleopatra* in the city. It was on the set of this epic movie that Elizabeth Taylor and Richard Burton's tempestuous love affair began and by the time the film was completed it was public knowledge. Naturally people were curious to see the world's greatest lovers, as they'd become known, on screen together. In retrospect, it wasn't the greatest of films, but, as a romantically minded young girl, I thought it was wonderful. Just at some dramatic moment with the entire theatre caught up in the plot, Mum began to laugh. The more I nudged her to be quiet, the worse she became, 'It's so awful, it's funny,' she giggled in a whisper. I was mortified.

Then there was the time she decided to go on a diet. It was on a weekend. She had cooked the Sunday roast with spuds, vegetables and gravy and it smelt fabulous. As we – Dad, the boys and I – sat down to devour our meal, Mum who'd eaten only two boiled eggs for breakfast, brought in her plate – with six prunes on it! We watched her eat them one by one while she watched us clean our plates.

Later that afternoon I was reading in my room when I heard a frantic kind of sound coming from the pantry. Thinking it might be a mouse, I snuck out to kitchen and flung open the door, only to discover Mum with her hand in the biscuit tin. 'I'm hungry,' she said plaintively. That was the end of her diet.

In the last weeks of her life – before she went to hospital, one of the nurses who looked after Mum told me how much she liked her. 'Your mother is a very nice woman,' she said. 'I've never heard her say an unkind word about anyone.' And that was true – except it must be said, when it came to Dad and Margot! But otherwise Mum was an extraordinarily kind person who always had time to help someone in need. She was too softhearted really and coping with the realities of life and the demands of a dominant man like Dad (something he occasionally acknowledged) was too much for her to handle. More often than not she turned to alcohol for solace. My mother's life was a sad one and much of it was wasted. She never really knew her grandchildren, for instance. I find it impossible to think about her without sorrow.

I'm not sure when I first started to seriously think the time had come to close down *ITA*, but in looking back I can see that it was on my mind. I gave an interview to Yvonne Preston for the *Canberra Times* in May 1994, in which I said,

'Once you get past fifty, you start to think. First you lose friends who die and then you become aware of how short the time span is that we have. Some of us exercise our options and take a different direction. Others can't because of financial commitments or we don't want to . . .'

A few days later in another interview, this time with Suzanne Daniel in the *Sydney Morning Herald*, I said: 'I want to write more, travel, garden and I guess have more pleasure time. Yes, I am getting ready for a new chapter in my life.'

In the end, I was not only physically but also mentally worn out. I couldn't keep going. I was utterly exhausted and my anger was increasing. I think I kept it mostly hidden and under control, but it was there. Sometimes I felt as though I would burst. There was no one I could talk to about how I felt.

I didn't consider for one moment lumbering the kids with my problems. Why should I? They'll have their own worries in the years to come; they didn't need mine. Kate was no longer living at home. Having graduated as an architect she now had a job and decided she'd like to flat with friends, something my own mother had forbidden me to do when I was twenty. She considered my wanting to leave home as a slight to her mothering skills and gave me such a hard time, I stayed at home. I've always regretted this, as I would have liked to have had some time on my own between leaving home and getting married.

Kate had worked for me for several months after graduating as an architect from Sydney University. The recession was in full swing at the time and there were few jobs for bright young architects. It was wonderful having her working with me – she is a natural with people and she quickly adapted to the business. Her logical mind and intelligence made her a delight to have on staff and many of our customers told me how much they enjoyed dealing with her, without knowing she was my daughter. She had seen for herself how tough business was and I guess, how hard I worked – she knew this of course, just from growing up with me, but working for me gave her a really good look at what I did when I was away from home.

I employed other people's children, too – among them Bunty Turner's daughter Sarah and my two nieces Angie and Rebecca, the daughters of my elder brother Julian. It was hard for young people, even those with ability, to find employment in the early nineties. I was happy to be able to give them a job and, especially with journalist Angie and artist/stylist Rebecca, to have a hand in their early training.

Ben was still at home and studying at university for his science degree. I often worked back, not getting in until eight. He would have dinner waiting for me. Sometimes I'd give him cooking instructions over the phone – other times he'd experiment with a dish that he had seen me cook. He always was interested in cooking and, when he was studying for his PhD and often up at Fowlers Gap, not far from Broken Hill, at the CSIRO research station doing soil research, was in demand as a cook by his colleagues. His culinary skills are highly regarded. I often brag about them to my friends and especially about the fact that he can whip up the best chocolate cake in the microwave. Both Kate and Ben knew that I was worn out, but I didn't tell them what I was contemplating.

One morning I awoke and knew that I was the only one who could make the decision to close the magazine and the company; that I not only had to make it, but make sure it happened. Once again, as I had when I was weighing up whether to stay at 2KY or keep chairing NACAIDS, I asked myself if I was doing what I'd choose to be doing if I knew I had only six months to live. The answer was no. I wasn't enjoying my life. Mind you, I didn't have any life apart from Capricorn Publishing and *ITA*. I was simply existing. I no longer wanted to go on this way.

Although Australia's recession was officially over, the economy was still sluggish. Business lacked confidence. Our advertising revenue was still poor and there was no indication that it would pick up. Our forward bookings were just about non-existent. We owed money to printers, contributors, and many other suppliers, all of whom were very patient with us. I could see no light at the end of our particular tunnel. Not even a flicker.

In the last few months of the magazine's life, the rage in me grew even bigger. I used to wonder if it was something menopausal or whether I was heading for a breakdown. I think it might have been a combination of both. I had this strange feeling – that no doubt a psychiatrist could explain – that I wanted to punish myself. Why or for what I do not know, but it was a very strong urge. There was only one thing to do. Pull the plug. Pay the bills and get my life back.

I went to see my 'Charlie' and, quite unlike him, he asked me to join him and another visitor for a cup of tea. I am sure I must have looked like I was carrying the problems of the world on my shoulders. I could barely listen, let alone make small talk. The visitor finally took his leave and I told 'Charlie' I thought we should call it quits.

Again he offered to keep the business going. What a man! He had invested hundreds of thousands of dollars and he still didn't want me to close down, in spite of everything. He often called *ITA* magazine his folly but, as a very young man, he had published books and had enjoyed the experience. His career had taken him down a different path but his very fond memories of his own publishing success influenced him in making the decision to support Capricorn Publishing.

We owed *ITA*'s printer, Hannanprint in Sydney, several hundred thousand dollars. But I had assured the Hannan Group's Managing Director, Michael Hannan, early in the magazine's life that whatever happened (there were often rumours that we were going to close and Michael, not unnaturally, must have worried that he might end up with an unpaid bill) my company would never go bankrupt, and that everyone would be paid.

Given the way things turned out and our constant cash-flow problems, it was lucky for me that Michael believed me. We never would have lasted as long as we did without his support. He even allowed me 120 days credit. It's something I'll never forget. When I announced we were ceasing publication of *ITA*, we owed Hannanprint almost $700 000. Before anyone else knew that we were closing, I rang Michael and made an appointment to see him. I told him what I was doing and assured him once again that he would be paid. Amazingly, he didn't even ask when. He just thanked me for letting him know.

'Charlie' and I called in the accountants to work out how much money we'd need to put into Capricorn to settle all the debts. We decided to publish our last issue – August 1994 – and keep it on sale for at least six weeks instead of the usual four. That particular issue had better advertising revenue than usual and money from sales of the magazine would help us settle our bills. We anticipated a bigger sale than usual, believing that people would consider the last issue would be a collector's item.

We knew I had to tell the staff face to face. We also knew that there would be a media circus to handle. Telling the staff was the hard part. The rest was relatively easy. The men and women I employed had worked energetically for *ITA* and most of them loved the magazine almost as much as I did. We knew *ITA* was a special magazine. We were also mindful that not enough people understood the kind of magazine it was because I was never able to promote *ITA* properly. There were a lot of misconceptions about it. Australia's magazine market was, and still is, very crowded. You do need to have plenty of promotional money to establish any magazine in such a marketplace. But in spite of everything, there had been some fun moments and the occasional triumph. We were proud of *ITA*. Some great professional associations had been established and friendships, too. We respected each other's abilities and the quality Australian magazine we had managed to produce against all odds!

All of these things were on my mind when I asked the staff to join me at 4 p.m., 11 July 1994. They had no idea what was going to happen. I could hardly get the words out. I was so upset that when I finally managed to tell them I was going to close the magazine, while at the same time thanking them for everything they had done to try to make it successful, I was stopped for words – it was too distressing for me. I simply couldn't go on. Thank heavens, Alan Mackenzie who looked after the production of our Program Publishing Division, came forward and hugged me. I managed to pull myself together. I thanked them yet again. There was a hushed, horrified silence. I went back to my office. I think everyone drifted off to the pub. They were in a state of shock. Thank heavens also for Ainslie Cahill, who came to Sydney and stayed with me for two weeks to help me with the many things that had to be done. Her support meant a great deal to me.

We had sent out a press release to coincide with my breaking the news to the staff. It wasn't long before the phone was ringing. Was it true? It couldn't be. Were we really closing down? The following morning, the TV crews had Capricorn Publishing staked out. It was awful. I tried to avoid them but it was impossible. I realise now that I just should have breezed past them, but I was feeling shattered and not thinking clearly. I drove around the streets of Redfern trying to find a sneaky way into the building. Silly me. Of all people I should have appreciated the persistence of the media. A Channel 10 reporter nabbed me on the back stairs. He asked me if I was upset. Fortunately, that meant I had only to give him the briefest of answers. 'Yes,' I said, and closed the door.

Announcing the magazine's closure didn't mean everything simply stopped. There were a million and one things for me to do. I had to write references, work out termination payments, inform the various authorities that a business is required by law to notify, deal with unions regarding termination payments, stop the phones, look after subscription refunds. Some subscribers wrote and said they didn't know what they'd do without *ITA* and told us to keep the money. There were hundreds of callers to attend to as well.

Most of the staff left the day I announced the closure. The cleaner was put off. That meant I often had to clean the office as well as the toilets at night. There was no one else. Ainslie was terrific as only she can be. She often lent me a hand with the vacuuming. I kept only a few people to help me wind up the business. I decided to sell everything that could be sold. I wasn't keen to have an auction, but as the auctioneer explained: 'Ita, if we hold the sale at your premises you'll make more money. People will come just to have a look'. He was right. They did. It tested my fortitude, but we did make more than we expected.

In the middle of the clean-up, *Sixty Minutes* rang to see if I'd talk to them about *ITA*. I was deluged with requests from the media and I figured if I gave one main interview then I'd be left in peace. *Sixty Minutes* filmed me as I was still feeling much anguish, not only at my decision to close, but also because of what I'd had to endure in the weeks afterwards. They were not around, however, when I called in the dump bins and filled them day after day with material that had once filled the pages of *ITA* – transparencies, layouts, hundreds of copies of old *ITA*s as well as countless unfulfilled hopes and dreams. The staff had left all sorts of junk behind in their desks as well. It all went into the bins in the office car park. The worst part of it all was the nostalgia evoked of the days gone by, plus the fact that to reach the car park meant going up and down three flights of stairs. It was a couple of years before my sciatic nerve recovered from the strain and loads of those hectic few weeks of clearance. Not one former staff member rang to offer to help. I wondered about this. But on the other hand, why should they have? They had to get on with their lives. The few people I'd kept were fantastic and, even though they knew they would soon be out of a job, remained incredibly cheerful. They were going through tough times too, and I knew that.

There were pluses, I discovered, in having a well-built, strong son like Ben and his equally strong mates. Because I knew I shouldn't be carrying heavy loads (I'd been warned before that doing such things weren't good for my back) I asked Ben if he could round up some of his mates to give me a hand. I offered to pay them. The boys came and did whatever I asked. Later that night, Ben told me the boys were happy to help and for no charge!

Then there were the people who owed me money. When you're a small, struggling business it seems that others are always prepared to take advantage of you. They know there's not much you can do if they are slow in paying or even don't pay at all – one prominent fashion company chose the latter option, even though *ITA* had done a great deal to help it grow its business by allowing the firm access to *ITA* club members.

More than two months after announcing the closure, half a dozen firms were still dodging paying us. I'd had enough. I placed the outstanding accounts in the hands of the meanest, toughest debt collection agency I could find and, on their advice, initiated proceedings against one company whose owner said he couldn't afford to pay but was still able to afford to travel overseas. He settled!

Even our landlord proved difficult. Having painted the premises, cleaned them beautifully, left him the alarm system and the blinds and given him the escorted tour, after which he said he was absolutely delighted with the way the premises looked, I said to him, 'You'll organise for the return of our bond, won't you?'

'Bond?' he said. 'Did you pay a bond?'

Oh no, I thought. I had another problem customer on my hands. I gave him a month and rang again to remind him.

'You have to understand Ita. I have a $20 000 overdraft and it's extended.'

'You have to understand,' I replied, 'I want to close my company.'

He said he'd get back to me. A few days later, he sent me a post-dated cheque for three-quarters of the bond. The remainder would come shortly, he said.

He expected me to accept this kind of shoddy behaviour and to be ladylike and polite about it, which is the way everyone expects Ita Buttrose to behave. As I wrote in an earlier chapter, there is an expectation of how Ita Buttrose should be. I am aware of it and try to behave as people expect me to.

Maybe I'm wrong. Maybe I should worry less about being the Ita Buttrose everyone expects me to be. But there's no getting away from the fact that when you're Ita Buttrose, people do have a preconceived idea of who you are and what you do and the kind of behaviour they expect from you.

As a result, I rarely tell people how I feel. I cope with major catastrophes, usually by myself. I did ring Kate when I got home in the evening, after I'd made the initial decision with 'Charlie' to close *ITA*, and told her what was happening. There was a knock at the front door within thirty minutes of me telling her. 'You can't spend this evening by yourself,' she said. 'I'm staying.' And so she did. What would I have done without her? She knew – because we are kindred spirits – exactly how I was feeling. There was no need for me to say anything further about that bleak day. Kate was there for me. That was all that mattered.

In looking back at this melancholy time I realise I had no time to grieve. I'd been expected to soldier on, to get the things done that had to be done. Ita the person had no time to grieve for *ITA* the magazine. A part of me had died, but I hadn't been allowed to go to the funeral.

I was furious about the people who wouldn't pay me the money they owed. As for the landlord, I felt like punching him in the face. There were times when I wished I hadn't been decent and left him the alarm system, the blinds and the industrial vacuum cleaner. Briefly, I felt like breaking in and taking them back again.

And then there was the insulting interview that *Sixty Minutes* did! I don't think I'll ever forget the moment when reporter Tracey Curro suggested that I was a failure. Heaven help me, since when does having a go equate with failure? I consider that I would have failed if I had not paid our creditors and my staff their full entitlements. I certainly wasn't about to hop on the plane to Spain like Christopher Skase! That would have been the easy option.

I've often thought *Sixty Minutes* had a wonderful opportunity to tell the behind-the-scenes struggles of a small independent publisher in Australia, but because they came with a preconceived idea of the segment they wanted, or perhaps because they worked for Kerry Packer, they didn't want to see the real story under their noses. They came with only one intention – to bury me. But I refused to let them.

Having told me I was a failure, Tracey insisted I was old, in a way that sounded as if I had a terminal disease.

'Don't you feel old?' she persisted.

I assured her I didn't. And then I asked her a question.

'What is old, Tracey?'

'Well,' she said, somewhat smugly, 'I know I'm not old.'

'Someone fifteen might think you're very old,' I suggested.

That stopped her – but only for a second. 'Well,' she declared, 'you're middle-aged.'

'These days,' I told her, 'middle age is sixty!'

Frank Devine, the columnist in the *Australian*, summed it up well in a piece he wrote not long afterwards: 'Age shall not weary her, but *Sixty Minutes* will.'

The Nine Network copped tremendous criticism over Tracey's interview. People were incensed on my behalf. I received hundreds of faxes and letters, which were very comforting during the days when I was winding everything up. Their protests must have really been something because it resulted in a call from Nine's then chairman, Bruce Gyngell, from Los Angeles where he was doing some business. 'I've received a great many calls,' he confessed. 'Have we upset you?'

Well, yes and no. Not that I said that to Bruce whom

I've known for years and with whom I've shared a drink or two, and some delightful times. 'Of course not,' I said in my best Ita Buttrose voice. 'It was an interesting experience.' But he knew that *Sixty Minutes* had bombed.

A number of the letters I received applauded me for 'putting Tracey in her place' about age and ageing. Australians generally have a peculiar attitude to age and growing older. I can only wonder why, especially given the fact that we are a rapidly ageing society.

After I'd closed the magazine, one of the readers wrote and told me that she thought it had been five years ahead of its time and that in five years time there would be an even bigger need for a magazine like *ITA*. I received many thoughtful letters from people who were genuinely sorry to see the magazine go. They were comforting. It helped to know that people were thinking of me. Phillip Adams got straight to the point in his letter:

> So your namesake journal is no more. But better the masthead bite the dust than its originator. I've no doubt that Kerry played a shabby role in all this. And Rupert too? No one will, of course, have the guts to publicly speculate on these possibilities. That's the consequence of having a media oligopoly.

Bob Carr, the New South Wales Premier (a former journalist, who had worked on the *Bulletin* when I was running the *Weekly*), wrote, 'Don't be disheartened by the fate of the magazine. It was a quality effort, deserved better and gave work to decent journalists'.

Carolyn Hewson dropped me a line, too.

> It was just two years ago when I locked horns with the editors of some of the weekly magazines, having stated that I thought they could do more to empower women and help them educate themselves on important issues such as health, family responsibilities etc, etc. Ita, you did just that. You produced a magazine free of the catchy, populist illusion and provided a solid, informative, interesting, fine monthly read. Thank you for trying – God help us if we lose people who are prepared to try and try again . . .

I also heard from Max Suich, who after leaving Fairfax had gone on to start his own newspaper, *The Independent*, in 1989. In 1993 he changed it to a magazine format, renaming it the *Independent Monthly*. Its circulation peaked at 33 000 – not enough to help it attract enough advertising or cope with rising print costs. It finally suffered the same fate as *ITA*. Max closed it down in July 1996. The *Independent Monthly* had a fine reputation for publishing stories and opinions other publications wouldn't touch – and like *ITA*, was also a valuable forum for many talented Australian writers, artists and photographers.

In an interview with *Media Australia Update*, Max said, 'One major reason why we've closed is my wife and I – a major part of the magazine – are just exhausted after seven years. If someone else had picked it up it would have been a considerable success but we just ran out of puff'. I knew exactly what he meant.

No one forced me to close *ITA*. Nor did I go bankrupt. Like Max and his wife, I ran out of puff. Working seven days a week and often late into the night had taken its toll. Whenever I did manage to get away I was in daily contact with the office to make sure the cash flow hadn't dried up and that our creditors were under control. There was never any respite from the day-to-day pressures. A couple of times I had appointed someone from outside as Editor for *ITA*, with me taking an Editor-in-Chief role, but time and time again, the staff resisted such moves, always finding fault with the incumbent and making the person's life a misery. They wanted only me as their Editor – which was gratifying, but eventually intolerable.

My workload was horrendous. Editing a magazine is a full-time job and in the past had given me joy and satisfaction. But this time I had to combine my role with running the company – another full-time job that included constant searching for new business, another demanding task. Consequently, I usually had to read *ITA* copy and page proofs in the evening or on weekends and because the magazine's editorial budget was tight, I often wrote some of its regular features – again after hours.

A great deal of my time was spent with our advertising team, which often felt demoralised by the lack of positive response, and required motivation as well as ideas for advertising prospects. Agencies and potential clients always preferred me (I think it makes them feel important when an Editor turns up) to call on them in the company of our Advertising Manager and these meetings were preceded by hours polishing up proposals and concepts. I used to enjoy this though. I would study a potential client's business including its plusses and minuses and then try to come up with a brainwave to increase sales. Sometimes a prospective advertiser would get so excited that I knew the business was in the bag. For instance, when I told Waterford Wedgwood that I was prepared to turn the first sixteen pages of our December 1991 Christmas issue into an elegant catalogue titled 'Timeless Gifts' promoting their products, the then managing director, Roger Little, couldn't resist an enthusiastic 'I like that idea'. I knew that no matter what his advertising agency said, we would clinch the deal. We did. Roger didn't even demur about the $50 000 I charged him for the project. I remember tearing back to Capricorn Publishing to let Ken Saville know of our success. When we shared our bottle of wine that night we were full of festive cheer.

The *ITA* Club, which I always thought was one of our better ideas, was fun but also taxing. Even though the Club had its own manager, the readers – not unreasonably – expected me to attend all functions and they were held throughout Australia. On those occasions that required it, I acted as MC as well. By anyone's standards I was working long and hard. By 1994 I was averaging only five hours sleep a night. Is it any wonder I felt worn out?

Whether you work for yourself or for someone else, sometimes the time comes when you know that in spite of your very best efforts a certain project is not going to prosper. It is at such a moment that a boss is truly put to the test. It does take courage to admit that a venture does not seem to be working, but it takes even greater courage to say that it must cease altogether.

But that is what management is all about. A boss has to be a person not only with a vision, who can motivate, share goals with his or her staff and who can command respect; a boss also must be a person who can make the difficult decisions, ones that sometimes mean staff won't like you. And, occasionally, a boss must be a person who is brave enough to pull the plug. If you can't take the tough decisions, then you shouldn't be in management.

Why didn't *ITA* work? I've asked myself that question over and over again. There was of course the recession but, putting that to one side, I'm convinced the magazine was ahead of its time. There is a different attitude to age now that didn't exist in 1989. If a woman picked up *ITA* she was admitting she was older and women weren't comfortable doing that. Age discrimination was something women were very familiar with – some had been thrown on the employment scrap heap in preference to bright young things. It would have been unheard of for a personality like

When I was the subject of Roger Climpson's *This Is Your Life* on Channel 7 in 1979, two of the surprise guests were my childhood next-door neighbours. I lived at number 9 Parsley Road, in the eastern Sydney suburb of Vaucluse. Trish Burns lived at number 7, and international film director Peter Weir resided at number 11. In 1997 Trish and I had a fabulous holiday in France. Our friendship began when we were eight!

My favourite photograph of Marj McGowen taken with Kate and Ben in 1980. They loved her, like all kids did. Sometimes when I was travelling she would come and look after them. She never quite got over our dog, Brutus, who liked to sleep beside her bed – and snored!

In 1985 I joined John Fairfax & Sons. My duties included feature writing for the now defunct afternoon *Sun* newspaper. I interviewed Michael Chamberlain – here with his daughter Kahlia – for a special series in July 1985 on one of Australia's most controversial murder cases. I also talked with Michael's wife, Lindy, in Berrimah Prison, Darwin, where she was sent after being found guilty of murdering their first daughter, Azaria.

Photograph courtesy of the Fairfax Photo Library

A proud mother. This is one of my favourite pictures. Ben and I were celebrating the Christmas festive season in 1987 with several friends at lunch at our home. I like entertaining and I love cooking because I find it very relaxing. Ben likes cooking, too. Sometimes I wish he'd get out of my kitchen!

On the AIDS campaign in 1985. As Chairperson of the National Advisory Committee on AIDS (NACAIDS) I often shared press conferences with the Chairperson of the AIDS Task Force, Professor David Penington. We both knew the importance of getting the correct educational messages out to the public.

Photograph courtesy of the Fairfax Photo Library

In 1995 I visited Nairobi in Kenya for World Vision Australia with Dr Brendan Nelson, now the Federal Member for the Sydney seat of Bradfield. We visited many villages throughout Kenya listening to the problems Africans face in combating the HIV/AIDS virus.

In June 1985 I joined 2KY to host their morning show from nine until twelve.
This shot was taken on my first day there. Radio is the most wonderful of mediums – it is
so instant and you never know what will happen when you take talkback calls. A few
months after starting at the station, I helped to talk a man out of committing suicide.

Photograph courtesy of the Fairfax Photo Library

With former Prime Minister Gough Whitlam at a Curran Foundation dinner in
Sydney in 1988. Gough was Chairman of the Australian National Gallery when
I joined the Council in 1990. There was never a dull moment. When he became
Prime Minister in 1972, he stirred a sense of patriotism that most Australians
never realised they had.

I went to The Lodge in Canberra in 1989 to interview Hazel Hawke, the then wife of the Prime Minister, for the first issue of *ITA*. Hazel has many admirers, notably for the dignified way she has handled matters through difficult times of her life – most especially when Bob left her after thirty-nine years of marriage for a younger woman, Blanche d'Alpuget, whom he married in 1995.

Photograph by Michael Jensen

Prime Minister Bob Hawke launched *ITA* Magazine at Parliament House, Canberra, on 15 February 1989. It was an unforgettable day. Bob kept telling me to relax because I was so nervous. By launching *ITA* he confirmed that his Government was genuine in its commitment to the advancement of women and that it believed in women having a go.

THE INTERNATIONAL MAGAZINE FOR WOMEN

*The exciting new
magazine for
The Woman Who
Wasn't Born Yesterday*

ISSUE 1 MARCH 1989
$5.00 • N.Z. $7.50 including GST

9 771032 563016

The cover of the first issue of *ITA* Magazine carried the line 'The exciting
new magazine for *The Woman Who Wasn't Born Yesterday*.' In hindsight, that was a mistake.
Many Australian women weren't ready to face the fact that they were getting older.
Like most other Australians, they think of ageing as something to avoid at all costs.
If only we could!

The family was out in force for TV's
This is Your Life in 1998. Here I am with
(from left, back row) brothers Julian, Will
and Charles and (from left, front row)
Aunty Billy, Kate and Ben.
Photograph courtesy Channel Nine

On the road again: as a journalist in 2001,
interviewing New South Wales
Opposition Leader Kerry Chikarovski,
and then Federal Democrats Leader Meg
Lees for *The Australian Women's Weekly*.
Photograph courtesy The Australian Women's Weekly

Breaking TV's female age barrier
with fellow 2001 *Beauty & the Beast*
regulars (clockwise from upper left) Prue
MacSween, Jeannie Little, Maureen Duval,
the beastly Stan Zemanek and Jan Murray.
This top-rating show has paved the way
for mature women on TV.
Photograph courtesy Foxtel

Maggie Tabberer to admit her age back then. But in an early 2001 issue of *The Australian Women's Weekly* Maggie happily admitted to being 64 (I remember when she didn't want anyone to know she had turned 50), and to being thrilled at having been asked to be the face of Foxtel's FX Channel for Women, an appointment that wouldn't have been considered as little as five years ago. In the past, television has been conspicuous for its absence of older women presenters. Pay-TV has led the way here. Foxtel's highly successful *Beauty & the Beast* with its controversial beast Stan Zemanek opened the doors for older female personalities who have delighted audiences around Australia with their wit and wisdom. When I made my first appearance on the panel in 1996 I had no idea that by 2001 I would be one of the five permanent regulars (four of us are 55 plus) signed for the year for the top-rating show, which is the only program to be screened on the same day on both pay and free-to-air television. I'm sure that if *ITA* were to hit the streets now its progress would be much easier.

There's no doubt in my mind though that the advertising industry had a part to play in our demise. Some in the industry openly bad-mouthed us for reasons that were never clear to me. Without essential advertising dollars, the magazine was never going to be profitable and there is a limit to how long a publisher can wait for this to happen. It was all very well for Harold Mitchell to talk about hanging in for twenty years, but such a proposition was hardly feasible. Our paucity of advertising pages also affected the look of *ITA*.

Women have been conditioned to see plenty of advertising in their favourite magazines. It's the way they find out about new products and something that not only gives them information, but pleasure.

Even when *ITA* had a larger circulation than it did when we closed, we were unable to get a healthy quota of advertisements. From time to time I heard the old rumour – they didn't want to support me in case they offended Kerry Packer. Maybe that was the case – but if it was, how gutless of them.

One of the other problems in being Ita Buttrose who once ran vast circulating titles like *The Australian Women's Weekly* is that many people expect me always to run a similar selling title. They couldn't or didn't want to see that a niche title like *ITA* was never going to be an immense circulation title like the *Weekly*.

In the five and a half years that *ITA* was on sale, it was apparent that the advertising industry still had a long way to go in accepting that there was an older market waiting to be properly recognised and addressed. Like the women who did not want to pick up *ITA* for fear of being thought of as 'old', the advertising industry was obsessed with maintaining its Peter Pan image. One day they'll learn that it's okay to leave boyhood behind. I know that is outrageously sexist, but then so is the advertising industry – and its decision makers are mainly men.

In the same year I closed *ITA* I accepted the position of Chair of the Seniors Media Network Council, an initiative of the then New South Wales Liberal Government, to improve the portrayal of older people in the media and in advertising.

Among other things, we conducted briefings at working breakfasts for CEOs of the top advertising agencies in Sydney. It was an interesting exercise. The CEOs, all men in their late forties and early fifties, listened politely to what we had to say. They considered the facts we presented about ageing, plus the fact that the baby boomers were quickly moving towards their fifties. (The first baby boomers started to turn fifty in 1996 – the world may never be the same again!) You could see the penny drop. You could almost see them thinking: 'Hell, I am one of the statistics of Australia's ageing society.' Yet at the same time it was apparent they were also thinking: 'But fifty isn't all that old. I'm still going to enjoy life the way I always have. Nothing will change.' If only they had realised this earlier, *ITA* might have survived.

But they didn't. In fact, many of the agencies seemed to be inhabited only by extremely youthful-looking men and women, the kind who believed growing older will never happen to them. I'd often convince someone that *ITA* could do an effective job promoting their product only to have some bright young ad exec talk them out of it.

This happened time and time again. Tom Hayson, Chairman of the Hayson Group of Companies, confirmed this when he wrote to me on 13 July 1994.

You should not feel too despondent that you have lost the fight to keep *ITA* alive despite the fierce competition from the mega media groups and the apathy of advertisers who should know better.

Yours was a valiant effort against impossible odds, and the fact that you tried so hard and so long is a tribute to your grit and spirit to succeed.

I have long regretted that I was one of those apathetic advertisers after you came to my office some years ago seeking an advertisement from us.

As I remember it, your advertising presentation was most persuasive and could have done a good job for us.

I was sold on your ideas but allowed the strong views of a young marketing manager, who should have known better, [to] sway me into using our funds to concentrate on a younger market, much to the detriment of our business.

I recalled that when Sir Frank Packer had started *The Australian Women's Weekly* back in 1933 he had had difficulty attracting advertisers to his new magazine. He sought out the biggest and best advertisers of the day and put a pitch to them. It worked for him. And two advertisers, Bushells Tea and Arnotts Biscuits, were still treated with reverence when I went to the *Weekly* in 1975 as Editor, because they had supported Sir Frank in his hour of need. He never forgot that. Whenever they advertised in the *Weekly* they were given priority treatment.

I decided to take a leaf out of Sir Frank's book. I made a list of the top twenty companies that would be suitable advertisers in *ITA* and I called on their CEOs. I appealed to the businessperson in them. I did a passionate support-an-Australian company pitch. I extolled the need for independent publishers. They listened politely and wished me well. Alas not one buck came my way. As a woman, I was not part of the old boys' network, which was then, and still is, the fundamental way of doing business in Australia.

Several wrote to say no, among them W. F. Sutcliffe, an executive with the National Australia Bank, who sent a rather old-fashioned style of letter, which reinforced two things – banks didn't know much about communication and, as his response showed, did not think much about women's potential as customers either.

I refer to your letter of 21st ultimo, also call on General Manager, Arthur Sanderson, with view to the Bank taking advertising space in 'Ita' magazine.

Thank you for making this opportunity available to the Bank, but after investigation we find that we do not have a product at this particular time which is directed to women specifically and for this reason regret we are not in a position to avail of your offer at present.

With that kind of communication it's hard to believe that the NAB is one of our top companies.

I did persuade a major skin-care company to sign up. At a discount, of course, and as part of the deal, I also had to address their company rallies in four States. Such is the price a small, independent publisher has to pay. But I was prepared to do almost anything – I did *so* want *ITA* to succeed.

There was another important factor that militated against *ITA*'s success – we couldn't afford to promote the magazine effectively. I don't believe small publishers can ever compete with the big guys unless they have megabucks to spend on regular promotion. The only effective way to sell magazines is to publicise content. Advertising agencies often persuade small publishers to promote their magazines by sponsoring film festivals, fashion events and the like – but such activities rarely result in circulation sales. People only buy magazines for their content. Editors should stick those words up where they can see them every day. Spending money on 'feel good' marketing is nothing but a waste of funds.

I did editorial comments for the Sydney radio station 2GB, where I subsequently got a full-time job in 1996 hosting their afternoon show from 12.30 p.m. to 4 p.m. I also did Sunday morning personality interviews for the station in return for on-air advertising for *ITA*.

But what *ITA* needed was television exposure. In the summer of 1991 I called on Steve Cosser, the founder of Australis, when he was boss of the TEN Network, which at the time was struggling in the ratings and for profits. I suggested to Cosser that what he needed for TEN was more publicity and that I would be happy to run stories in

ITA on TEN's shows and personalities in exchange for TV spots for my magazine. I explained to him how this worked. It was something I had learned when I ran the women's publishing division for Kerry Packer and had a close business relationship with Sam Chisholm, the then boss of Kerry's Nine Network. Sam is a genius. He ran British Sky Broadcasting for Rupert Murdoch from 1990 to 1991 and was tremendously successful in turning around this former loss-making enterprise.

Back in his Packer days Sam would ring me and say, 'I want to win the ratings the week after next. Can you help me?'

'What would you like me to do?'

'We need publicity for our movie. Can you give it a couple of upfront pages in the *Weekly* with colour photographs?'

I always did. And Sam would win the ratings. The *Weekly* had a lot of clout in those days.

This exchange of mediums worked both ways.

When we'd have a week of not-so-hot sales for the *Weekly*, I'd ring Sam. 'I need your help. Our sales are sluggish. Can you give me some extra TV spots for the *Weekly*?' And Sam would oblige.

I am not suggesting that *ITA* had the reach and influence of the *Weekly*, but Cosser was having problems getting any positive publicity for TEN. He could see the logic of what I proposed but he had too many other things on his mind – such as banks and other critics, who were not happy with

TEN's financial performance. He was a distracted man. He never got back to me. In 1992, Westpac took control of TEN and to my surprise – and pleasure – offered me a seat on the TEN board that I accepted.

After we'd closed, a reader wrote and said she felt we did not market *ITA* well enough. 'Not enough people knew about your existence. I never saw the magazine at hairdressers, doctors or on airlines.' Well, we did have *ITA* going into hairdressers but after only six months were told we were no longer wanted. We were to be replaced by titles from Murdoch magazines. And we did have *ITA* flying Qantas – both domestic and international – only to receive a letter saying we were not considered to be of general enough appeal. Yet *ITA* was an almost all-Australian content magazine with very little overseas material in it. We only published fiction written by Australian authors, too.

We later discovered we had been ejected from Qantas for magazines from Kerry Packer's company, many of which were filled with stories about overseas celebrities or happenings. I did think that Australia's own airline, which itself had modest beginnings, might have found a way to support one small all-Australian magazine. I rang up and did my best to get us back in the air, but I couldn't persuade Qantas that *ITA* was worthy of flying with the airline. Later, I managed to get *ITA* into some of our leading hotels only to be rung after a few months and told that we were being switched for magazines from either Packer or Murdoch magazines. Such is life for a small publisher – any small business, I guess.

We often came up with excellent marketing ideas and made them work for us, only to see them 'knocked off' by the major publishers. There isn't much loyalty in business and of course I knew only too well how big corporate Australia wouldn't wish to be on the wrong side of influential men like Packer and Murdoch.

Max Suich and I both know how difficult it is to be an independent publisher in Australia, yet independent publishers are needed. It is not in our nation's best interests to have only three big print publishing groups dominate the daily newspaper and magazine market.

We lack politicians with the guts to speak out – they're terrified that if they do, the media bosses will turn their empires against them. When Rupert was busily buying up Australia's newspapers – to give him control of more than 65 per cent of them – I ran into some leading Liberals at the Sydney Hilton Hotel.

'You guys should do something about Rupert. It is not good for Australia. No publisher should control so many of our newspapers,' I told them.

'Oh, Rupert's been pretty good to us lately,' said the leader of the group. 'We wouldn't want to do anything to upset him.'

Not enough Australians understand or seem to care that there is a lack of access to diverse viewpoints and alternative sources of news. A great many people think the only news that happens is what they read in the papers or see on TV. It isn't, of course. We need to be concerned about the news we don't hear about. The ABC often takes Australia by surprise when it runs stories about well-known figures and brings to our attention devious and sometimes dubious activities in which such people are involved. Some of these issues would never get the public scrutiny they deserve without the ABC.

The big boys have so much clout that they can make supermarkets toss a smaller publisher out, which is what happened with Woolworths and *ITA*. Early in 1990, without warning, Woolworths told us that *ITA* did not sell enough volume and that they were going to replace us with *NOW*, a new magazine from the now defunct publishing company Century Publishing, in which J.B. Fairfax had a stake. John Hemming, previously Managing Director of Fairfax Magazines, ran it for a short while. *NOW* didn't last much over three months! Woolworths, unlike Coles, did not feel it important to support an independent Australian publisher. No amount of phoning could persuade them to reconsider their decision or even see us to discuss the matter. The loss of Woolworths as an outlet was another setback for us. Woolworths mightn't have thought we sold enough copies but our sales had been increasing at the supermarket chain. Not being there affected our circulation.

Before I launched the magazine, I had gone to Melbourne to see Brian Quinn, when he was boss of Coles Myer, to ask for his advice and support in getting *ITA* to as wide an audience as possible. He was very helpful and offered me all kinds of useful advice. He warned me, too, to be on guard against what he described as 'the middle ground Turks' – the bright young men, burning with ambition with lots to prove, who would have little regard for an independent publisher. I encountered 'Turks' on many occasions and no doubt they were in plentiful numbers at Woolworths – but never at Coles Myer. Even after Quinn had left, Coles Myer supported us – they encouraged us, they met with us three or four times a year and frequently ran special promotions for *ITA* throughout their supermarkets. They never once wavered in their support.

Most people in the publishing and advertising circles were aware that the circulation of *ITA* had dropped in the early months of 1994. This was due to a cover price increase. We had remained five dollars for five years. We had to get rid of our accumulative debt; it was holding us back. Clearly, we were still going to have to be patient in waiting for increased advertising. I couldn't cut expenses further. They were stripped to the bone. I couldn't work any harder either. There was only one option left: put up the cover price. I was very apprehensive about doing this. I knew all about customer resistance to price rises having been through this situation many times at Packer's and Murdoch's companies. I was well aware that a drop in circulation always follows a cover price increase and that it could take several months, sometimes as much as a year, before circulation was regained. We were usually able to speed up this process by spending plenty of money on promotion.

This wasn't an option for *ITA*. I wrote to all our several thousand subscribers and told them I had a problem. I either had to print the magazine offshore to save money or put up the cover price. What would they prefer me to do? More than 80 per cent of those who responded said: 'Do not print outside Australia. Too many Australian products are going offshore. Stay here. Put the price up. We will gladly pay the extra money.'

Encouraged, but still worried, I did just that. But unfortunately, the reality was quite different. Our readers and subscribers baulked at the new $5.80 cover price. After I'd announced the closure a reader wrote to say how sorry she was. 'The women of Australia have let you down.' I think they did. Our sales plummetted. Alarmingly. There was nothing else for me to do but drop the cover price, which I did, to $4.95. Psychologically, I thought it sounded better than $5. But rapid cover-price changes confuse readers. They wonder what the hell is going on and lose confidence. Sales began to lift slowly but not quickly enough for our cash flow needs. The moral of the story is: the customer doesn't always speak the truth and much and all as many Australians like to say they would prefer to support Australian products, at the end of the day, price is the influencing factor – which is not all that extraordinary, is it?

But for me, it was the last straw. Our media knockers were howling that *ITA* was on its last legs. No matter that even with a circulation of 35 000 we were still doing as well as *HQ* and *Mode* (two magazines then owned by Australian

Consolidated Press), which were not singled out as 'failing' in the way *ITA* was. Yet both titles had enjoyed significantly greater circulation a few years earlier – just like *ITA*. It seemed there was one rule for *ITA* and another for other magazines. I had nothing more to give. I made the only decision I could under the circumstances and I know now, as I did then, that it was the right one.

Would I ever do it again? No, I don't think so. Once is enough. I don't ever want to have the worry of running my own business again or practically non-stop week after week. I do not ever intend to short-change myself on life again. I have worked and supported myself since I was fifteen. I decided it was time to do some of the things I never had time to do.

I started my company because I wanted to make my own decisions and set new standards in journalism. I had to have a go at producing *ITA* because I would hate to finish up as a little old lady wondering if I could have done it. I have no intention of ending my life with unanswered questions. *ITA* was a quality magazine and an intelligent read. I believe Australia is the poorer for its loss. I was a truly independent publisher and such publishers are needed to keep the other bastards honest.

Running my own publishing company was an amazing experience – a significant chapter in my career. I do not think I failed. Nor do I consider the magazine a failure. I had a dream and I had a go at getting it. I learned a great deal in those turbulent six years.

I learned how to run a business extremely leanly and meanly; how essential it is to have multi-skilled employees, especially in a small business; how important keeping up with technology is for survival; how vital it is to spend the best money you can afford on a good accountant and financial advice; and how to keep a smile on my face, maintain my enthusiasm and motivate my team, even though all the odds seemed stacked against me at all too frequent intervals.

In the weeks after *ITA* had closed, people would come up to me and touch me on the shoulder or squeeze my hand, as if a member of the family had died. I suppose in a way that was correct. *ITA* the magazine was certainly a big part of my life.

But it was only a part – not the sum total. I had a dream, but nowhere is it written (that I know of) that a dream has to last forever. When one dream ends, it is time to go and find another. Which is what I have done. I have an abundance of dreams. Perhaps not all of them will come true, but some of them will.

I grew as a person and a boss while I was running Capricorn Publishing. I aged a bit too! But I also found in me a strength that I didn't know I had. In the years to come, when I look back on crucial turning points in my life, I know that the time relating to *ITA* and Capricorn Publishing will be a very special one for me, and something that I wouldn't have wanted to miss.

8

IN SEARCH OF A NEW DREAM

I don't think Ita is manipulative enough for politics.

RICHARD WALSH, FORMER MANAGING DIRECTOR OF
AUSTRALIAN CONSOLIDATED PRESS

Less than three weeks after announcing *ITA*'s closure, I was
approached to enter Federal politics. This was not the first
time. Over the years I've had many offers to go into politics,
the first in the late seventies when I was running the *Weekly*.
I had a couple in the eighties too. I always said no, because
of the children. Kate and Ben were always my number one
priority (they still are, even though they're adults!) and I
didn't want to be separated for long periods from them,
which is what would have happened if I'd gone to Canberra.
From what I've seen of politics, it doesn't allow politicians
much time with their families. But I never closed the door
on a political career. I thought perhaps the day might come
when an opportunity would present itself and, if the timing
was right, I'd head for Parliament.

I almost made it to Canberra in an advisory capacity in 1993. Federal Opposition Leader John Hewson, whom everyone expected to be Australia's next Prime Minister, asked me to become one of his special advisers to keep him directly informed on the needs of women, family and community health. I was one of 'a gang of six' which is how Sydney's *Telegraph-Mirror* (now *Telegraph*) dubbed us. Most other papers described us as Hewson's 'Kitchen Cabinet'.

The other members of the 'gang' and their policy areas were Sir Arvi Parbo, the mining industry chief – Australian industry and international competitiveness; Professor David Penington (the former head of the AIDS Task Force), Melbourne University Vice Chancellor – education and training; the late Aboriginal activist Charles Perkins, the former public servant – Aboriginal issues; Professor Judith Sloan, the labour market economist – unemployment; and Dick Smith, the publisher/explorer – environment and development.

Hewson said his reason for appointing us was to make sure that he and his team, as well as the bureaucracy, did not become isolated from the community. He also pointed out that many of us had 'already served governments of both political persuasions in an advisory capacity. The role of special advisers will not be to defend existing Coalition policy'.

Membership of Hewson's 'Kitchen Cabinet' was honorary but that was fine by me, because to have the ear of the future PM was the opportunity of a lifetime. In retrospect,

I think Prime Ministerial advisers are worth some kind of recompense. No one – not even Paul Keating – expected Hewson to lose. My appointment was only a few hours old when women's organisations began ringing me about issues they wanted raised on their behalf.

Keating attacked Hewson for our appointments saying the reason for the 'Kitchen Cabinet's' existence was the deficiencies in the Opposition Leader's own front bench. Hewson responded by saying that he would put his advisers up against Keating's advisers – and he singled out Bill Kelty, Wally Curran and John Halfpenny – any day. It's no wonder so many people in business hesitate about getting involved in politics. Suddenly our names were being booted around like political footballs.

I thought Hewson's plan a good one and I still believe it is. Governments do get out of touch, something that was very apparent during Keating's term as Prime Minister, especially during the recession, when it was clear that the Government and its public service advisers didn't have a clue how tough it really was for so many Australians. Keating still hadn't got the message when he again went to the polls in 1996, and the Australian people voted him out, fed up with an arrogant Prime Minister who seemingly had forgotten the people on struggle street. Keating had a reputation for being the kind of man who holds a grudge. Late-night calls with him abusing – complete with expletives – journalists who had written something he didn't like were legendary.

In November 1993, my three-year term as a member of the Council of the National Gallery was due to expire. I expected to be appointed for another term. It was acknowledged practice that Council members, except artists, were given a second term. As well as being member of Council, I was the Chair of the Program and Marketing Committee and knew that I had helped set up a more effective publicity machine at the Gallery. What's more, as a founding donation member of the Gallery, I've always had its interests very much at heart.

I discovered my term hadn't been extended after another Council member phoned me at the end of October and asked me if I'd read the latest Council papers. When I did, I found that my name had been deleted as a member of Council. A few days later, I received a letter from Lionel Bowen, our Chairman and former Deputy Prime Minister, saying he had 'ascertained' my term had not been renewed. I rang and spoke to Lionel, and told him how puzzled I was at the way I was being treated. Lionel is a decent man – it was obvious he was embarrassed at what was going on.

Of course, the media got a whiff of things and rang me. When asked if I'd thought the Prime Minister had had a hand in my removal from Council, I said yes. Later Bob McMullen, the Minister for the Arts, in an interview with Laurie Oakes on Channel 9, denied that Keating had anything to do with my non-appointment, but I didn't believe it for one moment. Lionel Bowen had expected me to continue – we had already talked about detailed 1994 plans for the Gallery.

I knew the kind of tough game Keating played. I'd learned all about the way men do business when I worked for Packer and Murdoch. If I wasn't wanted at the National Gallery, so be it. I thought that at least John Hewson would ring to say he was sorry I was being given such rotten treatment, but there was only a deafening silence. However, a few weeks after the story broke, I saw him across a crowded room at some function in Sydney. 'Oh hi,' he called out, 'I meant to give you a ring about the National Gallery matter, but I've been busy.'

Is it any wonder John Hewson lost the election everyone thought he would win? He was a man of ability but as a communicator had much to learn. That was painfully clear when it became apparent that he wasn't able to explain to the electorate the benefits of the GST, which John Howard successfully introduced in 2000. At least Hewson had the guts to tell us the truth about what was needed in Australia before he went to the polls, a trait that is rare in most politicians.

My friend the late Sir Peter Abeles was overseas at the time of the election. He was on his way home the night the votes were being counted and when his plane stopped over in Singapore, rang a friend in Sydney to get the results.

'How big is his victory?' he asked, assuming that Hewson had won.

'Keating's won comfortably,' said his friend.

'Don't joke,' Peter said.

'I'm serious. Hewson has lost.'

'I tell you Ita,' Sir Peter said, when we lunched not long after his return, 'I couldn't believe it!'

Without a doubt, politics is an uncertain life. Nothing, even something that looks like a sure thing, can be guaranteed. Yet I am often urged to go into politics. People write to me saying I should. When I give speeches and afterwards take questions, members of the audience often ask if I would consider a political career.

So there I was, still organising refunds to subscribers and cleaning up the *ITA* offices on 10 August 1994 when Tony Staley, the Federal President of the Liberal Party, rang. Tony, whom I've known for years, asked if he and New South Wales Liberal Party Director Barry O'Farrell (new Deputy Leader of the New South Wales Parliamentary Liberal Party) could come and see me. 'Privately, quietly', he said. 'Perhaps we could share a sandwich lunch in your office?'

That suited me. Under the circumstances, I didn't particularly feel like going out. After their arrival, we exchanged pleasantries for a few minutes and then Tony explained what he wanted. The Liberals wanted me to run for the Party in North Sydney. The popular and well-respected Independent, Ted Mack, had held the seat for six years. I didn't have to make up my mind right then and there; I had a few days to do that and if I said yes, I'd have to go and meet some 200 people, important to the preselection, straight away. If

I got preselection and ultimately won, I'd have to leave the eastern suburbs and relocate to the electorate. It was a lot to digest over a sandwich!

I don't know whether Tony Staley thought I was manipulative enough to be a good politician, as Richard Walsh suggested I wasn't, because I didn't bother to ask him. I've always thought that integrity and commitment were far more important attributes for politicians to have. Richard Walsh's 'not manipulative enough' remarks, made in an interview with the *Sydney/Melbourne Weekly* in 1996, reveal more about him than me.

I was tempted to say yes to Staley, but timing is so important in life, isn't it? It was less than a month since I had closed *ITA*. I'd had no time at all to consider my future, let alone mourn for what I had lost. My good friend British author Shirley Conran had written to commiserate and advised me 'not to take the first thing that comes along. Give yourself time to make the right decision'. She needn't have worried about that. I knew I didn't have the energy to go shake twenty hands, let alone 200. I really didn't know what I wanted to do. I was very uncertain. For the first time in my life, I had no other job to go to. Nevertheless I declined the Liberals' offer.

Strange how things turn out – before the election, Ted Mack surprised everyone by unexpectedly announcing his retirement. North Sydney reverted to being the safe Liberal seat it had always been (before Ted Mack won the seat, it had been held for ten years by John Spender, former Liberal

Attorney General in the Fraser Government and later
Australia's Ambassador to France). Lawyer Joe Hockey,
previously policy adviser to the former New South Wales
Liberal Premier John Fahey, ultimately won the seat for the
Liberals. I sat next to him at dinner not so long after his
victory, and it was obvious that he was enjoying Canberra
and the cut and thrust of politics; I doubt he had any idea
that his seat had once been offered to me!

A week after Staley's visit Bob Sessions, the Publishing
Director of Penguin Books, rang and asked if he, too, could
call on me. Just like Staley, Bob Sessions got straight to the
point: 'It's time you wrote another book, and I'll publish it.'

It was a suggestion that appealed to me because it was
a long time since I'd written a book – my first two books,
First Edition, My First Forty Years and *Every Occasion: Your Guide
to Modern Etiquette* had both been published in 1985. But
remembering Shirley Conran's advice, I told Bob I'd think
over his proposal and get back to him when I'd finished
tidying up all my business affairs and taken a holiday. I kept
reminding myself of the need to take only one step at a
time.

There was still a great deal for me to do – including
hosting a couple of *ITA* Club lunches and fashion parades
for which we had sold tickets and felt obligated to hold so
that we could thank, in person, the subscribers who had
supported us. These were sad–happy occasions. The subscribers told me they didn't know how they would manage
to get by without *ITA*.

I had other responsibilities to consider as well. My work as Chair of the Seniors Media Network Council was moving along at a fast pace. There were a number of initiatives we wanted to establish within a tight timeframe. I also had my responsibilities as a director of Prudential Assurance, something I took very seriously. I was the first woman to join the Prudential board in 1990, and did so at the invitation of the then Chairman, Sir John Mason, a charming Englishman who had previously been the UK High Commissioner to Australia. Before I was appointed, he took me to lunch at his Sydney club and said the board wanted someone with commonsense and he thought that I had it in abundance.

My fellow directors – all men – were a charming bunch and most welcoming, although after a couple of meetings, one of them did confide to me that my presence at the board table had changed the way they ran their meetings. 'In what way?' I asked. 'We can't swear or tell jokes,' he replied. I know he meant it more as a comment and not a criticism. I also knew he had a wife who had never worked and that women like me were perhaps not what he had been conditioned to expect in the boardroom. When it comes to the advancement of women, both sexes are still on a sharp learning curve.

I told him I loved jokes and that anyone who has ever worked for Kerry Packer has heard every swear word imaginable. I don't think I've ever worked for anyone with such a foul temper or mouth as Kerry.

On 30 August 1994 I closed the door on Redfern, locked

the car park and went home to ponder my future. It was all very well to tell myself that I'd take one step at a time, but I was feeling a little frightened. After all, I was over fifty and knew plenty of people my age who couldn't get a job. I liked working. I enjoyed the routine of going to the office every day, doing my best to produce the greatest magazine or newspaper. If I couldn't get a permanent, full-time job, what would my life be like? We define our worth by the work we do. Maybe people would think me worthless? Worse still, maybe I'd think of myself as worthless.

I kept telling myself that of course I'd find a full-time job, that ultimately I'd find some little spot in publishing somewhere. I love publishing so much that I often think I must have printer's ink in my veins. I couldn't imagine not having something to edit. I looked in the newspapers for jobs that I thought might be suitable. I even wrote off for a couple. I didn't get a reply! I'd heard about this indifference to job applicants but it wasn't pleasant experiencing it. It doesn't take long to tell someone their job application has been unsuccessful. Surely there's still time for manners in business, no matter how busy people think they are.

I had always kept my hand in on the public speaking circuit, mainly through the Saxton Agency, Australia's first-ever speaking agency, founded by an enterprising British woman called Joan Saxton. When Joan retired in the early nineties, Winston Broadbent took over Saxton's and in 1997, bought out Harry M. Miller's speaker's bureau, giving Saxton's an important base in Sydney. Winston was particularly

kind to me when *ITA* closed. He knew that I no longer
employed any staff – not even a secretary – and that people
still rang me with all kinds of requests, assuming that I had
several helpers to give me a hand.

Even though Capricorn Publishing was officially closed,
I was still getting at least forty calls a day with inquiries
about the magazine, usually something to do with a subscription. I'd had *ITA*'s phone number diverted to my office
phone at home, and it took me hours to attend to all the
calls. Winston said Saxton's would be happy to help
monitor my calls and to handle some of the secretarial
work. I appreciated his thoughtfulness because I did need
assistance and there were frequently times when I did feel
very much alone.

One thing did please Winston (although he was genuinely sorry about *ITA*'s demise) and that was that I now had
more time for public speaking and I could take engagements
between nine and five. When I was running *ITA* I only
accepted bookings for evening or weekend functions, and
then only if I could fit them in with my publishing
commitments. After *ITA* closed, Winston would ring tri-
umphantly almost every day to announce he had another
booking. He got me half a dozen or so in what was left of
1994, and in 1995 I had a record year of speech making.

It's something that gives me pleasure because it allows
me to travel around Australia. It also enables me to meet
people and find out about other companies' businesses and
their problems. It's quite a challenge to try to tailor a speech

and offer constructive solutions, based on your own experiences and interpretation of a particular target market. My
journalistic training comes in useful because it's usually necessary to do research and ask questions, all of which I've
been trained to do. The topics I'm asked to address are
extremely varied, too, and in recent years have included such
things as 'Managing Change into the Twenty-first Century',
'Redefining Work in the New Millennium', 'How Superior
Service Can Make a Difference and Win Customers', 'How
to Effectively Market to Women', 'The Need for Men's Liberation', and 'Why Bullies Have No Place in Our Schools'
(this last in my capacity as Patron of Safety House Australia).
Sometimes I'm asked to tackle lighter topics such as 'Hairdressers Are Better for You than Doctors', which is a
refreshing change of pace.

There's rarely a dull moment on the speaker's circuit. It's
wonderfully unpredictable, always a learning experience and,
occasionally, offers overseas travel. In the last few years, I've
had engagements in Bali, Las Vegas, Hong Kong and on the
Cunard Liner *Caronia* cruising the Mediterranean. It's hard
to take, I tell you!

As 1994 drew to a close I had a call from Glenda Orland,
the Media and Promotions Manager for World Vision
Australia, she said they were looking for someone who
understood the media well to take on a consultancy as
Communications Strategist. Would I be interested in the
job? Yes I would, I told her.

I already had an involvement with World Vision through

my role as National Patron of its Women of Vision program, which encourages Australian women to financially support women and girls in the Third World. I am a keen supporter of the program because I believe women need to think globally in their fight to advance the rights and welfare of their sisters. One way of doing this is for women in more affluent countries like Australia to help those in Third World countries become educated, because it's only through education that they will ever achieve any kind of equality.

In order to understand the need for the Women of Vision program I had gone on a fact-finding trip to Bangladesh with Glenda in 1993, and subsequently wrote in *ITA* about my visit and the women I'd met. Bangladesh was a real eye-opener. I had never seen such soul-destroying poverty before, nor had I ever encountered the kind of spirit displayed by the Bangladeshi women I met. In spite of their harsh life, they have an unshakeable belief that better things lie ahead – if not for them, at least for their children, especially their daughters.

Many remarkable events occurred on that trip. One in particular has stayed etched in my mind. I was in the capital, Dhaka, and had been taken to the most foul-smelling slums situated in the mud of a riverbank. The only way to reach them was by rowboat as the river had swallowed up the walkways.

We passed many shanty huts, some of them half submerged, and yet somehow people were living in them. As I walked along followed by several bright-eyed and curious children, I saw through the open door of a rattan tent the tiniest baby lying on a small piece of matting placed over the mud floor. A kneeling woman – presumably the baby's mother – was fanning the baby, trying to keep the child cool in the overwhelming heat. It was at least 40°C with humidity around 100 per cent.

I couldn't help stopping to take in the beauty of what I was seeing. I remember thinking, 'My God, the miracle of life against all odds'.

Right then and there I made a commitment to myself and, I guess, also to God, that I would try to do more to help people in the Third World. I hoped that if that tiny baby was a girl, she would be wanted and loved. So many girl babies in the Third World are not – boys are still the preferred sex. Malnutrition is the biggest health problem affecting women in Bangladesh, because at mealtimes the best food is given to boys and men. Girls and older women sometimes just have to go without.

Most women's lives in Bangladesh and other Third World countries is tough from birth to death. A woman has no rights. If she has a job, the money she earns belongs to her husband. However, the range of jobs available to her is minimal. She can work as a servant – the more houses she cleans the more she earns, the usual rate is $2.50 per house per month – but the odds are she suffers from malnutrition and therefore doesn't have the kind of energy that Australian women take for granted.

She might get a job chipping bricks, a mind-numbing

task. Working outdoors, with no protection from the sun she chips away at the bricks until they are reduced to rubble and able to be used for roadworks. For this she receives the princely sum of 60 cents a day. The other major area of employment are the garment factories (hours 7 a.m. to 5 or 6 p.m.). Bangladesh supplies some of the French couture houses with silk shirts and other fineries, such as exquisite embroidery. There's a big risk, though, that in the factories, where hundreds of workers are crammed into hot, sub-standard buildings, the male bosses will force her to have sex. If you're an unmarried woman, forced sex means you are forever 'spoiled' and the likelihood of getting a husband is reduced. Women are not safe on the streets, either, espe-cially at night. Definitely not, I was told – a woman could be abducted – and raped.

When I returned to Australia I spoke at special fundrais-ers, and I did television, radio and magazine interviews that World Vision organised. I made TV commercials for aware-ness campaigns and also endorsed print promotions. I even managed to talk about World Vision's work at my regular Saxton speaking engagements and still do so whenever an opportune moment crops up.

Glenda took me to see a variety of projects being run by World Vision. I was impressed with the things they were doing, such as teaching women how to write and to budget; showing them how to make garments that could be sold to get money to buy food for the family; instructing them about hygiene – even something as simple as washing their hands before and after preparing food, helping them set up savings groups – many villages in Bangladesh have all-women credit unions that allow members to take out loans to build another room on to their one-roomed huts, encouraging them to save to perhaps buy a cow, then to use some of the milk for their children's needs and sell the rest. The aim of every lesson is to help the women and their families stand on their own feet and be independent.

These fact-finding missions are no holiday, nor is the accommodation five star, as money is never wasted on such things – something I'm sure World Vision's supporters would be pleased to know. World Vision works a visitor hard. We went by an open boat to see projects, we walked and we travelled by car. We went to bed early and we got up early. No time was ever wasted.

Bangladesh was memorable for a number of reasons, not the least of which was my stopover at a monastery run by the Sisters of the Poor Clare in Mymensigh, a three-hour drive north from Dhaka. It was considered the only safe place for Glenda and me to stay. The other members of our team – all men – dropped us off at the front door of the monastery, an ugly grey concrete building with high walls decked with barbed wire. We rang the bell and almost at once a small, bright-eyed nun with a wide smile appeared at the door. 'I'm Sister Aloysius, you must be the Australians,' she said. 'Are you from Perth?' Somewhat taken aback, we both said no. Sister Aloysius then explained that back in 1982 she had accompanied a nun in need of an operation to Western Australia, where she stayed at a convent in the Perth suburb of Subiaco and had what I think might have been the best six months of her life.

She invited us in. 'I know you Australians,' she said. 'You have your main meal at the end of the day and you're big eaters.' Before arriving at the monastery, however, Glenda and I had lunched late with villagers who were part of a World Vision project. They had gone to a great deal of trouble to give us a substantial meal with lots of rice and vegetables. They had even cooked a chicken, which is considered a luxury in Bangladesh, and we were duly appreciative of the honour they'd paid us.

Glenda and I tried to explain to Sister Aloysius that we weren't really hungry and asked her please not to go to too much trouble. She just smiled as she showed us to our room, which had two iron beds in it and not much else. The floor was concrete, as was the adjoining cold-water-only shower. This wasn't a problem, however – it was so hot and humid that a cold shower was bliss.

At dinnertime, we discovered Sister Aloysius had been busy. 'Australians like roasts, don't they?' she said. She did us proud – soup, roast chicken with gravy, baked potatoes and string beans, and paw paw for dessert. She insisted we have a second helping of the main course! We could hardly walk from the table to our beds – we were so full.

Sister Aloysius was the only nun we met, although we could hear the others singing in the chapel. I went and listened for a while outside the chapel because the singing was so lovely. American nuns from Cleveland, Ohio, founded the Sisters of the Poor Clare in Bangladesh in 1893. It is an enclosed order and the nuns pray twenty-four hours a day, even in the middle of the night, with three shifts of nuns taking it in turns to go to the chapel to pray. Sister Aloysius told us her day began at 4.30 a.m. and ended at 10 p.m. She joined the order when she was sixteen and had been there for forty-one years and had come from Southern India from a poor family who were unable to afford a marriage dowry. Religious life offered her a certain kind of security.

We learnt all this the following morning at breakfast when Sister Aloysius had a cup of tea with us. She explained that she and her fellow nuns had taken a vow of poverty. But there was something incongruous about talking to a nun who had taken a vow of poverty, while outside the monastery walls people lived in fearful poverty with no choice available to them to do anything else.

Her smile when I asked her what she most remembered about Australia lit up her face. 'Ah,' she said, 'Kraft Cheddar Cheese slices! I think that cheese must be made in heaven'.

When I returned to Australia I rang the marketing manager at Kraft in Melbourne and asked for his help in getting some cheese to the nuns at Mymensigh. It had to be in tins, I told him, explaining that food in cardboard boxes goes mouldy in Bangladesh's high humidity. Kraft was fabulous. The company donated a substantial selection of their cheeses that, with World Vision's help, arrived safely at the Sisters of the Poor Clare. Not long after I received a charming thank you note from Sister Aloysius. I sent it on to Glenda in Melbourne where she lives, with a PS on it: 'Oh, what a friend we have in cheeses!'

There were many unexpected happenings on my visit to Bangladesh. In the rural village of Savar, I met thirteen-year-old Taslima, who was married at twelve to a man aged twenty-two. He worked in a shoe factory. Through an interpreter, she whispered the facts of her brief life. Three months ago she had stopped menstruating. She thought she might be pregnant.

The interpreter explained this by saying: 'There is a problem.' That was something of an understatement.

Taslima's family hadn't yet paid her entire dowry and unless they did she wouldn't be permitted to go to her in-laws, which is the custom after a woman marries. Her father, a labourer, had to raise $1400. Although Taslima said she was sure he would be able to do this, the interpreter didn't share her confidence. She was such a pretty little thing and so young, that I couldn't help but wonder what would happen to her and couldn't get her out of my mind. No doubt this had something to do with the mother in me! How would I feel if my daughter were in a similar situation? At thirteen a girl is still a child – not ready to be married, let alone a mother.

To cut a long story short, I arranged to sponsor Taslima through a special arrangement with World Vision and thus resolved the problems of her dowry. She was able to go and live with her husband and his parents but shortly afterwards lost the baby. Because she was so young and not well nourished, it took a while to get her health back.

World Vision have since advised me that Taslima and her husband have decided to put off having a family until she is older, something I was pleased to hear, and that, with some of the sponsorship money I had sent, Taslima had bought a cow that I sincerely hope she didn't call Ita! When last I heard, the cow had turned out to be a good milker and Taslima and her husband were very happy.

The people who ask me why I would bother about someone like Taslima, or for that matter anyone in the Third World, surprise me. I often think how I would like to be treated if I had been born less fortunate than I was, or if I were blind, deaf or incapacitated in any other way. None of us chooses to be born disabled or into poverty or to have few privileges. That is a circumstance beyond our control – but I know if that were my lot back in the eighties I would hope that someone, somewhere would consider my plight and give me a helping hand.

I was still giving breakfast and lunchtime talks about Bangladesh when Glenda rang with the Communications Strategist offer. She wanted me to go to Africa for World Vision in November 1994, however it was later decided to defer the trip until 1995.

This suited me, as there were other commitments I had to fulfil. Harry Czeiger and I had decided to continue our fashion collaboration and I went over to New Zealand to launch 'Ita's Collection'. It was well-received and as the New

Zealand economy was then performing better than Australia's we had excellent sales as well. That same year we also managed to get the after-five component of 'Ita's Collection' into David Jones. This was an exciting development.

When I returned from New Zealand I received a surprise phone call from Les Thompson, the Program Manager at Sydney's 2GB, the former highly rating Fairfax radio station which had been sold off during Warwick Fairfax's futile takeover attempt. Ron Casey, the afternoon presenter, had suffered a heart attack and the station urgently needed someone to do his slot while he recovered. Les, Ron and I had all worked together at 2KY back in the eighties. I loved radio and thought it would be marvellous to be back on air. I'd been on air for a couple of weeks and when Les called into the studio one day to say he thought I hadn't lost my broadcasting skills. 'You still have what it takes,' he said.

Poor old 2GB, though, wasn't like the glorious radio station I remembered when I had filled in there several years earlier. By 1994, 2GB in Sydney's Sussex Street was run-down and shabby looking. Everything reeked of decay. But the men and women who work in radio are so addicted to the thrill of broadcasting that everyone was prepared to overlook the deficiencies of the place.

The year 1995 was a busy one, the legendary TV producer John Collins asked me to become a regular commentator on the Seven Network's *John Mangos Show*. For five and sometimes eight minutes I could talk on any topic I chose and there was nothing I couldn't have my say about.

I had a ball. John Mangos is one of the nice guys of television and it was very agreeable working with him. He didn't mind either if I gave the occasional plug to World Vision.

It was during this time that I finally set off on my next fact-finding trip for the organisation, this time to Kenya and Tanzania. A few months earlier, I had been asked to put together a list of influential people whom I thought would benefit from knowing more about World Vision's work and ultimately act as ambassadors for the organisation. One of my recommendations was Dr Brendan Nelson, the former President of the Australian Medical Association, who had just won preselection for the safe Liberal seat of Bradfield in New South Wales and is now in Federal Parliament. He'd resigned as AMA President and had some time on his hands waiting for the election to be called and didn't need much persuading to accept World Vision's invitation to travel with me. As I was going to Africa primarily to look at HIV/AIDS education programs, I thought Brendan's background would perfectly equip him to find out first hand about the difficulties doctors face in places such as Africa. I also pointed out to Glenda that long term it probably would be in World Vision's interests to have someone like Brendan know about the organisation's scope and responsibilities.

He was a young man in his late thirties, entering politics in an extremely safe seat. Unless something goes horribly wrong he is likely to be in Parliament for a long time and as a man of some ability, should go far. I was sure that he had the potential to be an important voice for World Vision in the future.

Just as I had been in Bangladesh, I was struck by the confidence and determination of African women. Brendan commented on it, too. Fed up with seeing their husbands and families die from AIDS, they are the driving force behind AIDS education programs in their country's rural villages.

Neither of us will forget the hospital we visited in Arusha in Tanzania though, where we saw two patients in each bed, even in the maternity wing. We were also alarmed to see lines of disposable plastic gloves washed and hanging out to dry so they could be reused, especially as this is a country where the HIV/AIDS virus spreads so rapidly. But Africa is so poor, and its hospitals have to manage with such limited funds – sometimes none at all – that even disposable gloves have to be recycled.

There was one wonderful, hilarious moment at the Tanzanian/Kenyan border. As we walked back to the car after completing customs and immigration, Masai women and boys and girls, insisting we buy souvenirs, mobbed us. We escaped into our car and locked the windows. They tapped on them saying, 'Please buy'. It was so hot, we finally had to open the windows again.

A young man addressed us in French. We told him we were English-speaking.

'Where are you from?' he asked.

'We're from Australia, mate,' Brendan replied.

The boy took a good look at him. 'Do you think Paul Keating will win the election?' Brendan was stunned. How had Keating done it? He couldn't believe it. The boy then explained that as a member of the Kenyan running team, he had visited Australia and met Prime Minister Keating. He'd been following events in Australia ever since. Brendan was relieved. For a moment, I think he thought he'd encountered some kind of Labor Party spy!

Shortly after returning home I met an enterprising South African called Clive Barrett, and we began a highly successful partnership. He introduced me to the Ita Treadmill. After trying it out and realising its health benefits, I agreed to endorse the product. At first this was mainly on TV, and primarily on Channel 10's morning show hosted by Bert Newton who is a brilliant salesman. We've always worked well together and sales of the treadmill soared.

Australia was ready for the Ita Treadmill. Many men and women have heard the health messages and accept that keeping fit and healthy is an individual responsibility. Women are also aware that exercise is one of the best ways to avoid osteoporosis in their older years. In a little over twelve months, we sold hundreds of thousands of treadmills. Women liked the Ita Treadmill because it allowed them to exercise in the privacy of their own homes regardless of the weather and, most importantly, they didn't have to worry about their safety.

The treadmill was still selling its socks off when Clive came up with the idea of marketing a similar treadmill around the world. After all, if the Ita Treadmill was such a success here, why wouldn't something just like it do just as well in other parts of the world? With the help of the Sydney-based celebrity manager Max Markson (who had negotiated my contract with him and often handled sponsorship and advertising deals on my behalf), Clive signed up supermodel Linda Evangelista, not only for the rest of the world but also for Australia.

The Ita Treadmill was still being sold here and suddenly there was another treadmill – that looked very much like mine – being promoted by the gorgeous Linda. Sales of the Ita Treadmill came to a halt. No wonder, really. The market was confused and that's something successful marketers should try to avoid.

There wasn't much I could do about it – the decision to sell two comparable treadmills concurrently had nothing to do with me and, besides, I had other things on my mind. I was back at 2GB full-time. The station was about to be taken over by John Singleton and when I officially joined, was being run by his good friend Ian Kennon. I knew Ian reasonably well from the days when he and I worked for Kerry Packer and he was ACP's advertising chief, before leaving to run his own advertising agency.

There were many rumours about the station's future but I trusted John and I knew Kennon was a man of his word. A permanent position had been offered to me after I had filled in again, this time for four weeks over the January 1996 holiday season. At the completion of my last shift, I was asked if I'd like to stay and do the 1 p.m. to 4 p.m. program on a regular basis permanently.

If 2GB was shabby when I filled in for Ron Casey in 1994, it was now in a far worse state. The studio chairs were nearly all broken. The microphone covers were torn. The headsets were tacky too and some were unusable. The staff kitchen was so filthy and inhabited by so many cockroaches that, if the health department had called to inspect the place, I'm sure it would have been condemned.

It was common to have cockroaches in the studio, too. On one occasion I was interviewing the soprano Yvonne Kenny when I noticed one heading towards her. She was talking enthusiastically about her work and I wasn't quite sure what to do. The microphones were on. Just as I was about to say, 'Excuse me, Yvonne, there is a cockroach heading towards you', the wretched thing gave a little leap and disappeared into her dress. Heaven knows exactly where it went – I just hope it didn't give Yvonne too much of a fright when it decided to emerge again!

Derryn Hinch was signed to do mornings up against John Laws, and Mark Day took over the drive shift. Clive Robertson, who had been with 2GB for a number of years, remained in the breakfast shift. Not long after Derryn, Mark and I began, there was a power coup and Ian Kennon left, with management responsibilities being taken over by Ian Grace, a former disc jockey who'd had some success in repositioning 2GB's sister station, 2CH. He appeared to be out of his depth running 2GB, though, and he also had to cope with a cashflow problem that would not have made his job any easier.

I had only to look at the faces of the people in the accounting section to know the strain they were under. After *ITA*, I was an expert on cashflow difficulties. At 2GB, I often wasn't paid on time. A station that isn't able to pay its on-air presenters punctually has big problems. On one occasion, when my pay cheque was two weeks overdue, I had to drop Grace a note saying that while I liked working at 2GB, I couldn't go on doing so for no recompense. Could he please arrange for me to be paid? He apologised by return memo but another two days went by before my cheque turned up.

All sorts of promises were made and broken. I was assured that an experienced radio producer would be assigned to my show as well as back-up support plus pro-motion, but it never eventuated. From time to time, 2GB advertised for producers but there was always some reason as to why no one was suitable. I ended up with a young twenty-something journalist, formerly from the country, who hadn't been in Sydney long. He had worked in 2GB's newsroom which John Singleton closed down because, he said, it cost too much money to run. The lad was competent, but in no way could he have been described as an experi-enced radio producer.

Derryn and Mark weren't happy about the lack of pro-motion either, and we were all conscious that the station had no direction. It had been through many changes in its on-air personality line-up in the couple of years before 1996, and just as it looked as though it was going to settle down, the newsroom was axed. This again changed the sound of the station which was still called 2GB News Talk – but without a newsroom, it was more of a news minus! It's a wonder any listeners remained loyal, but some did. Ian Grace decided to do some research to see what the listeners thought of the new line-up of presenters. 'You know,' he told me after he'd received the findings, 'you were the big surprise. The listeners actually liked you, the men as well as the women'.

Well, that was a relief and told me that I was on the right track in the kind of show I was putting on. Ian Grace told me not to change anything that I was doing – he thought my program was sounding good.

Ian Kennon had said that Singleton was in for the long haul and that he knew it could take eighteen months to two years to get 2GB re-established. I don't think any of us kidded ourselves that we didn't have a mighty task ahead of us. In order to have as much time as possible to devote to the cause, I gave up some of my other commitments. I resigned my directorships with Prudential, and HopeTown Special School for mildly intellectually disabled children at Wyong, and also my position as a Trustee of the Centennial Park and Moore Park Trust.

In June, 2GB's ratings had slipped overall by 0.4 to 5% but as I pointed out to *Media Week* when they rang for a comment, 2GB had made changes, either in personnel or programming, in every survey of 1996. 'People resist change and it takes time for an audience to settle down,' I explained. In July, it seemed as though the station's fortunes were looking up. Ian Grace told Carolyn Beaumont of the Sydney *Sunday Telegraph* that in just six months 2GB had been turned from a business losing $4 million a year into a station in profit. (I took a look at the faces in the accounting section the following morning. They still looked stressed out to me.)

In her article, Carolyn pointed out that since it had been relaunched as a talk station, 2GB had been in a very strange situation. Although it had an excellent on-air team, executives in other radio stations wondered why this very strong on-air team (as they considered it to be) was radio's best-kept secret. It was something Mark, Derryn and I often mulled over, too.

And try as hard as he could, Derryn Hinch just didn't seem to click with Sydney audiences in the way that he had with those in Melbourne, where he had once been a top-rating personality. There was a strong rumour that he was going to be asked to leave. I figured I might as well throw my hat in the ring for the morning slot. I suggested to Max Markson that if he ran into John Singleton (they were doing something together for Variety Club) to please tell him that I'd like to be considered.

I'll never know exactly what happened but a day or two afterwards, Max asked me to call into his office on my way home from 2GB. He seemed very upset. 'I don't want to tell you this,' he said, 'but I've spoken to John and he wants you to leave 2GB. He says you're not rating well enough.'

It was true that the surveys so far had been disappointing, but I didn't feel it was entirely my fault. There had been management changes as well as the axing of the news – which 2GB listeners liked – plus no promotion at all, not only for me but for the station generally. And it didn't help that Derryn wasn't rating well. In spite of all this, I felt that my show was starting to come together and that I was getting a better feel for the 2GB listeners. I didn't think it reasonable or fair that I be judged after only six months on air. It takes more than six months to turn around a station that had been performing as badly as 2GB. I felt I was at least entitled to a year to show what I could do, and said so to Max.

'It's no use. No,' Max said, 'John wants you to go straight away.' I was stunned.

'I won't,' I replied, 'and I won't be the scapegoat for the bad management of the place either. I'll finish the current survey and leave when it's over.'

I went home distraught and opened a bottle of wine. I even had a little weep. The wind had been well and truly knocked out of me. I simply couldn't believe what had happened. I never thought John Singleton would treat me so shabbily. This was, after all, the man who once sent me a note saying I was his 'best bird mate'. I felt as though I'd been plucked!

I told no one what had happened. I worked my hardest over the next few weeks and I prayed to God to give me a good survey result. The station had agreed to say that I had resigned. On my last day, I found a lavish arrangement of flowers waiting for me on my desk with a card saying 2GB wished me all the best. It was enough to make me chunder, to use a word that Singleton no doubt knows intimately. What hypocrisy. I gave the flowers to my junior producer.

When, later in the afternoon, I went to say goodbye to Ian Grace, he told me that he was impressed with the way I had conducted myself. 'Most people in your situation behave badly,' he said. It reminded me of the conversation I'd had with Chris Anderson when I left the *Sun-Herald*. Once again, I think, I was being told that I had behaved in a professional manner.

2GB was required to pay me three months notice, but Ian Grace told me that because of cashflow problems (I wondered what had happened so quickly to that profit he'd been bragging about) they wouldn't be able to pay me the entire sum on the day I finished up. They would pay me out over three months. As I expected, the first month's payment was late and I had to send Grace a fax asking him where it was.

When the ratings did come out about ten days after I'd finished, I had gained more than 2.7 percentage points in audience share, the largest rating increase 2GB had experienced all year. My rating went up to 5.5, which meant I outrated Derryn as well. You bet I gloated.

When I'd got the axe via Max Markson, I had written to Singleton telling him that I thought the least he could have done as a 'mate' was to tell me face to face that he wanted me to leave. I didn't hear a word from him for some weeks. When he did finally call, he said he'd been overseas and only just read my letter. He denied telling Max that he wanted me to leave. He said Max misunderstood him. He claimed that Max had said his advice to me was that I should leave 2GB, and that he (John) had said, 'Well, if that's what Ita wants to do . . .' Naturally, I passed John's comments on to Max, who stuck by his version of events. I didn't know what to think. Only one thing was certain – I was without a full-time job again.

I was hurt and absolutely furious. I wanted to get even. I remembered something my *Women's Weekly* colleague, Nan Musgrove, had told me about settling scores. Betty Keep had done it when she was editor of the *Weekly*'s fashion pages and Sir Frank had told her that he was going to bring out the Irish fashion personality, Sybil Connolly, to guest edit them. Betty didn't think this was a good idea at all – she didn't want some overseas personality tampering with her pages. She wrote Sybil Connolly's name down on a piece of paper and stuck pins in it. Then she put the paper in her bottom drawer. Not long after came the news that Sybil Connolly had fallen down some stairs and broken her leg. As a result, she couldn't come to Australia. Everyone on the *Weekly* was most impressed at such an effective way of disposing of 'the enemy', but this was one handy hint that the magazine didn't pass on to its readers.

I wrote Singleton's name on a piece of paper and stuck pins in it and put it in the bottom drawer of my desk. Every time the ratings came out and 2GB lost points, which they kept doing, I put another pin in. In August 1997, 2GB had its worst rating result since the radio industry began compiling ratings records in 1958. The once dominant network now only had a 3.7 per cent share of Sydney's listening audience. Revenge was sweet, but I figured enough was enough. I returned the pins to my pin box and threw out the paper with Singleton's name on it. As far as I was concerned he was yesterday's news. And so it seemed was 2GB. At the beginning of 2001 it was still struggling in the ratings and had hired yet another new array of presenters to try to improve its fortunes. One of them was Channel Nine's former Midday host Kerri-Anne Kennerley. I sent her a congratulatory fax warning her to make sure her contract was iron clad. Time will tell if she took my advice!

As often happens, before I'd finished up at 2GB, something new came my way. A Sydney-based group, Publishing Partners, was going to produce a magazine for the Jewel supermarket chain and asked me to edit it. With another Sydney journalist, Louise Di Francesco – who also runs her own PR company, The Write Communications Group – and art director Valeska Dominguez, I formed Three Dimensional Publishing.

Lou and I had known each other for some years. She is one of Australia's best public relations practitioners, and I've often recommended her to organisations like the Sydney Festival and the National Gallery; she worked with me on some of *ITA*'s promotions, too. Like me, she loves print and the thought of working together on a magazine was something that appealed to us both. She introduced me to Valeska.

We all hit it off well and approached our new task with much enthusiasm. We each worked from our own office, emailing the copy back and forth to one another. *Jewel* magazine was a friendly magazine with recipes, handy hints for new mothers, budget fashion, decorating tips, relationship stories, travel stars, and a monster crossword. It was the ideal magazine to take home after doing the shopping and to sit down and read while enjoying a cup of coffee.

We had published only two issues before the Jewel supermarket chain was taken over by Davids Holdings, which in 1997 revealed that because of over-expansion it had serious financial difficulties. For reasons that are now entirely clear, they did not want to continue on with the magazine. The three of us were devastated, but, as luck would have it, while we were working on the second issue of *Jewel* magazine, we'd been invited by the advertising agency Saatchi & Saatchi to put in a tender to provide editorial services for the *David Jones Magazine*.

Condé Nast, the publishers of *Vogue*, had produced it for a couple of years but David Jones wanted a new direction. We beat a lot of competition for this job including Australian Consolidated Press, although it was very close. At one point, David Jones couldn't decide between the two of us and had suggested that ACP produce the magazine and Three Dimensional Publishing act as consultants to the project. It was an arrangement that simply wouldn't work. Some of ACP's team weren't at all happy about the thought of taking any kind of direction from consultants, especially when one of them was Ita Buttrose.

In the end, David Jones decided in our favour because they liked our creative concept better. We were cock-a-hoop about our victory and thrilled to have such a prestigious client as David Jones. Because Lou had too much other work on her plate she dropped out, so Valeska and I formed Buttrose and Dominguez Design and got to work. I had spent hours in David Jones looking at how it operated. How did it talk to its customers? What were they really like? What went on in the store that would interest readers of the magazine? Valeska had strong ideas on how she wanted the magazine to look. We agreed that everything we did in the magazine had to entice customers into the stores. We had been flat out for three months working on our first issue when, about a week before we were due to send all the material to the printer, Mark McInnes, David Jones' Marketing Director, asked me to meet with him.

My gut instinct told me the news was going to be bad. I was right – it was. Our first issue of the *David Jones Magazine* would also be our last! McInnes said the magazine no longer fitted in with David Jones' future directions. I told him that Valeska and I wouldn't have taken on the job if we'd known it was to be for only one issue. We both found the decision difficult to understand especially as, in his column in the magazine, Peter Wilkinson, the Managing Director of David Jones, had written: 'This is the first issue under Ita's direction and I am sure you will be as delighted with the results as we are. We want you to think of the *David Jones Magazine* as a friend, here to help you with the best activity of all – shopping!'

On the day the *David Jones Magazine* went into the stores, Valeska and I received a fax from John Recek, the Managing Director of the fashion company Simona. 'I would like to congratulate you on the new *David Jones Magazine*. I received my copy today and I think it is fantastic, informative, well presented and a pleasure to read!' We both hoped he'd sent a copy to Peter Wilkinson.

If I hadn't had this book to complete I might have had some time on my hands, but Bob Sessions and his Penguin team made sure I was kept occupied meeting their deadline. I might also have wondered why doors kept closing in my face. My father told me when I was a junior reporter that there were always plenty of opportunities to be grabbed in life. 'Keep knocking on the door of opportunity,' he always told me, 'and if it seems closed keep on knocking until it opens.' Well, I certainly did my fair share of knocking in the nineties and no one can accuse me of not trying to make the most of the opportunities that presented themselves to me.

But the fact is that the way we work has changed forever. My experiences in the nineties reinforce this. Nothing much is long-term any more. Work comes in fits and starts. Work might be a three-month contract and then there might be nothing specific to do for a couple of months, before another short contract turns up. People will need to learn to be careful to put money aside for non-working periods.

This kind of work pattern gives a whole new meaning to the word 'budget'.

Back in March 1997, I had taken a step in another direction. I had my first piece of fiction, *Interlude in New York*, published in *The Australian Women's Weekly*. It was a romantic short story and my heroine, Catherine Walker, was a successful career woman in marketing and public relations. Like many other journalists I'd always had it in the back of my mind to write fiction, but I wasn't sure if I was a good enough writer to do this. I wasn't certain I could handle dialogue.

It was Sydney literary agent Selwa Anthony who suggested that I should have a go at writing something fictional. She knew that some of ACP's magazines were looking for romance stories and was so persistent I said I would. Nene King, the then Editorial Director of the *Weekly*, liked 'Interlude in New York' and published it. Mind you, Nene cheekily promoted it on the cover as 'Ita's racy romance' and in the same way on the *Weekly*'s TV advertisements, giving the impression that my fiction was my own personal story. It wasn't – but lots of people didn't believe me when I kept repeating it was make believe, not fact! To be honest, their reaction gave me a bit of a buzz.

And so did the response of Julie Gibbs, Penguin's Executive Publisher, who read 'Interlude in New York' on a plane somewhere over Australia. Almost as soon as it had landed she was on the phone excitedly predicting great things for my story's heroine Catherine Walker.

'Penguin thinks Catherine has a glittering future,' Julie said. 'We want you to write a novel about her.'

We agreed to meet and Julie arrived practically waving an enticing advance cheque in my face! She made me such an attractive offer that I simply couldn't say no. But, as I soon discovered, writing a blockbuster romantic novel of 130 000 words is quite different from a 1500 word story, especially if you have to write it while fulfilling other work contracts. Unfortunately, Penguin's handsome advance was not enough to enable me to give up my other income-making commitments. Very few authors in Australia can afford to do that. The market here is just not large enough to generate the kind of sales that would make this possible.

I transformed Catherine Walker into a magazine editor with media-mogul ambitions, and then I let my imagination run riot. I don't find writing easy, because I am my own worst critic, but that doesn't mean I don't like it. I do very much! I even enjoy the isolation that comes with it. Actually no fiction author could ever be lonely because the characters become friends, taking over your mind morning, noon and night. Mine even disrupted my slumber on several occasions.

Coming up with the book's title was another difficult task. Nothing I thought of sounded right. One morning I was walking my splendid black labrador, Humphrey, at one of our favourite ocean-side parks when inspiration hit me. My book was all about love – the title had to convey that. Two of my nieces Elizabeth and Evie, the daughters of my brother Will, often asked me for advice about their love life during their teens and early twenties. Invariably the conversation would get around to me asking: 'But, darling, do you really love him?' And each of them would always respond: 'But, Aunty Ita, what is love?' I dedicated my book to the pair of them!

What Is Love? was published in October 2000 and Nene King, who has retired to Noosa, on Queensland's Sunshine Coast, flew down to Sydney to officially launch it. Within six weeks *What Is Love?* had been set as prescribed text on the popular fiction course at the University of Tasmania and I had completed a marathon Australia-wide author's tour. This included speaking at breakfasts, lunches and dinners – sometimes all on the same day and well into the evening; book signings in major retail outlets; and inter-views with the media. These days it's not enough for an author just to write the book – marketing it is essential and a condition of an author's contract. This is exhausting work and requires an author to have remarkable stamina. It was around about this time that the best-selling Irish author Maeve Binchy announced her retirement from writing because she said the thought of having to endure another author's tour was too horrible to contemplate. Penguin felt confident enough about my novel's potential to print a large initial print run. By the end of the year some booksellers had already sold out which thrilled me no end.

Before *What Is Love?* was released, Julie Gibbs had been

to see me with yet another advance cheque and a contract for the sequel. I've already thought up the title and, unlike Maeve Binchy, I'm looking forward to my next author's tour!

Catherine Walker promises to add an exciting dimension to my life and I have great plans for her future. I suspect that she was also responsible for my return to *The Australian Women's Weekly* as a columnist in 1998. In April of that year Nene King rang and told me she had an exciting idea that she'd like to discuss. Over coffee, she asked if I would consider writing a column, 'Modern Manners', for the magazine. Back in 1985 I'd written *Every Occasion: Your Guide to Modern Etiquette* and it has been reprinted several times since then. Nene was familiar with my book and believed that I was the ideal person to advise the magazine's readers on manners – something she believed was sadly lacking in the Australia of today.

I couldn't believe my ears when Nene outlined what she had in mind. The thought of ever returning to my beloved *Women's Weekly* had never crossed my mind. Nothing will ever take away the special place the *Weekly* has in my heart. Nene suggested that perhaps I might like to go away and think about her proposal. No way! I accepted at once. It was as though I'd been asked to come home.

9

MATESHIP VERSUS FRIENDSHIP

_____

It is great to have friends when one is young, but indeed it is
still more so when you are getting old. When we are young,
friends are, like everything else, a matter of course. In the old
days we know what it means to have them.

NORWEGIAN COMPOSER, EDVARD GRIEG

When I was hosting a talkback segment one afternoon on
Sydney's 2GB in 1996, a woman rang in to tell me how
lonely she was. She had no friends. Although she'd had a
long and satisfying career, it was only in retirement she
realised that because of the demands of her job she had
never had the time to nurture friendships or to make new
ones. She was always too busy. This has to be one of the
consequences of Women's Liberation that no one ever
considered.

I sympathised with her because it was a problem I had
identified in my own life a few years earlier and I knew that
I would have to do something about it. Friendship is a fragile

thing and like everything else that is important in life it needs to be worked at. You can't simply take your friends for granted and the older I've become the more I've valued the friendship of women.

It was something I discussed with Hazel Hawke in the first issue of *ITA* in 1989, when she was still the wife of Prime Minister Bob Hawke. 'I have enormous respect for women,' she said, 'but it was something that didn't develop until middle age. I didn't realise the great resource women are to each other until I was in my forties.' This was the time of her life when she was pretty much on her own raising three children while Bob Hawke was preoccupied with his work for the trade union movement.

'Women understand each other,' she said. 'Often, their experiences have been very similar. The friendship, the understanding, the strength, is very special. Women can learn from each other and support each other too. There is a special feeling of camaraderie.'

There's no doubt that the friendship of women is very special. Women instinctively know what it is to be a woman physically and emotionally and what it is to be a wife and mother. They understand the experiences. They feel the nuances. They speak the language. A good friend will listen, sort out the wood from the trees, pour another cup of tea and send you home feeling all right with the world once more, knowing you would do the same for her.

In recent years I have renewed my friendship with Trish Burns (formerly Byrne), now the Executive Director of the

Curran Foundation in Sydney, my old childhood chum from my Parsley Bay days. When we first married, Trish and I saw a fair bit of each other, but then I went to England and although we kept in touch we each were busy raising our families (she is Kate's godmother). In recent years, we've been making up for lost time and in 1997 Trish suggested I come with her to France for a holiday. It was just marvellous – the first time that I can remember going on holidays and not having to worry about what was happening back home at the office. I felt totally free for the first time in my life! Trish had asked three other women, too – all friends of hers. It turned out to be one of those holidays where that camaraderie that Hazel Hawke spoke about was very evident.

We shared the rental of a charming farmhouse in the beautiful Loire Valley and each day, after a breakfast of croissants and tea or coffee, would head out sightseeing. In the evening we'd eat dinner in the kitchen in front of a big log fire and talk, sometimes until quite late, about our dreams – the ones that had come true and the ones that hadn't. We discussed men, too – some of us had been married, some not, a couple were widows; I was the only divorcee. As all of us are fifty plus, we're reasonably realistic about the shortage of men for women in our particular age group. But those of us who are 'available' agreed that we would be happy to be in a relationship – and in spite of the odds, hope one will eventuate.

By the end of our time in France new friendships had

been made, and even if we don't meet up for another five years, we know that we would only have to sit down and start talking, to take up where we left off. I've always thought women have a language of their own, and that holiday in France confirmed it yet again for me.

While I am sure men share great friendships, too, it seems to me that Australian men place more importance on mateship than friendship. You rarely hear men talking about their best friends, but you do hear them going on a great deal about their best mates. Mind you, a great many Australian men call anyone and everyone 'mate' – the man next door, the bloke they went to school with, their colleagues at the office, their fellow worker in the factory. There are new mates (men you meet for the first time) and old mates (men you've known for a long time). The garbo can be a mate, the butcher, the baker, the bus driver and definitely the taxi driver. Good guys are mates, bad guys are mates. Even law-breakers like Alan Bond – 'Bondy' to his real mates – is called 'mate'. The greatest accolade a man can give another man is to begin a sentence by saying: 'Well, Fred's a mate of mine . . .' Anyone who's a mate must be okay. I can't help thinking that 'mate' must be one of the most overused and least understood words in Australia.

What exactly do men mean when they call each other 'mate'? Perhaps communication between the sexes would be improved if women understood the meaning of mateship better than they do. Is a mate a friend in the true sense of the word? For women, friendship is never one-way traffic. One person supporting another through a bad patch, but never able to reveal anything of herself, is not a true friend. Friendship is a mutual relationship in which giving is as important as receiving. Is that what mateship means too?

At *Cleo* and *ITA* we continually tried to discover what men were really like. How did they view friendship? Did it mean the same thing to them as it does to women? At one *ITA* session, a thirty-five-year-old businessman told us:

Mateship is superficial. When I talk to a mate we talk about football and have a lot of laughs. We are loud. Then I listen to my wife when she talks to one of her friends and suddenly she is telling her all sorts of things that she never tells me. Women's friendships are more important to them.

Men say, 'Yeah, I know, mate' – but we don't talk about the real problem. Or we say, 'Yeah, mate, I understand' – but that's as far as we go. Men are zero on communication.

When I get on the phone I talk about sport because it's all part of our conquest mentality. It's more natural to talk about these things than to talk about personal problems. But my wife gets on the phone and talks to her best friend and I hear her say, 'I'm taking the wrong pill, it's giving me PMT', and I'm aware the other woman is listening and

sympathising and offering support. I often ask myself
if I'm listening enough.

Perhaps that man put his finger on the problem. Men
don't listen enough. Listening, true listening, has the ability
to touch emotions from time to time. Women know this but
few men do. Most men are conditioned not to show weak-
ness, not to cry, that kind of thing – they have no option
but to bottle up their emotions and feelings.

When Penguin Publishing Director Robert Sessions
approached me to write this book, he told me not to worry
about what people might say about anything I wrote. 'It doesn't
matter what people say about you,' he insisted. He must be
joking. Of course it matters. I've been let down on numerous
occasions by 'friends' who have said hurtful – often outrageously untrue – things about me to journalists. These 'friends'
are always anonymous. Sometimes I don't recognise the Ita
Buttrose that I see described in some articles. Neither do other
people. I gave a speech in Brisbane in September 1997, and
afterwards a man came up to me and said: 'Listening to you
speak today changed my perception of you. From what I'd
read about you in the media, I thought you were a stuck-up
bitch. I now know that's not true. You're all right.' And then
he shook my hand. I simply thanked him.

Over the years, plenty of people have claimed to be my
friends only to turn out to be opportunistic friends of
convenience. As my career has had its ups and downs, so too
have some of my friendships. Even so, occasionally I have

been surprised at people I had thought of as true friends who have disappeared out of my life merely because they have decided I am of no further 'use' to them.

I've sometimes confused them by turning up from time to time in what are considered to be 'positions of power', only to find them wanting to reclaim friendship. I don't have any illusions about power. It is meaningless. Power comes and goes. It can turn you into a person that others loathe or ridicule. It rarely brings you long-term friendships and it doesn't necessarily make you happy or bring you content-ment. Power is for the moment, not the future.

It's my experience, too, that power is far more acceptable in a man than it is in a woman. That's another thing I often wonder about. I am constantly told that men find powerful women frightening and yet, as far as I know, women don't fear men with power; instead, they find powerful men attrac-tive. It is one of life's great mysteries.

When I was a young girl attending a convent school the nuns used to tell me, every time I queried something in religion classes, that it was a mystery and that I would find out the answer when I died and went to heaven. It seems a long time to wait. I would like to find out why men find powerful women frightening before I die!

Maybe my two dear friends Marj McGowen and Nan Musgrove have already discovered the answer to this great conundrum. Their deaths, three years apart, gave me enor-mous cause to reflect on friendship and the role it plays in supporting us and keeping us sane through the vicissitudes of life. I am sure they will pardon my levity, but it was somewhat inconsiderate of them to go and leave such a big hole in my life. They were friends of such rare quality that I could tell them anything about my life, knowing that they would keep my confidences to themselves. I am sure that it is this quality of shared experience and frank discussion of life's joys and setbacks that men lack in their lives.

There have been big gaps for me in the friendship department since Marj and Nan died. I shared so many confidences with them. They can't be replaced, I know that; but I do sometimes wish they were still around, because I miss their sound advice and laughter.

I met Nan very early in my career. When I started as a teenager at the *Weekly* she was a senior journalist whom I addressed as 'Miss Musgrove'. There was none of that nineties first name stuff from juniors in those days. She was a tall, well-groomed woman, and wore her hair swept up into a splendid French roll. She looked very efficient but had a twinkle in her eye and seemed always ready for a laugh. I arrived at the *Weekly* with those skills that my parents had stressed were so important for a girl to have. I could type and do shorthand but the other copygirls could not. I was therefore deemed to be 'useful'.

Nan was putting together a medical book for the magazine and needed some help. She was told that the new copygirl (me) could type and that she could 'use' me to help her get the job done on time. I was terribly excited about all of this and considered it an important break. I was given a desk and a typewriter. Whatever Nan gave me I typed as speedily as possible, and generally tried to make myself helpful.

Many years later, Nan told me that I was noticed for the good work I did on the medical assignment. Of course I knew nothing about this at the time. That was 1957! Imagine how I felt when I returned to the *Weekly* in 1975 as Editor to find Miss Musgrove still there. As a former junior on the magazine, now the boss, I felt it only polite to ask Nan – and other colleagues of her generation – if they minded if I now called them by their first names. There were no dissenters.

Unlike some of the *Weekly*'s long-time staffers, Nan gave me a very warm welcome. It was just like the old days when I was fifteen. She was willing to give me a chance to see what I could do. It didn't take me long, however, to find out that Nan's talents were not being properly used. Although she was doing the TV column – an important assignment, because Kerry Packer also owned Channel 9 and the *Weekly* was beneficial in promoting the channel to its huge readership – and doing it well, she was such a good writer that I felt sure she could do more challenging stuff.

Nan was a brilliant observer of people and so shrewd in her judgment. She could pick a phoney in a flash. She had a fabulous enthusiasm for life plus a wonderfully inquiring mind, something she never lost and which is an essential requirement for a journalist. I gave her more profiles to do and the *Weekly*'s readers wrote to say how much they enjoyed them. Nan had an excellent news sense, too, and was always coming up with first-rate ideas for stories. About twelve months after my appointment as Editor I made her News Editor. Her management skills had just been waiting to be noticed. She flourished in her new role and, in it, made a significant contribution to the success of the *Weekly*.

There was much I was yet to find out about her however. On one particular occasion, early in my editorship, I was invited to the world premiere of *The Return of the Pink Panther* movie in Switzerland. I would love to have gone, but it was only a few months after we'd changed the size of the *Weekly* and this was not the time for me to leave my desk. I knew there would be some terrific opportunities for interviews with celebrities which magazine readers love so much.

I asked Nan if she'd like to go in my place and was stunned to find out that she'd never been outside of Australia. She was then over sixty. I just couldn't believe that in all her years at the *Weekly* she had never scored an over-seas trip. She returned in high spirits and dropped names with disgusting pleasure. She'd met Peter Sellers, the star of the film; Blake Edwards, the film's producer-director and husband of Julie Andrews (who was there too); and the biggest names of all – Richard Burton and Elizabeth Taylor. We were all suitably impressed and the *Weekly*'s readers loved Nan's account of the event. I believe it is essential for journalists to travel, and I've helped many get to places they might otherwise never have seen. It's also one of the best ways to say thank you to an employee for a job well done.

Ultimately, I persuaded Kerry to appoint Nan as chief of our London Bureau, which meant she looked after all publishing interests for ACP, not just the *Weekly*'s. She went with her partner of many years, Ken Kennedy, whom she referred to as 'Meaningful'. This name had come about following a long discussion we'd had about the names people give their partners when they are not married. The *Weekly* was doing an article about the growing numbers of people living together without marriage. We felt that introducing someone as 'my de facto' or the 'person I live with' could be improved upon. Nan said she always told people that she was in a meaningful relationship. Almost instantly, Ken was dubbed 'Meaningful'. Nan was a great letter writer and often closed her notes to me with the line: 'Meaningful sends his love'.

It was fantastic having Nan in London. Her personal, weekly letters to me included amusing tales of the goings-on of the royals and other public figures. We'd publish one story in the *Weekly* and I'd get the other version, which was of course not for publication. We always knew the 'real' gossip about the royal family because Anne Matheson, the *Weekly*'s long-serving Royal Correspondent, would lunch with Nan on a regular basis and tell her 'all'. That's one of the big differences between the women's magazine market then and now. Then we didn't print all the gossip and dirt on the royals – now they do, and sometimes I do wonder how and with whom facts are checked before publication. Mind you, even off the record in the seventies, we didn't go in for the kind of dirt that some women's magazines now dig up.

During my time with the *Weekly* we only once published a story about the royals that did not please the Queen. I received a letter from Buckingham Palace to say she was not amused with something or other we had published. I can't remember what it was now. We didn't intentionally set out to upset the royals and it was just a short story – only one page – pretty harmless by today's standards. But when the Palace notified Nan that we were about to get a black mark, she rang to tell me as though the end of the world had come. Anne Matheson, who was almost as 'royal' as the royals, was not at all amused either – she hadn't written the offending story (of course) – we'd bought it from an agency. It would not do for the *Weekly* to be out of royal favour! Nor was it in the interests of our readers either – they relied on the *Weekly* to tell them about the royal family and we were often given a newsbreak over other magazines because the Palace liked and trusted us and thought highly of Anne Matheson. I wrote to the Palace apologising for our misdemeanour and the *Weekly* was reinstated back into the royal good books.

I'm sure the Palace no longer writes to magazines that have earned its disapproval. It simply wouldn't have the time to comment on all the mainly unsubstantiated rubbish that has been published about the royals. In the latter part of the eighties and the nineties, the traditional women's magazines in Australia went almost feral, sinking to the lowest level of reporting. 'Best friends' of various members of the royal family seemed to be able to provide them with all kinds of salacious material, much of which was obviously downright rubbish.

It was apparent, after Princess Diana's shocking death in a car accident in Paris in 1997, that the world had grown weary of and dismayed by the way magazines and news-papers kept invading the Princess's life. Magazine editors may deny this, but significant drops in circulation of tradi-tional women's magazines in Australia indicate otherwise. After the incredible display of grief Britons and the rest of the world showed at her funeral, editors – including those in this country – promised to mend their ways and to act more responsibly in what they publish and in the methods used to acquire stories and photographs of famous people. Standards have certainly improved and thankfully Prince William was left in peace during the remainder of his school days – but even so, I think it will be many years before the women's press regains the esteem and respect that it once enjoyed, as well as its high readership. Of course, it might never do so. Once you alienate your marketplace, future prospects are always doubtful and official circulation figures released in 2001 show that the former big-selling women's magazines are still struggling to regain their lost circulations.

There are still question marks about the reputation and standing of the royal family. It might never recover either. While many stories published about them during this chaotic time were liberally laced with fiction rather than fact, some articles were accurate. There seems little doubt that Diana was left to sink or swim by the royal family and its advisers. Why did 'the firm' treat the gauche young woman so thoughtlessly in the early days of her marriage to Prince Charles? We'll never know for sure, but perhaps having procured a healthy female of good genetic stock for breeding purposes, the royals didn't give a damn about much else. When I went to London in 1981 to cover the wedding of the ill-fated couple for Network TEN and the *Sunday Telegraph*, I wrote that I doubted the world would ever again see a ceremony of such pomp and circumstance. Now, I think what we were witnessing was the beginning of the end of respect for, and influence of, this most British institution. When I returned home, I found a note waiting for me from Nan. It said she had heard from one of her former Palace contacts that Charles had only married Diana because the family had ordered him to do so.

Nan died of cancer. She was working for me at the *Sunday Telegraph* as a features writer when it was first diagnosed. She thought she'd beaten the damn thing. Doctors say that if, after treatment, you can survive five years with no further sign of cancer, it usually means you're conquered it. Nan was just a few months short of the five years when, on a routine check-up, there was an ominous black spot near the cervix. The cancer had reappeared. I was very concerned about her. She was worried, too, but in her typical Nan way, not so much for herself but more for 'Meaningful'. She didn't like to think of him alone without her. Although she maintained her usual optimistic outlook, she was now on the downhill path.

When Nan died in 1991, she was a valued contributor to *ITA*. When times were particularly trying for *ITA*, her counsel always stood me in good stead. Even now, I can still hear her no-nonsense voice which always signalled she was going to lay something on the line. 'Now listen, Boss . . .,' she'd begin – and I always did.

Nan was always candid. I was having trouble writing a speech one day when she rang.

'What are you doing?' she asked.

'I'm writing this bloody speech and I don't know what to say. They want me to talk about Ita Buttrose, the person, and Ita Buttrose, the personality, and I'm finding it difficult. I hate talking about me.'

Nan didn't hesitate. 'Tell them you are the most maligned person I've ever met. And that's because you have talent and good looks. Everyone is jealous of you. Men are jealous of your talent and want to get it off with you and can't. Women are jealous of both and reckon you must be sleeping with someone to become the success you are.'

And so that's what I told them. Nan's contribution to my speech brought the house down when I delivered it.

I can't remember exactly when Marj and I became friends. I do recall our first lunch. She was then working as public relations manager for Sekers, the textile and fabric company in Sydney. I was Women's Editor of the *Daily* and *Sunday Telegraphs*. Marj had a business proposition she wanted to put to me and had booked a table at Primo's, a trendy lunch spot of the day. At first we were polite and formal. Then, almost simultaneously, we confided our mutual dislike for big lunches. Our friendship was cemented over what we hoped was a slimming mushroom omelette, and we never looked back.

Friendship and business combined beautifully when Marj joined me at the *Weekly* in 1977 to become my Executive Assistant. It was Kerry's idea that I should have such a person to help me with my workload, which had grown tremendously. In 1976 I was appointed Editor-in-Chief of ACP's Women's Magazines, and in 1977 became Publisher of ACP's Women's Division, but running the *Weekly* was my major responsibility. I not only determined its editorial content and direction but also fronted its TV and radio commercials every week and wrote a weekly column.

For better or worse, I had become a 'celebrity' and my life changed forever. I lost my anonymity and became public property. Marj understood the extraordinary change that had happened in my life and was aware of how fiercely I tried to protect Kate and Ben's privacy. Occasionally, when I was away for a week or more she would come and stay with them, even though I had live-in help. They loved her like all kids did. Marj had a special knack of getting on with young people.

It was agreed that her main role would be to make my professional life run as smoothly as possible. I also told Marj I wanted her to help me with special promotions and marketing activities for the *Weekly*. The magazine's readers always had high expectations of the *Weekly*. They counted on it to set an example and occasionally to show the way. People who are only familiar with the magazine as it is today (it is now also a monthly, a transformation that took place in 1983) might find it difficult to appreciate what an influential and revered magazine the *Weekly* once was. When I was in charge, almost four million people read it every week. Australians trusted the *Weekly*. If it said something was true, they knew it was. The *Weekly* played an influential role in reflecting community standards and concerns.

In the seventies parents were beginning to worry about the growing use of drugs among young people. A director of one of ACP's subsidiary companies had lost a son to a drug overdose and he had heard about an excellent drug treatment program, Odyssey House, in the United States. He thought it was needed in Australia and he came to see me to enlist my support. I agreed that the *Weekly* would do whatever it could to get Odyssey House up and running in Australia. Marj and I worked hard to bring this about. The *Weekly*'s clout enabled us to organise free air travel to bring the American founder of Odyssey House, Dr Judianne Densen-Gerber, here so she could talk about her work and help raise the necessary money to establish Odyssey House. We organised lunches at which she spoke, including one with Tamie Fraser at the Lodge in Canberra. Prime Minister Fraser joined us for coffee. Naturally, there was a great deal of publicity about Judianne and Odyssey in the *Weekly* and we were able to organise interviews on TV and radio, too. It was an extremely successful trip. Support for Odyssey House grew and it was soon established in Australia and is still going strong as, unfortunately, drug addiction in Australia continues to increase.

Anything to do with children always had the *Weekly*'s attention. When researchers at Sydney University approached me with news of a significant breakthrough into the causes of cot death that was being held up due to lack of funding, I sent Marj to investigate. She reported back that the research seemed promising. I agreed with her and brought the matter to Kerry's attention because the sum of money needed was substantial. He agreed with our recommendation that the *Weekly* support the research and okayed the payment of the $50 000 that was needed.

Our *Women's Weekly* Health and Beauty Seminars, which were held in capital cities throughout Australia, were another triumph. We knew that our readers were looking for fashion advice and information about health and beauty, so we devised a weekend treat which included a fashion parade, guest speakers, wine tastings, and a dinner followed by a late film preview. While we were dispensing advice, we also encouraged women to take some time out for themselves and to enjoy the friendship of their sisters.

We encouraged our readers to think of people in need, too. I had read about the success of a London charity that had raised funds by selling other people's junk. I told Marj that I wanted to do something similar here to raise money

for The Smith Family, the Sydney-based welfare organisation. (I became a director of The Smith Family in 1997.)
Jumbly, as we called it, was a huge undertaking and would
never have been the triumph it was without Marj's careful
eye for detail and organisation. Jumbly couldn't happen
today because people now sell their second-hand goods at
their own garage sales and pocket the money themselves,
but in 1980 people had plenty of unwanted items. They
were happy to get rid of it by sending it to the *Weekly*.

The biggest problem we had was getting all the jumble
to Sydney and we decided the best way to do this would
be to set up collection centres around the country and then
find a way to transport everything to Sydney. I went to see
Sir Peter Abeles, then the Managing Director of TNT and
Ansett Airlines, to see if he would consider donating the
services of his company, Comet, to bring our junk to
Sydney. He listened and then asked: 'Is this something that
you think I should do?' What else could I say but yes! It
didn't take long for the spare floors at ACP to fill up with
clothes, toys, furniture, and even an extra-large electronic
sign that explorer/entrepreneur Dick Smith had made for his
office that flashed 'yes' or 'no', if a special button was pressed.
It used to have pride of place in his office and he enjoyed
surprising his staff with it when they'd come and ask him
for pay increases. We auctioned it at Jumbly and I bought
it for Kerry who was delighted with his new toy!

Jumbly dawned on a fine, sunny day and Marj and I decided
to walk the couple of blocks from the *Weekly*'s offices in Park

Street to Sydney Town Hall where we'd spent the last few days erecting stalls to display all the goods we'd collected. I'd managed to persuade the Lord Mayor to let us use the place free of charge. Marj and I were nervous, what if Jumbly was a flop? But when we were close enough to see the Town Hall's front door, Marj stopped. 'Ita, look!' There was a giant queue, stretching all the way down George Street as far as the eye could see. We were beside ourselves. Later, police had to close George Street to traffic – there were so many people trying to get into the Town Hall. Jumbly was a fantastic event and raised more than $50 000 for The Smith Family.

We did so many things together that sometimes I still find it hard to believe that Marj is no longer here. Occasionally we would spend the cocktail hour with each other – on the phone – in our respective homes and each with a gin and tonic because we both had mothers who said nice girls never drank on their own! Marj fought cancer of the liver for three years, putting up a tremendous fight. I never heard her complain. Towards the end she admitted to pain, but only in a matter-of-fact kind of way.

By this time, she was working as executive director of the Shepherd Centre for Deaf Children in Sydney. I'll never forget the day she found out what was wrong. She had been off-colour for twelve months. Her GP kept telling her she had a virus. I got angry. For heaven's sake, I told her, no one has a virus for twelve months. Tell your doctor to do some tests and find out what's wrong.

She did.

The results arrived a few days later, not long before we were to have dinner at the American Club with her boss, Dr Bruce Shepherd. I picked her up. One look at her face and I knew the news wasn't good. She was with me but she wasn't. She was somewhere far away, wrapped in her own thoughts.

The 'Good Shepherd', as we affectionately called Bruce, asked Marj what her doctor had said. I kicked him so hard under the table it's a wonder he ever walked again without a limp. He got the message. Marj's answer was evasive. We changed the subject.

Next morning I rang her front door bell and demanded to be let in. She was still in a state of shock.

'Tell me what's wrong,' I said.

'I have bowel cancer,' she replied. I was relieved. Bowel cancer! Doctors can fix that, I told myself.

'But,' she went on, 'the cancer has spread to my liver.'

We both knew what that meant, but neither of us wanted to believe it. Let alone accept it.

Marj didn't, until six months before she died, when doctors told her there was nothing more they could do. She was such a good woman, an exceptional human being, about whom I have never heard anyone say an unkind word. That's quite something in a society like ours where so many take delight in muck-raking – especially after a person has died.

At Christmas in 1987 when I knew – and she knew – that she was dying, I realised that I had never told her just how much our friendship meant to me. It wasn't that I took it for granted, but expressing feelings about friendship isn't often done – or at least that's my experience. I am grateful that God inspired me to tell her that Christmas how much her friendship meant and how much I admired her determination to beat the cancer that finally killed her. I loved her. I told her so. She thanked me, and for a while we said nothing. We were lost in our memories.

Many involved our days together on the *Weekly*. How we'd laugh when we recollected our treasured trip in 1980 to London where Nan had booked us in for a treatment at one of that city's newest health and beauty sanctuaries.

When we arrived we could see only naked people – sunbathing, swimming, having treatments. We were shown to lockers and told to take all our clothes off. We looked at each other. We were desperate. How could we escape?

We composed ourselves, went upstairs and told the receptionist that we had to make an important business call and would ring later if we had time for another appointment. As boss of ACP's office in London, Nan had pulled all sorts of strings to get us into the place, which was always booked out. She was very annoyed with us when we turned up at the office and told her we'd decided not to stay. All that nudity just wasn't us.

There was our unforgettable stopover in Paris, with a lunchtime trip on the River Seine where we splurged on a magnificent and expensive bottle of Chateau Margaux. Marj always claimed I ticked her off for spilling a drop of this pricey vintage.

There was one memorable Christmas shopping spree when we organised a hire car – well, if I must be honest, I organised it, I was always the extravagant one, not Marj – and did our Christmas shopping in comfort. We filled the boot with goodies and then went to Beppi's, our favourite Italian restaurant, for a quick bite of lunch (with the car waiting outside) before returning to the office. The same year, Marj gave me a recording of the Salvation Army band playing Christmas carols because I had told her I adored band music.

There were shared confidences about our romantic hopes and ambitions. When I had marriage problems, Marj listened and offered her opinion. It was always astute. We often went to the opera, ballet and theatre together. On that remarkable visit to London we went to see the musical, *Chicago*. Years later, when it opened in Sydney I rang Marj and asked if she'd like to go.

'Love to,' she said.

It was a great show.

'Did you like it?' Marj asked.

'Fantastic,' I replied.

'Do you remember seeing it before?'

'Nope.'

'We saw it together in London. You slept all the way through it.'

Who else but a best friend would tolerate such sloppy behaviour?

I cried many times for her and sometimes for myself

during the three years Marj was ill. She kept working and refused to feel sorry for herself. She didn't give up her job until about a month before she died.

At the time Bruce Shepherd, the founder of the Centre, told me I was at the age when people I know will die. 'Maybe,' I wept, 'but I don't have to like it'.

Nan knew, of course, that Marj's death caused me immense sadness. We often talked about the old days when the three of us worked for Kerry Packer and the *Weekly* played such a big part in our lives. Both Nan and Marj 'suffered' because of their friendship with me. Kerry felt they had let him down. Well, I think that's what he thought. He treated them both pretty shabbily after I'd told him I was leaving Australian Consolidated Press.

I had stayed with Nan in London in 1980 before coming back to resign to take up Rupert Murdoch's offer. I had phoned Marj from there to ask her to make a time for me to see Kerry on my return. Once I'd decided to accept Rupert's offer, I knew that I had to give notice to ACP as soon as possible. It was the ethical thing to do. News Ltd and ACP were fiercely competitive in magazines and television. As a director of ACP, I felt obliged to let Kerry know my decision without delay.

I had no idea that he was going to behave in the appalling way that he did. He told Marj there was no future for her with the company and abused her for not ringing him to tell him why I wanted to see him. Mind you, Marj did not know what Rupert had offered me because I didn't tell her, not wanting to compromise her, although she was aware I'd lunch with him.

Kerry had conveniently forgotten that I had been to see him before I went overseas to say that I needed some new challenges, and that he had told me he was happy with me where I was. He failed to remember my disappointment when he said 'no' to Bruce Gyngell's suggestion that I become the anchorwoman on Nine's *Today Show*. He also forgot his 'no' to the suggestion – I think from Sam Chisholm – that I join the *Sixty Minutes* team; and he'd forgotten about his 'no' to my becoming an author when British author, Shirley Conran, asked me to write the Australian version of her best-selling *Superwoman*.

It never occurred to him that I was feeling as frustrated as hell – that much of it was his fault, and that the reason I'd been susceptible to an offer from Rupert was because I felt blocked at ACP. Much as I enjoyed running the *Women's Weekly*, I knew I could still manage it and do other things, too. How could a man with Kerry's kind of entrepreneurial spirit not appreciate that I had some, too?

If I had thought for one moment that he would take my departure out on Marj and Nan, I would never have stayed with Nan in London nor asked Marj to make the fateful appointment. It is something I regret deeply. But what woman will ever understand the male ego and the complex workings of the male mind?

Kerry didn't content himself with just giving Nan and Marj a hard time either. Ainslie Cahill, who was my Senior Secretary, was singled out too. She and I were only work colleagues then, but our relationship has developed into friendship, as Marj predicted to me it would not long before she died. After telling the staff of my 'defection', Kerry called Ainslie to his office. It was years before she told me what had happened.

Trevor Kennedy [he took over the women's division after my departure] was standing behind Kerry's chair. He offered me a promotion. It was some kind of marketing executive role, and clearly a job replacing Marjorie. I was not interested in taking on the position, as I knew Marjorie was being unkindly dumped.

KP knew you'd asked me to move to News Ltd. When I told KP I'd be going, he 'turned'.

'So when will you be leaving?' he asked.

I replied that I would expect to tidy up my work at ACP before I moved on.

'And what work is that?' he asked.

I began to list several outstanding matters. And when I got to correspondence – as you know the mailbag was always HUGE – he retorted, 'Fuck the correspondence, we want information!'

At the time I remember thinking, 'Oh gawd, get out the bright lights and the machine gun'.

Heaven only knows what information Kerry was looking for from Ainslie. I hadn't told Rupert any ACP secrets and I never did. It is not the way I operate. But when Kerry realised he wasn't going to be able to persuade Ainslie to change her mind about leaving, he turned his attention to Nan and Marj.

Nan, whose company he used to enjoy, was treated with anger and rudeness. It wasn't long before she was recalled to Australia and, as she had reached retirement age, was told she was no longer needed. There was no grand farewell, as was customary for someone who had served the company as long and as loyally as Nan, no thank you. She was being 'punished' for no greater crime than being my friend.

I presume this was the reason why I heard from so few of my *Weekly* colleagues and other friends at ACP after I had left. They were fearful that Kerry wouldn't like it if it were known they kept in touch. It is sad to think that people can be so scared – but then Kerry always was a bully. If he didn't get his way, he'd simply lose his temper. For this I blame his parents. They were always too busy doing their own thing to spend time with him and to give him the care and attention a young boy needs if he is to grow up into a well-rounded adult. Sir Frank was preoccupied building his empire and Kerry's mother led the typical, carefree life of a society woman with lots of parties, good times and plenty of champagne. It doesn't take a child long to find out that a tantrum or two always grabs attention.

He told me once that his mother used to call him stupid.

Even when he was an adult, I could see it was still a painful memory. I am sure Kerry must sometimes wish his mother – and indeed his father – could see him now! In their wildest dreams they would never have believed, I'm sure, that Kerry would become the success that he is – one of Australia's most famous citizens as well as its richest. It must give him a certain satisfaction. Whether it makes him happy is another matter.

Kerry's treatment of Marj, too, was very mean-spirited. She, like most people who worked at the *Weekly*, loved her job, loved the magazine. She was an asset to the company. She would have been an excellent support to Dawn Swain who was Editor of the *Weekly*. I have always thought that the shock and despondency Marj suffered at being kicked out of her job for no good reason put undue stress on her, and that this was possibly responsible for her cancer. I've read that such anxiety can trigger cancer and perhaps this was so in Marj's case.

A few months before she died, I told Marj I wished there were something I could do to help her. 'There's nothing anyone can do, Ita,' she said.

During some of the more difficult times of her illness I had lent her (for as long as she wanted) a small scapular with a relic of St Therese which I've carried with me for years. My late great Aunt Una, who was a Carmelite nun, gave it to me. I asked Marj if she'd like it once again. She said yes.

Marj died about 4.30 on a Sunday morning in April

1988. For some reason, I woke up at that time. I looked at my clock and wondered why I was awake. I swear I could hear Marj telling me that I could have my scapular back. No, I can't explain it, but I know that she was saying goodbye. Death has not ended our friendship. It will always remain. Death has simply taken away the time we might have spent together.

A few days after Marj died, a reader sent me some words on death written by Canon Henry Scott-Holland who lived from 1847 to 1918. They were very comforting then, and still are today.

Death is nothing at all . . . I have only slipped away into the next room . . . I am I and you are you. What-ever we were to each other, that we are still. Call me by my old familiar name, speak to me in the easy way which you always used. Put no difference into your tone; wear no forced air of solemnity or sorrow. Laugh as we always laughed at the little jokes we enjoyed together.

Play, smile, think of me, pray for me. Let my name be ever the household word that it always was. Let it be spoken without effect, without the ghost of a shadow on it. Life means all that it ever meant. It is the same as it ever was; there is absolutely unbro-ken continuity. What is this death but a negligible accident? Why should I be out of mind because I am out of sight?

I am but waiting for you, for an interval, somewhere very near just around the corner . . . all is well.

Much and all as I miss Marj and Nan I am in no haste to join them, which I am sure they would understand. I'm pretty sure, though, that they have a bottle of champagne chilling in the ice bucket awaiting my arrival. That's the kind of friends they are!

10

HAVE MEN LOST THEIR WAY?

When you are young and want to get married, men are
important, but later your work and your children and other
relationships become more important and men become more
marginal to your concern.

AMERICAN AUTHOR MARILYN FRENCH – *ITA*, MARCH 1994

Men are in need of help. They are confused in their relationships with women; many of them resent the lack of
choices in their lives; and their health leaves much to be
desired. What men need is some kind of male Germaine
Greer who will make them sit up and take a good look at
themselves. They need to campaign for better information
and more money to be spent on men's health and for the
needs of men on the political agenda. Male Liberation is
long overdue.

In 1995 Bruce Ruxton, the President of the Victorian
RSL, invited me to speak at his organisation's annual State

conference. I told the delegates that I was becoming increasingly worried about Australia's silence on matters that should concern us. I said we'd become a nation of wimps. I now believe this silence has spread to all kinds of men's issues, too – their rights, their health, their education and their employment.

Alarm bells should be ringing for men, but they're not. Generally speaking men have been unbelievably quiet about what is happening to them. Women seem more concerned about their problems. How can this be? Why are men so reluctant to raise their voices? Can't they see what is going on? What sort of a future do they think awaits their sons? Where are their leaders? Why aren't they more concerned about their health? Why are they falling behind in education and employment?

Some men have begun to speak out in recent times, like Tasmanian psychotherapist and author Steve Biddulph. In his book *Manhood* he acknowledges that:

> most men don't have a life. Instead, we have learned to pretend. Much of what men do is an outer show, kept up for protection. Most women today are not like this. They act from inner feeling and spirit, and more and more they know who they are and what they want.

'A man,' writes Biddulph, 'feels that there must be more, but does not know what that more is. So he spends his life pretending to be happy – to himself, his friends and his family'. Authors like Biddulph are rare and the issues he raises are an important breakthrough for the opposite sex. But there is little evidence that enough men are heeding his message. Unlike the women in the seventies who took to Women's Liberation as though they had individually discovered it, there is no evidence yet that large numbers of men have been caught up in anything so revolutionary.

As far as their health goes, not all men are indifferent but far too many are. When the ABC presented the four-part series *The Problem with Men* in 1997, they cleverly used humorist John Clarke and his offsider Bryan Dawe to give viewers what the *Bulletin* described as 'a Clayton's kind of program – the men's health program you are having when you are not having a men's health program'. The show, which featured prostate cancer, included the American Gulf War hero, General Norman Schwarzkopf talking about his battle with the illness. It rated its socks off.

Yet it would be hard to imagine a National Prostate Cancer Day to coincide with Breast Cancer Awareness Week, which is organised annually by women throughout Australia in October. Men have a long way to go and unless they wake up to the fact that they must take charge of their lives, will continue to be left behind. This is something that concerns and depresses me.

Men are losing out in their relationships with women, too. So many of them worry that whatever they do is wrong. 'I just don't know what my wife wants any more,' one man told me on radio 2GB's open line in 1996, 'and she doesn't seem to be able to tell me either'. Men regularly admit that they don't understand the woman in their lives – 'She says one thing and means another'. Why do men find it so difficult to communicate? Has it something to do with the way women rear their sons? Do women spoil them too much? Do mothers tell their boys how essential it is to listen? Do they talk to them explicitly enough about good sex and how to satisfy a woman? I am not for one moment blaming women for the problems men face, but I am suggesting that perhaps women need to be more constructive if we want men to regain their self-esteem.

Women's lives have changed dramatically since World War II and, for the most part, for the better. Men have not been able to keep up. Women now have different expectations. We have dreams and expect to achieve them; we have choices and exercise them. Women are also more self-sufficient than men. They view power differently, too and are not prepared to sacrifice choices, freedom, families and friends in the pursuit of power. Women look after their health because they want to enjoy their older years doing the many things they haven't had time to do. When they talk about the importance of a quality lifestyle, they mean it. No wonder many men envy women and the way they have structured their lives.

I am not alone in my observations that all is not well with the opposite sex. Ever since the mid-nineties commentators have been sending out distress signals. In April 1995

Geoffrey Maslen wrote an article, 'Boy, You're in Big Trouble', for the *Bulletin*, in which he outlined some of the massive problems facing Australian men.

> During the past ten years men have become the second sex – they were always more prone than women to diseases of the heart, liver, stomach and lungs, to cancer, strokes, stress-related illnesses and car accidents. They were always more likely to become alcoholics, drug users, criminals and murderers. But now they appear to be losing out to women in the intellectual stakes as well.

Maslen's article, which the *Bulletin* said included a 'growing body of surprising data', drew attention to the feminisation of higher education in Australia. It's apparent, and has been for some years, that women are increasingly outperforming men in higher education. It will be years before men catch them up – and then it will depend on whether they have the willpower to do so and the right leaders to show them the way.

Men are in trouble, but few of them realise it. They are coming off second best. We are producing a generation of men in Australia who are lost and hurting. They are confused about themselves, their lives and their place in society. In the early nineties, the magazine *New Woman* launched a 'brother' publication, *New Man*. In the first issue, the editor justified the need for a magazine for the 'new' man by arguing that the changes in women's lives posed a problem for him, because 'the new woman is assertive, self-confident and knows what she wants from life'.

Great, but what does it all mean for the modern male, asked Dr Anthony McMahon of Melbourne's Monash University in his article, 'Can Men Be Equal Too?' published in the university's *Montage* magazine. McMahon pointed out that the second issue of *New Man* did not appear. 'Most similar attempts to address "new" men have also failed,' he wrote. 'In fact, women make up the main audience for discussions of men and change. Perhaps this is not all that surprising, when one asks who benefits from change. Do men have as much to gain as women, or do men have something to lose?' In *Manhood*, Steve Biddulph contends that women have probably come as far as they can without some comparable changes in men.

In 2001, the image of the stand-alone, rugged Aussie male – so typified by the heroics of Anzac Cove, and enshrined in our culture through the myriad sporting icons that fill our newspapers and TVs every week – may be crashing down around us.

Former New South Wales Premier, Neville Wran's famous maxim, 'Balmain boys don't cry!', may be meaningless in the coming years to the Australian male. Some will argue that even Jesus wept, but I am not sure the feminisation of the Australian male has been a good thing. Men appear to be losing their way in unprecedented numbers. As someone who has always enjoyed the company of men – after all, they are not the opposite sex for nothing – I have seen first-hand the changing Aussie male, from slightly fragile (but nevertheless strong) rugged rascal, to little boy lost in the cosmos. Many believe that the Australian male has been emasculated by the revolution of the last forty years, and worse still, he has participated in it.

For instance, in her article 'The Man Who Wasn't Born Yesterday' for *ITA* in June 1989, Anne Musgrave quoted Sydney University researcher, Dr Alan Bowen-James:

> In holding themselves responsible for injustices suffered by women in the past (before today's male was even born) many men today are becoming excessively wimpish. Middle-class males are actually colluding in their own emasculation, yet there's a defensive position that the modern male seems quite justified in adopting. 'Why should I be held responsible for past injustices? Life's bloody hard for me, too.'

Life has been tough for men. After all, it's been okay for us girls, as we've been the ones driving the change and – even if there still are some areas left to tackle – we know the day will come when nothing is beyond our reach. Men have had to endure this torrent of change, unsure of what it all means.

Anne Musgrave quoted a top company executive in 'The Man Who Wasn't Born Yesterday' article as saying,

'The women's movement has been a terrific thing. It has helped men discover a side of us we didn't know existed – a softer, more female side'. That doesn't sound like something the average Aussie male would have said in the sixties and seventies and it's certainly not something the average Aussie male would have even thought in the forties and fifties.

I certainly can't imagine my father or brothers even mouthing those words. Some men may just be more in touch with their feelings, but do women really want a generation of men who can't fill a room with the smell of testosterone? Don't women need a strong, rugged bloke from time to time? Or have women become so dominant that they have overpowered men? Anne Musgrave concludes, 'In fighting for a fairer deal, did we give much thought to the effect of this enormous social upheaval on our generation of men? Isn't it time we welcomed them in from the cold? We've been swept up and along by a very positive, dynamic, highly-publicised on-going movement of change'.

What has happened is that we have enshrined feminism in our culture and condemned our men to be politically correct wusses. What Australian man would dare to say out loud that due to the advancement of women, men are being shoved aside; that they are being denied their equal rights; that they are being disadvantaged? Not many – if any – I suggest.

John Bednall, headmaster of the Hutchins School in Tasmania, told a meeting of Canberra educators in 1995 that it was now politically incorrect to encourage boys 'to want to lead, to want to make significant decisions, to want to be powerful. What has made us nervous of putting "boy" and "power" in the same sentence?' What indeed?

My friend, Dr Brendan Nelson, who easily won the seat of Bradfield not long after our World Vision trip to Africa in 1995, says 'there was a time when masculinity was considered a virtue but now it seems to be an obstacle to overcome'. In 2000 Prime Minster Howard asked him to head up the Federal Government's national inquiry into the education of boys, a task that has required Brendan and his committee to spend more than twelve months examining the social, cultural and educational factors affecting boys.

I interviewed him for a column I wrote for *The Australian Women's Weekly* in September of that year in which I asked were we turning boys into sissies? More than 50 per cent of the *Weekly's* readers who responded to my column said 'Yes!'

'Fifteen years ago it was recognised that the education system had to be changed to accommodate girls and to encourage them to study subjects other than arts, ones that were seen as boys' subjects like Maths and science,' Brendan told me. 'In 1980 the average tertiary scores for boys and girls were the same. By 1990 girls were four marks ahead; by 1996 they were 20 marks ahead and by 1998 girls out-performed boys in 64 out of 70 subjects and in the best 100 achievers only one in three were boys.'

The situation has continued to deteriorate for boys since then. In 1999 the retention rate to Year 12 was 78.5 per cent for females, but only 66.4 per cent for males – the largest gap for 23 years. Given that the evidence of boys' decline has been obvious to all, including education authorities throughout Australia, we can only puzzle why they failed to act. God knows what triggered the Howard Government to find out why boys are underachieving but, when it does, let's hope quick action is taken to remedy the situation.

I wouldn't be surprised if the way boys are being taught emerges as one of the major contributing factors to their lack of achievement. It's almost as if there is a silent conspiracy going on in our schools to make boys more like girls and that the education system is trying to behaviourally modify boys. Is it any wonder they're becoming increasingly confused as to what's expected of them?

The 'transformation' attempt begins at pre-school when little boys of three and four are told to sit quietly and concentrate even though lads this young find it almost impossible to stay still and listen, look and learn like little girls do. Why should they anyway? Their attention span is short because their minds are so active. Boys learn best by touching, experimenting and exploring. Even in the playground the odds are stacked against small boys where they are encouraged and, in some schools coerced, to play the same kinds of games girls do. How frustrating it must be for a boy to be compelled to play this way. The noisy rough and tumble and the occasional thump that boys delight in giving each other is their way of bonding.

Could this preference for co-ed team sport have anything

to do with the severe shortage of male teachers? As only one in five primary school teachers are men it seems highly likely. Naturally, the female influence is important in a boy's upbringing, but it can not, and never will, replace the need a boy has for a strong role model. That's something boys need desperately of course because they learn about masculinity from men. Fathers have a vital part to play, but they're also often in short supply. So many dads are too busy to spend much time with their sons. Many boys are being raised in single-parent households headed by women and have little meaningful contact with their fathers and men generally.

The lack of male teachers, not just at primary levels, but also at secondary worries Brendan who says there is a strong feminist agenda in our schools. 'Boys are being taught like girls – but boys are boys and have different requirements,' he says. Dr Ken Rowe, principal research fellow at the Australia Council of Educational Research, refers to education's 'feminised curriculum'.

Psychologist Bettina Arndt – and occasional fellow *Beauty & the Beast* panelist – writing in the Melbourne *Age* in December 2000 related the story of a Victorian history teacher struggling to come to terms with the humorous conversational style of her male students during class discussion. 'In a debate on some serious historical event she'd find the boys competing to express their views with a witty *Roy and HG* satirical edge. At first the teacher found it confronting "How can I get them to be serious?"' she wondered. 'But she has learnt to enjoy and appreciate this style, which she now sees as a valued part of the Australian male language. Yet, when it comes to written assessment, it doesn't translate – it's not easy teaching such boys to express their view in a style acceptable to examiners.'

Brendan Nelson says boys predominate in special classes for emotional and behavioural disturbances and that they are more likely to be early school failures and truants. They are abandoning learning and leaving leadership to girls. In 1998 a Queensland headmaster of a country school told me that only one boy had put his name forward that year to be a prefect. On discovering that the other twelve contenders were girls, the lad withdrew his name. This is not an isolated case. In an attempt to stop the rot one Sydney co-ed high school now offers leadership classes for boys. Girls are not allowed to attend. Brendan insists boys' self-esteem is linked to their education. 'Anti-social behaviour relates to the first seven to eight years of a child's development,' he says, pointing out that the role of the parents – both of them – at this time is also important.

As Australia heads into the 21st century with all its promise, it's sobering to know that our young men are committing suicide at a rate seven times higher than that of girls: we have one of the highest youth suicide rates in the world; young males have a 300 per cent higher death rate from motor accidents than young females; drug and mental health problems among men are on the rise; they are more likely to be the non-custodial partner in divorces involving children, to be imprisoned, and to be victims of deaths in custody.

In the workforce, younger men feel overwhelmed and overpowered by young women's push for career and financial success. They feel inadequate – and this feeling of inadequacy flows over into their personal lives. They hesitate, unsure of how to find or approach a woman about marriage for fear they will not measure up to young women achievers' high expectations of them. Ironically, many young career women in their late twenties and thirties now complain how difficult it is to meet a man, let alone find one to marry. Tim Fischer, the former Federal National Party Leader, says women need to give blokes a fair go. He says men would rather cut lawns than tell their wives, 'I love you'. How sad, and how well it illustrates just how confused modern man is.

Our men can no longer express themselves openly to women – not that they are much good at it anyway – but do we really want them to be closed and cornered in our society, to flounder in a no man's land? Do women really want this new species of male that they forced into existence? Do they truly want a man who is not able to speak his mind for fear of being labelled a male chauvinist or too macho? On the other hand, do they want a man who is so emasculated, feminine and weak that he can no longer be master of his own domain? Have women's efforts to 'civilise' men merely made them more disenchanted or simply disenfranchised them?

I am pessimistic about the future of the Australian male. Is there one with enough ambition and drive, and enough of a voice, to lead a revolution for men? As in most things, men will probably passively let things happen around them.

One of the inevitable consequences of the feminist revolution has been the fragmentation of society. The demand for equal rights, equal opportunity and all the rest inevitably leads to a new form of discrimination in which the needs of the so-called afflicted minority (i.e. women) take precedence over the needs of the alleged oppressive majority. This is true not only of women's issues but of every so-called special needs group in society and has been one of the trends of our age. Never before in the history of the world have special interest groups and minorities wielded so much power and influence.

Perhaps that is merely part of a new equilibrium, but we nevertheless must be aware of the implications for the new disenfranchised. Men used to have some power; now they feel they have none at all. Indeed, they feel as if they have lost their voice altogether. Is this what women have been aiming for – a new fragmented society in which only they have power? Is that not to replace one tyranny with another? Do two wrongs ever make a right?

I am convinced that success in personal relationships, raising families and in the workplace comes from having equal input from both men and women. There can be no argument that the differences between the sexes, properly harnessed and motivated, can do wonders for all organisations. It always has been the imbalance that has pushed women to strive for their rights. If the balance has now changed in women's direction to the detriment of men, then I don't think it will be of long-term benefit to either sex, professionally or personally.

It is odd, but research shows that although men control the decision-making of health and education, these are the two areas where women seem to be getting a better deal. The fact that working men between the ages of twenty-five and sixty-four have a death rate twice as high as women of the same age doesn't seem to have registered with many men, nor do they seem to think it alarming that women outlive them by some six to seven years. In 1900 it was only by one year. A 21st-century woman would not be so complacent about such a situation were the tables reversed. But our men go on like lambs to the slaughter, never asking why the same number of research dollars spent on breast cancer in women are not invested into men's health research – yet prostate cancer kills almost as many men per annum as breast cancer does women. One in sixteen men will get it, and each year 5000 new cases are diagnosed, resulting in 2000 deaths per annum.

Carmen Lawrence, the Federal Health Minister in the Keating Government, officiating at the first-ever national men's health conference in Melbourne in 1996, said: 'Men's health and early mortality are issues that affect us all. These men are our partners, our sons, our fathers and our friends, and they are dying in the prime of their productive lives. The cost is enormous – not only to families but also to the community as a whole.' Women used to say exactly the same thing about the consequences of breast cancer.

Wherever you look, the outlook for men's health seems grim. Recent Australian research suggests that men have a decreasing motility in their sperm. Impotency clinics claim to be treating hundreds of patients each week. Other research indicates that men's testes in Australia are both smaller and weigh less today than in years gone by – a deadly cocktail of societal stresses, pollution and radiation is killing the male's fertility. Yet men are silent. Could the Australian male be any more emasculated than he is today? Is it their conditioning that makes men accept their lot without questioning?

Do men feel they have to just grin and bear it, tough it out, take it like a man? For example, men are dying unnecessarily from testicular cancer and prostate cancer because men, out of some mistaken belief system, will not see a doctor. An article in Sydney's *Sun-Herald* in February 1997 referred to men as an 'Endangered Species'. Anna Patty wrote:

If there is something wrong with your genitals, the thinking is there is something wrong with you as a man. Some men express embarrassment or homophobic fears about being examined by a male doctor. Men are brought up to believe they should always be able to cope and to be in control. Not having been taught to accept their own vulnerability, men are more likely than women to use alcohol as a coping mechanism.

There's very little discussion about this major health problem for men, probably because it concerns alcohol and we all know how the Aussie male feels about his alcohol. One in six male employees in Australia is drinking at harmful or hazardous levels. The figure for women is one in ten. Alcoholism in the workplace is a sensitive issue. It would be. Employers and unions do not want to confront it, but alcohol-related problems cost Australia $10 billion a year. It is one of today's most important issues facing industry and government, but it is not being addressed.

Men don't seem to know or care either that women are outnumbering them at our major universities and are more successful academically. Monash University researchers pointed out in 1995 that significantly more women than men were gaining access to Australia's top universities, and that at six of Australia's eight major capital city universities, women made up well over half the first-year intake. In fact, there are fewer female than male freshers at only five out of thirty-six public universities. And not only are women surpassing men in their studies – they seem to be advancing beyond them in gaining key professional credentials, with university-educated women being more successful in finding jobs than their male counterparts. As the Monash researchers point out: 'Historically, graduation from these institutions has opened a pathway into a social, economic and political elite.'

I discussed the research with my fellow (male) directors at Prudential and one of them was staggered at the implications. 'My God,' he said, 'our days are numbered.' He said it without thinking, but his words reflected the way that many men feel. It's ignorance, though, that makes men think this way. They don't know what benefits are yet to come through the participation of well-educated women in business and community life. Working together, with equal input, it's possible that women and men might be able to create a far better world than the one we know today.

I feel sorry for men because it seems to me that the odds are stacked against them from day one. There's no doubt many fathers miss out on the real joys of parenthood because of career responsibilities. Women are only too well aware of the difficulties in combining work and family – men have the same problems. But with things like affirmative action, awareness-raising of women's issues, and childcare, men's needs have not been as carefully considered.

Paul Gollan, a lecturer in management at the Graduate School of Management at Sydney's Macquarie University, believes that fatherhood has been forgotten. 'The prevailing view of many fathers is that to be successful you must put your career first,' he says. Gollan thinks there are plenty of rules laid down for motherhood but no such rules are laid down for fatherhood. 'One of the major policy problems over the past few years is that men's interest in undertaking family work has been greatly inhibited by the fact that most discussions and debates on work and family issues have been part of a women's agenda.'

That's true, but why were men so silent? Men didn't even try to communicate how they felt about the need for paternity leave, or time off when the kids are sick, or shorter family-friendly hours. Women got tired of waiting for male-dominated businesses and unions to understand their needs as working mothers, and joined together to bring about the reforms they wanted. Men need to follow women's example and get with it!

British evidence suggests that three out of four men consider that their family relationships have been damaged by their working lives. 'The emphasis in recent years on justice for women has masked an important truth,' writes Gollan, 'that, in terms of the work–family dilemma, men are losers too, most obviously in their relationships with their children.'

Gollan says men don't value themselves at home either. Fathers, he says, need to recognise the positive aspects of fatherhood; and for men to achieve a more effective work and family balance, there must be widespread acknowledgment by men and women that fatherhood and supportive family-friendly policies are not only good for the family but are also good for business. But it is rare for senior managers to have an understanding of the dual-career, that is, combining work with family responsibilities. As Gollan points out, there is a lot of rhetoric about family-friendly policies but the reality paints a different picture. Recent Australian Bureau of Statistics figures show that less than one in ten parents receive help from their employer with childcare arrangements.

To understand something of where men are today, it is

worth looking back to the place from which the Aussie male has come. Peter West's informative book, *Fathers, Sons & Lovers*, details the story of the Australian male from the 1930s until today. It provides a fascinating insight.

In the thirties, boys looked forward to being a man. The male and female spheres were nearly mutually exclusive; so most boys seem to have modelled themselves on their fathers. Fathers set a pattern for boys and played an important part in their discipline.

The pattern for male behaviour, according to West, was to be tough. For a boy to be called a 'girl' or 'sissy' was the ultimate put-down. These images of toughness were learned both at home and at school. West also identifies something crucial in understanding the modern Aussie male. 'Some of the most perceptive comments on men come from women. We don't encourage males to analyse themselves.' Perhaps men do not think as deeply about things as women do, but that doesn't mean that men are not as bright; it does, however, suggest that perhaps their emotions are not as engaged as women's are. Many suspect that this is not a biological phenomenon but merely a reflection of the fact that by the time they are between four and six, we have trained young boys to mask their emotions.

Very little appears to have changed for men in modern times, except in one area.

... families are busier and there aren't always two parents to keep children in check. This makes the school's task more difficult. The Christian churches don't have the authority they once had. In sum, there seems to have been a decline in the authority structures that once held society together. Another change has been the declining role of the father.

In summing up the problems confronting boys, West writes:

They have to face up to becoming a man, and there is some tension around that, for there is always the possibility that people will find you not enough of a man. There seems to have been more certainty about this in the past, when being a man was an honourable position. The males of today are much more guarded – they have to say the right things to girls, they can't say this or that about women. Gender lines are less clear and argued about. So boys are uncertain about what they have to do to stay out of trouble.

'Indecisiveness' and 'confusion' appear to be the two words which most accurately define the current generation of men.

There's no doubt that it used to be much easier to be a male because roles were very sharply defined in pre-war Australia. Men were the breadwinners. They were strong

and worked hard to break the back of an unyielding continent to provide for their families as husbands and fathers.
Of course, that lent strength to the position of male dominance in Australian society. They had economic, legal and
sexual control and everything was well defined and neat.

I remember my own father having a strongly defined
sense of where he stood in the world, even if things were
not always rosy at home. Dad knew best. His word was law.
He was the supreme authority. If Dad said something, Dad
was right. It was important that he approve of the way we
cleaned our shoes, did our homework and played sport. If
Dad said it was time to learn to swim, it was. The best way
to learn was for him to throw you in the water and make
you fend for yourself. We were never to annoy Dad. If he
wanted to listen to a Wagner opera on a Sunday afternoon,
we had to keep quiet. The same rule applied when Dad
wanted to listen to the 7 p.m. news on the ABC. Dad was
also the ultimate threat. 'Wait until your father comes home!'
Mum often warned.

But no matter how busy he was, Dad usually had time
to help my brothers and me with our homework. When I
was at high school and studying home economics, as girls
did then, homework often included cooking a meal for the
family and asking for parental comment. Dad always took
this duty seriously and would write something thoughtful in
my cookery comment book. It was a great treat to take
Sunday afternoon walks with him and have his undivided
attention. Mealtimes were usually pleasant family times,

too – Dad always came home for dinner, even when he was working shiftwork on newspapers. Sunday lunch was another enjoyable family occasion, although I'm not sure Mum always relished cooking a roast dinner on a hot, summer's day! My brothers and I thought Dad was 'God'. As kids, we tried hard to win his praise. And did so right up until his death at 89, in June 1999, only 11 days short of his 90th birthday. The family had been planning a major celebration and some weeks earlier Dad had begun issuing instructions about who could and couldn't come. It wasn't fair that he didn't last the distance.

In the last few years before his death he had become increasingly frail and my brothers and I were concerned about him living alone. But Dad was adamant that he wanted to remain in his own home. I organised carers to be with him throughout the week and generally organised his life. Every weekend for almost five years I would drive the thirty minutes or so from my home to his to cook Dad a hot meal and stock up his fridge and pantry. He loved my dog Humphrey who thought Dad's pool was his personal pond. Sometimes Dad and I joined the dog for a dip. 'Bloody decent of your dog to let us use the pool,' he'd quip.

Unfortunately, in his eighties Dad was afflicted with macular degeneration, the debilitating eye disease that affects so many elderly people. It resulted in him no longer seeing well enough to read, a blow for someone like him who, for as long as I could remember, had started his day by reading the newspapers. Later, he suffered from intermittent dementia, something that often took my brothers and me by surprise.

The first day it happened was a frightful shock. Dad called me, and then my brother Charlie, to say he couldn't find his pyjamas. He was extremely agitated.

'Where are you?' I asked.

'In Bourke, where do you think,' he snapped.

'What are you doing there?'

'Attending a conference.' The tone of his voice indicated that he considered me a fool for even asking and he hung up. He'd done the same thing to Charlie.

We both drove quickly from our respective homes to Dad's place to find out what the hell was going on. He was sitting in the kitchen still fuming about his lost pyjamas – which he happened to be wearing! Physically, he was fine, but mentally all was not well. I took Dad home with me to keep an eye on him and a few days later he was back to his old self. It was a while before he had another spell of confusion. This pattern continued until his death.

It was manageable most of the time, but upsetting because we didn't like to see Dad this way. He'd always told us what to do. Now the boot was on the other foot. These are difficult times for families trying to do the right thing by a parent. Somehow we coped and Dad was happy in the strange planet he often inhabited. And when he was back in the real world he seemed content. He loved to walk around his garden; he enjoyed his tucker and the occasional glass of red, and took to napping in the sunshine on his front verandah in the afternoon. All things considered, I think Dad's last years on earth were pleasant and comfortable. He was pleased when my youngest brother Charles finally married in 1995 and he and his wife Leanne gave him two more grandchildren – Charles III and Alexandra – bringing the total to nine. He was tickled pink when granddaughter Elizabeth and her husband John Spira presented him with a great-grandchild, Andrew.

In the last twelve months of his life Dad seemed to be constantly in and out of hospital, but when in May 1999 he was admitted to the Sanitarium, the private hospital in Sydney's North Shore suburb of Wahroonga, it wasn't long before I knew he wouldn't be going home again. Like most hospitals, both private and public, the Sanitarium was short-staffed, and didn't even have anyone to help Dad feed himself. It's hard for an elderly man with poor vision to find things in places that are unfamiliar to him. What's more people who suffer from dementia become very disoriented when their routine alters in any way. When I explained this to the hospital supervisors and also that Dad would need someone to assist him at meal-times, they said as the hospital was short-staffed it couldn't supply anyone and suggested that I get the carers who had looked after him at home to come to the Sanitarium to feed him. I was outraged! I protested that Dad had been in a health fund for something like forty years and that as he was paying for his treatment we expected the hospital to make sure he was at least fed. The hospital was sorry, but such assistance was beyond their means. Australia's health system is in a terrible mess. I hate to think what happens to elderly patients who don't have families or the means to pay carers to feed them.

On Dad's last day, I arrived around seven in the morning. He was conscious, although he couldn't talk. He took my hand and kissed it several times. I told him Kate and Ben sent their love and his eyes acknowledged that he understood. I prattled on about other family news and then sat beside him, holding his hand. As he dozed, I reread his book *Words and Music* that he wrote in 1983 about the ups and downs of his life and career. Dad was by no means a perfect parent, but he wasn't a bad one either. And for a boy who left school not long after his fifteenth birthday and helped support his mother and his four brothers and two sisters after their father shot through, leaving the family in hard times financially, he had led a full and fascinating life. It was comforting to read his book, with its wickedly sharp anecdotes about people and events. My brothers arrived throughout the day and we were all there when Dad died late that night. Afterwards we said a prayer at his bedside.

I went home and howled my eyes out. Dad and I were very close, kindred spirits really. As he wrote in *Words and Music* we had a complete understanding of each other's character. I could talk to Dad about almost anything and sometimes it seemed Dad thought the same about me. When he was in his eighties he told me what a wonderful woman my mother was and how beautiful and sexy she had been. Even adult children like to think of their parents as happy people, so perhaps I imagined it – but I'm sure Dad regretted that he and Mum hadn't stayed married.

Sometimes I drive past his old home and like the fact that it looks the same as it ever did. I find it strangely sooth-ing. I miss Dad. When the feeling becomes too unbearable I put on a CD of something by Wagner and let the mem-ories take me over.

Nothing was the same in Australia after World War II. It changed men as well as women and forced boys to grow up quickly into men, to take up the slack of the men who had gone off to fight. Peter West writes:

> The war removed men from the fairly tight bonds which had enclosed them – nuclear and extended family, the church, and long hours of work, usually forty-eight hours a week or more. Men were thrown close together, without close scrutiny from women and the churches, and especially in the presence of danger and death, met a range of people outside their previous experience. There were possibilities of having sex – with women and with other men – without the usual restrictions.

But back home women were enjoying the experience of earning their own money in the workforce. Suddenly, an element which had been strictly reserved as a piece of male identity, was being stripped away. Work and economic power were no longer the exclusive preserve of men. Family life changed, but the male model for life continued to be taught, even in the face of sweeping change. By the eighties and nineties though, men clearly seemed to be ill at ease with the model; yet it is the only one society has offered them, and they have been made to feel guilty for following through on it.

It seems most men lead their lives according to a script. As Peter West explains, it's one that emphasises toughness, strength, hard work, sport and – in many cases – drinking and sex. But a rethinking of masculinity has begun as a result of feminism. Men are feeling the strain of change, and are having their behaviour feminised by society. This is causing stress in their lives, but they feel 'powerless' to do anything about it. Who would ever have thought such a word would be applied to the Australian male?

Men seem to be losing their way more with every year that passes. Perhaps that is not quite the right way to look at it; perhaps the more accurate statement is that women have driven the massive change in society, assuming that men would come with them, but men simply haven't been able to keep up with them.

One thing that has not changed over the years – and never will – is a boy's need for a father. Boys don't cope well with divorce and family break-up and in the rearrangements that follow, they are often left in the care of their mothers, which robs them of a significant role model to help them to handle life in the modern world as well as understand and function with some form of masculinity. However, when Brendan Nelson commented about the high number of boys being raised in families headed only by women, he was immediately accused of conducting a witch-hunt against single mothers. However unpalatable the truth may be to some feminists, fathers (or father figures) are essential to a boy's healthy upbringing.

But researchers have also discovered that even boys who are lucky enough to have fathers who live with them barely speak to them because their dads are too busy. The average boy gets less than fifteen minutes a day with his father. Not surprisingly, sons often feel bitter about this. Having a distant father is not a pleasant thing for a young boy, particularly as so much of his socialisation depends on it.

I am thankful that when Ben was growing up, I was able to keep strong male role models in his life to ensure that he didn't lack for male input into his demeanour and persona. For this reason, I sent him to a single-sex school (I favour single-sex schools for both boys and girls) and I also made sure that he regularly saw his father. It took considerable effort on my part, but I am confident that Ben is better equipped to face the world as a man because of it.

Peter West writes:

Many boys in recent times show a desperate search for a father's love. We must try to get those fathers who are in touch with their sons to share their feelings with them. We have to encourage men and women who separate or divorce to maintain contact between father and son. We have to give males the message that being a father is a wonderful thing.

Like Brendan Nelson, he worries that, 'Schools are becoming increasingly feminised. Schools need to have men who are available to boys'. Roughly, only a quarter of those going into teacher training are men. The numbers of male teachers over the next few years will drop alarmingly because of retirements, exacerbating the problem further.

Somehow we must address this problem in our families and schools. Perhaps there is also room for some kind of responsible 'big brother' or 'surrogate father' scheme in Australia, something like the scheme Legacy began after World War II when men who had made it back from the war acted as surrogate fathers to the sons and daughters of servicemen who did not.

Of course, the current danger would be how to keep the rampant Australian paedophile out! Paedophilia is a community issue which has received widespread coverage in the media on an almost unprecedented scale over the last few years, and was brought out into the open by the Royal Commission in New South Wales into police corruption. Evidence produced in court demonstrated all too well the dangers young men face, often from people in authority whom they had every reason to trust. Once again we have let our boys down.

Sport appears to be the last great domain of the Australian male. He still gets it mostly his own way in the newspapers, and on radio and TV. But this too may be changing. Every year that passes sees the breeze of change grow stronger, along with the chorus of catcalls from some women to tear down this last male bastion. But we can't overlook the fact that men get much of their identity from sport, which probably is something to do with a very deep need in them for combat and conquest. 'Sport is something of a passing rite to manhood in Australia,' Peter West writes. 'Football was widely seen as the test of orthodox manhood.'

But the feminisation of the Australian male is apparent on the sporting field too. In recent times, there has been so much twaddle trotted out about competitive sport being harmful to children. Of all things, there are suggestions that playing competition sport may damage boys by making them less sensitive to the needs and feelings of others. Is there any part of life that is not marked by competition? I certainly wish that people felt this way when I was struggling against the 'old boys' power brigade at News Ltd. Wouldn't it have been terrific not to have had to struggle and compete? But, at the end of the day, doesn't competition make us stronger and develop our will to win? Surely we do not really want to feminise the Australian male further by taking away his sport, too? Testosterone, like it or not, drives men on in these matters and that not only makes it biological but healthy too. Certain life skills are learned through sports and competition, even if the Aussie male does take the 'biffo', as Channel 9's Paul 'Fatty' Vautin calls it, a bit too far.

There is a wonderful line in the film, *City Slickers*, where one of the characters in this feel-good, nineties-male-introspection film admits that the only time he felt he could be close to his own father was when they were sharing their interest in sports. They couldn't talk otherwise, but they could about baseball. That was their chance to bond, the chance for a son to become close to his father. The same is clearly true in Australia. For boys, sport is very much a father–son thing, where boys learn to bond with their fathers, and, rightly or wrongly, to please them and make them proud through conquest.

But even this seems to be changing in Australia. Peter West writes:

Boys seem unsure about how to make an acceptable masculinity. They seem to be turning increasingly to highly masculinised sports such as martial arts and bodybuilding in an attempt to prove their masculinity. They want to be close to strong, physical masculine figures; they find them reassuring. So it is no surprise that the sport of bodybuilding is booming among adolescent boys. It probably shouldn't come as too much of a surprise either to learn that the incidence of eating disorders is growing in young men. More and more of them are suffering from bulimia and anorexia nervosa and both are very much linked to poor self-esteem.

There seems to be a feeling among men that life nowadays is all too hard. Nothing is the way they thought it would be. The new, powerful women cannot be tempered or appeased – which might explain why so many women say a good man is hard to find. But that aside, in these days both men and women admit to being lonely and often wish they could meet 'somebody nice'. In spite of all the problems, men and women still wish to share their lives. Surely we are our own worst enemies?

Sydney psychologist and matchmaker Yvonne Allen who occasionally appears on *Beauty & the Beast*, told the *Australian*'s Jill Margo in February 1997:

Through the rise of feminism, women's roles and expectations have altered and with this, long established wooing rituals have been swept away. There are no clear guidelines any more and many of my male clients report feeling intimidated. In the old days a man would send flowers and would go on several dates before he held her hand. Things would happen step by step. Now men don't know what to do.

Allen says that she believes numerous men live alone because they fear handling today's woman.

I don't think they are reading the situation properly. They assume such women have plenty going on but they should look beyond the surface and realise that more often than not, eligible women go home to an empty flat and eat a takeaway in front of the television. These women are not in a position where they can say: 'Hey, I'm available.' They are trapped by their roles, by the very gains they have fought for in terms of feminism. It is a sad irony because these women have much more to offer as a result of these gains.

I know from personal experience what Allen means. Her remarks confirm for me that the major problem men and women have is communicating. It's easy to shift the blame on to men and say they don't know how to talk to a woman or how to listen, but somewhere along the way both sexes have forgotten how to talk properly to each other; and women are as much responsible for this as men are. Maybe it's the listening part of communication that stumps us.

In her 'Man Who Wasn't Born Yesterday' article, Anne Musgrave asked if men have become confused because women do not know what they really want. I believe there is an element of truth here. Women seem to have arrived at a crossroad, too. Perhaps we are no longer sure of the way ahead either. Yet we have forced men to march with us into the brave new world, without telling them much about the direction in which we were heading and without even giving them a compass. But as pioneers we weren't always sure where our path would take us. Was it our responsibility to show men the way? Surely not!

It may seem strange to some of you that a woman should raise such male issues, especially a woman who has strived for so long for equality in a profession that is often described as a man's domain. And in spite of women's progress, the media remains pretty much a man's world. Women's issues will never get much space while men mainly decide what's of interest to them as readers, viewers and listeners. Not that men's issues get much airing either – not the kind of topics that I've written about in this chapter. Little constructive advice is ever given to men on how to handle the myriad problems they face. I am sure they often read women's advice columns looking for solutions to their problems, with the result that their thinking is coloured by what they read. It doesn't help to solve men's problems with female solutions.

It would be nice to think that we can see a refreshing honesty and clarity of perspective in the new generation of young men and women. They do seem to have an easier, less complicated way of doing things together, like sharing apartments, cleaning duties and the grocery shopping. Girls pay for their own dinner when they dine out with boys and often buy their own drinks. If they like a boy they think nothing of ringing him up, telling him so and asking him out.

But it seems to me that so many young adults, in their twenties and thirties, are yearning for one-to-one, meaningful relationships as many older Australians are. They seem frightened to make a commitment and they are just not sure how to communicate what it is they are looking for or what they feel they need. Some say the 21st century will be the Golden Age, and I hope it will be. Even though few of us believe in fairytales, that doesn't mean we have to live without the possibility of happy endings. But, as Prime Minister John Howard once reminded the nation, loneliness is a great problem for many men and women in Australia.

If we want that happy ending in the new millennium, we have to find a language that will allow men and women to honestly express what they want from each other.

11

THE FAMILY: WILL IT

SURVIVE?

Woman knows what Man has long forgotten, that the ultimate and spiritual unit of any civilisation is still the family.

CLARE BOOTH LUCE

My family is the most important thing in my life. Not just my children, but my brothers and their kids, my uncles and aunts, nieces and nephews, and cousins. Whenever I have problems I look to the family for support. On those occasions when everything was crumbling, or temporarily seemed to be, my family was my rock. I know my brothers are proud of me and interested in what I'm doing. I also know if they believe someone has 'done me wrong' that they are prepared to seek retribution on my behalf. 'Toots,' Will says, 'it might take time, but we'll get them in the end.' The simple truth is my family means more to me that any career success I might have.

Like other Australian families, we've changed along with the times, but my brothers and I have raised our children pretty much the same way we were brought up: with love, discipline and an appreciation of the work ethic. Charlie's children are too young to determine just how they're going to turn out, but present indications are looking good. Julian, Will and I are very proud of our kids, who are all doing well in their chosen careers and, when family get-togethers occur, seem to enjoy each other's company. It's good to see.

Changes in family life were influenced by the decline in home ownership in the seventies when people decided to lead a domestic life in the suburbs.

Twenty per cent of people did not marry, which was a dramatic shift from the fifties and sixties when almost everyone married. In the seventies, one in three marriages ended in divorce and the birthrate fell. By the mid eighties more than half a million children lived with only one parent because of divorce, death or unmarried motherhood. In the nineties, about eight per cent of all marriages ended within five years. And by 2001, the *Australian Year Book* released by the Bureau of Statistics to coincide with Australia Day, showed that our marital state was still in decline with 52 566 divorces granted in 1999. Forty per cent of marriages now end in divorce. Family breakdown costs the nation around $3 billion per annum.

During my days at *Cleo* in the seventies, I observed the changing role of women unfold – changes which were to have a significant effect on families. Like innocent bystanders, I suppose, we had no idea of the long-term effect of what was happening, even though we were emotionally involved. We were primarily spectators whose main job was to face the changing climate with an appropriate product to meet a growing need. It gave me a unique position, for which I am eternally grateful, to witness the revolution firsthand and to feel its effects in the things we wanted to think and talk about.

Similarly, during my days at the *Weekly*, I was struck and alarmed by facts and figures about the changes – and sometimes problems – relating to family life, which kept coming my way. Every month research would land on my desk and beg to be read. As a single working mother (for part of the seventies) I had a great interest in all of this.

In the seventies, *Cleo* asked the great Australian poet Judith Wright if she thought there was any possibility of the complete erosion of marriage. Judith said:

It will probably end. And I'd be for it, because you do change if you are going to be a person at all. The person you are at twenty is very different from the person you are going to be at thirty if you're growing mentally and emotionally – and you might well grow in different directions.

Marriage should not be something that you take on as a lifetime job necessarily. It's very seldom, I think, that a marriage lasts satisfactorily for a lifetime.

This ought to be accepted more. Divorce shouldn't be an agonising tearing apart. But you should accept that if you want children you should stay together and bring them up to the stage where they can stand on their own two feet. If you want to go on living together, then well and good. It should be accepted that marriage is a job and love can be something quite different.

Perhaps not all of us would agree with Judith Wright's views, but there can be no argument that in these days love and marriage no longer go together like a horse and carriage, to quote the old song that Frank Sinatra sang in the fifties. Because love and marriage have changed, so too has the family – and this includes the definition of the family. Historian Richard Waterhouse, author of *Private Pleasures, Public Leisure: A History of Australian Popular Culture since 1788*, says, 'There is a lot of nostalgia in Australia for the family of the fifties. The family of the fifties seems more secure; there was a mum and dad who were always there . . . domesticity was enjoyed'.

But the fact of the matter is that Australians do not live that way now and probably never will again – the images of today's family are diverse. Even so, everyone knows who his or her family is. It isn't something that has to be constantly defined. There is no such thing as the perfect family or, for that matter, the normal family. There is only our family – the one each one of us knows, loves and cares about. I believe everyone determines what is a family by their own family. If a person has a mother, divorced Dad, a drunk for a brother, and three sisters – that's family. The notion that a family is a mother and a father and two children is sadly very out of place nowadays. I know very few families of this persuasion.

The last two decades have been affected by extreme change. In the last twenty-five years there has been an increase in one-parent families. Of all families with dependent children in 1991, almost 17 per cent were one-parent families compared with 9 per cent in 1974. This is not all that unusual, as Peter McDonald points out in his book, *Families in Australia*, reminding us that one-parent families were equally common just over a hundred years ago. In Victoria in 1891, almost 17 per cent of all families with dependent children were one-parent families, but the proportion of one-parent families headed by men was higher in 1891 at 38 per cent as compared to 1991 at 12 per cent, reflecting the higher levels of maternal mortality at the time.

When I learned this, I was surprised. We tend to think that the family has always been two parents and a clutch of kids. History tells us otherwise. Has the romanticised version of marriage and family been to the detriment of modern relationships? Have we been trying to live up to something that never existed in the first place?

It isn't easy (but what is these days?) to be a one-parent family. We live in a society that places great importance financially on the two-parent income; and even socially, couples are preferred. One-parent families are much more likely than couples with children to fall into the low-income categories, and are also far more likely to be renting their accommodation than couples are. Fifty-four per cent of single-parent families are renting as compared to 20 per cent of couples with children. Fourteen per cent of one-parent families live with another family; mothers who are sole parents are less likely to be employed and are less likely (79 per cent less likely) to have a car.

In 1994, the Year of the Family, a great deal of time was wasted on trying to define 'what' the family was. We can't look back to what the family was or what we wish it was. We have to look at the family as it exists in the times we live in, and then we have to work out the needs of the family in the 21st century. In 1992, I convened a national summit in Canberra – Australia's first National Family Summit at Parliament House. Marriage guidance expert, Dr Warwick Hartin, referred to the nostalgia for life in the fifties when marriage rates in Australia were high and stable. He told Summit delegates:

> The longer perspective of history has shown that the short period of the fifties and sixties was an aberration from longer historical trends and that what has happened since is a return to pre-existing trends, which were forming at the beginning of the century.
>
> If we look closely, we can see that singlehood is about the same now as it was at the beginning of the

century, remarriage rates are the same now as they were in England three centuries ago; the duration of marriage for a sizeable proportion of the population is now as brief as it was for many people two or three centuries ago; and de facto relationships were more common than they are now.

According to Dr Hartin three startling changes affected marriage in Australia in the 20th century – the advent of the universal accessibility of divorce; the big increase of married women in the workplace; and a dramatically increasing life expectancy. It is obvious Australia's politicians and leaders have underestimated the massive social changes caused by longevity. Many of the problems we face today – budget deficits, compulsory superannuation, threats to the pension and Medicare – are a result of our low birthrate and ageing population. We are living in history's first mass-longevity society.

Many of our current problems didn't exist in earlier times when life was much shorter. It may not be entirely coincidental that the steep rise in the divorce rate roughly corresponds with the greatest ever expansion in life expectancy in the history of the human race. Longer life expectancy for women in particular, coupled with smaller family size, means that women no longer spend their entire lives with children, in the home. As a result women have become free to enter the workforce in increasing numbers, which they have done. Fewer children and longer life spans mean couples spend far more time together, on their own, with no distractions – like kids, for instance – to keep their minds off any problems in their relationship. As the relationship between the marriage partners becomes more central, deficiencies are magnified.

The seventies also brought a change in our attitude to marriage. The transformation of Australia's divorce laws, that came into effect in 1975, were greatly responsible for the rapid increase in divorce and around the same time, more and more people began to live together in de facto relationships. In 1975, 16 per cent of couples marrying had lived together beforehand (the Pill had removed any fears of unwanted pregnancy).

By 1991, the number of people in de facto relationships had risen to more than 50 per cent. De facto relationships are more prominent among younger people – in 1992, 69 per cent of people in de facto relationships were aged less than thirty-five, compared with 38 per cent of married couples. By 2001, cohabiting parents are so taken for granted that their unmarried status is no longer considered cause for comment. But de facto relationships break up at roughly twice the rate of married couples and, when cohabiting couples do marry, they are more likely to divorce. This instability has a detrimental effect on any children the couple may have – from their own relationship and also previous ones. Many such children end up living with only one parent, usually the mother.

As statistics repeatedly show that children living in sole

parent (and larger families) face a high risk of poverty, the future for these youngsters is unpromising. As a director of The Smith Family, Australia's largest independent welfare organisation, I was regularly reminded of the struggle that many families undergo trying to make ends meet. In November 2000, The Smith Family released its 'Meeting the Challenges of the 21st Century Australia Report' which uncovered a worrying new phenomenon – the growing ranks of the working poor. The assumption has always been that having a job was all we needed to pay our way. In this century that's no longer the case; being employed is no longer a guarantee that a person won't live in poverty.

It's hard to accept at first, isn't it? But The Smith Family's report uncovered facts that should make us question why and where we're going wrong. Too many Australians are now classified as disadvantaged. About 1.7 million adults live in poverty – for couples that is $406 a week or less, and for singles, $225 or less. Even though some 42 per cent of poor families have one or both parents working – they still can't make a go of it, because the cost of living is so high and, at the same time, there has been a rise in part-time and casual employment and falling earnings for the lowest paid sections of the labour force. In the last years of the 20th century Australia's poorest became worse off and the gap between the rich and poor widened.

What particularly concerns me is the number of Australian children growing up in deprived circumstances. An estimated 732 000 (14.9 per cent) of dependent children live in poverty in this well-to-do country of ours. Statistics like this make me feel ashamed.

Former Prime Minister Bob Hawke made an election promise in 1987 that by 1990 there would be no children living in poverty. It was a worthy ambition and deserved to be praised. Instead, people criticised the Prime Minister for making a promise that proved impossible to fulfil. Hawke's intention was right, and if well-off men and women, corporations and trade unions had listened to what he said and had then put their hands in their pockets, his vision could have become a reality. Corporations don't think twice about giving $300 000 to something like the Sydney to Hobart Yacht Race, or half a million in sponsorship to (say) the Three Tenors concert. Why not spend such sums on improving the lot of children living in poverty?

It's not as if we could plead ignorance of the plight of Aussie children. As long ago as 1986, a study on eight comparable OECD countries revealed that Australia came second only to the USA in having the highest percentage of children living below the poverty line. In 1991 the Henderson Report disclosed that 17 per cent of our children lived below the poverty line. While circumstances have improved a little since then, we still have one in four children living in poverty. But when such figures appear in our newspapers, there's not much evidence of community concern which is something that always mystifies me. But then, as a nation we don't get too stirred up about anything, do we? Except perhaps sport – and in recent times, taxes.

What a pity we aren't capable of channelling some of the fervour we displayed during the 2000 Olympics or the rage that small business displayed over the GST/Business Activity Statements into demanding a better go for our disadvantaged children.

When Bob Hawke said he wanted to wipe out child poverty, the media mocked his promise. In its customary way it preferred to knock the Prime Minister, rather than look at the real issue: the future of Australia's children. It was as if children were not considered important – 'getting' the Prime Minister was a much better pastime. Yet as noted American author Marilyn French told *ITA* in 1994:

The question of how we create the next generation
is a crucial one for society as a whole. It should
matter to people who don't have children as much as
it matters to those who do. It should matter to men
as much as it does to women.

But many women today are choosing not to have children at all, not wanting to impede their career options or 'spoil' their lifestyle. In the past, few women would have made such a choice – having children was a priority. I know that I wouldn't have missed the experience for quids. Of course, a successful career is satisfying, as is winning accolades, but I can't see myself sitting in my rocking chair one day reflecting on past joys of scoring points at a board meeting. There comes a time in most people's lives when work loses its significance in the scheme of things and the value of human relations, not only family but also friends, becomes more important.

It was inevitable that the ever-increasing numbers of females in the workforce would bring a gradual transformation to Australia's laws. In his paper, 'Changing Law in a Dynamic Society', Professor David Weisbrot, the Dean of the Faculty of Law at Sydney University, pointed out that a variety of laws have changed to acknowledge women's changing role.

Domestic violence, for instance, has been identified as a serious matter in criminal law, even if occasionally some male judges neglect to take it seriously. There was a huge protest from women around the country in 1993 when Judge Derek Bollen of the South Australian Supreme Court told the jury in a marital rape case that: 'There is nothing wrong with a husband, faced with a wife's initial refusal to engage in intercourse, in attempting in an acceptable way to persuade her to change her mind, and that may involve a measure of rougher than usual handling.'

The law may have changed but domestic violence still affects a great many Australian families. In 1997 I helped the Sydney City Mission with a fundraising appeal. The Mission urgently needed money to increase accommodation facilities for victims of domestic violence. In August of that year, they were turning away sixty women and children a week because they had no room available for them.

As Anne Summers wrote in her column in the *Sydney*

Morning Herald in October 1997, 'Prime Ministers Hawke and Keating said all the right things and devoted some dollars to various campaigns and publications, but so far no government has ever taken the political plunge and decreed that this is a scourge that must be eradicated. Whatever it takes.' Anne said she was shocked when she worked as a consultant to Keating in 1992 to discover that women placed violence as the third most important issue (after childcare and women's health) of concern to them. She listed findings from the 1996 ABS Study, *Women's Safety Australia*, which showed that 271 000 women had experienced some form of physical violence at the hands of a partner or date in the past twelve months, some badly enough to end up in hospital or the morgue.

But the following month Prime Minister John Howard left no one in any doubt where he stood on the issue of domestic violence. He told the nation that 'real men don't hit women' and pledged $25 million for more than three years to fund programs around Australia aimed at stamping out domestic violence. 'It's a question of educating boys and educating men that violence against women is morally and socially unacceptable,' the Prime Minister said. His government, he said, is determined to eradicate domestic violence and in October 1999 he announced additional funding of $25 million up to June 2003. But in spite of the Prime Minister's best intentions domestic violence is still prevalent in Australian in 2001. Domestic violence is a major problem for indigenous women too. In the years between 1990 and

2000, Aboriginal women's deaths from domestic violence have been at least 30 per cent higher nationally than black deaths in custody for the same period. Compared to the rest of the population, indigenous men are ten times more likely to kill their spouses and, in some Aboriginal communities, family violence is so prevalent that women expect to be bashed. Excessive alcohol consumption is usually the cause.

Men have been affected by changes in law in the 20th century, too. Male homosexual conduct has been decriminalised everywhere, including Tasmania in 1997. De facto relationships have been recognised in law. Anti-discrimination and equal opportunity laws have been created to protect vulnerable members of society, although one has to wonder if 'vulnerable' includes children.

The *Family Law Act* of 1975, introduced before the dismissal of the Whitlam Government, was one of the most significant legal changes for the family. Its amendments to Australia's divorce laws were far-reaching, granting ease of access for couples to divorce after twelve months' separation. Possibly no other law has had such wide ramifications for the family than this one. Children have been the unfortunate victims of the failure of Australian marriages and so have men and women, although it has been only more recently that many people have begun to realise this.

Dr Don Edgar, the former head of the Australian Institute of Family Studies, has often talked about the impact of changing laws upon the altered role of women in Australian society. He argues that this was given structural support when the social engineering of not allowing married women access to jobs in the public service was abolished, in equal pay and anti-discrimination legislation, in the *Family Law Act*'s assertion of no fault, of equality before the law, of joint parental responsibility for children.

In *Families in Australia*, Peter McDonald writes:

The *Australian Family Law Act 1975* describes the family as the natural and fundamental group unit in society, but despite the level of importance it ascribes to the family, the Act does not tell us what the family is. The Act apparently presumes that what is meant by family is so well known that there is no need for a definition.

It would be inappropriate to pass sentence on the *Family Law Act* and lay the blame for the destruction of the Australian family on it. The law was simply a reflection of the new role of women in society. They were taking their place at the table as equal members who worked, paid taxes and refused to be silent any longer. Women wanted to have some say in their destiny and were no longer prepared to put up with unhappy marriages, philandering husbands, alcoholic or violent husbands or to be considered possessions of men.

Men were content to participate in this makeover of

Australia's culture from the fifties throughout the sixties and seventies because the movement of women into the workforce not only allowed them more economic autonomy from men, it also provided the family with a second source of income. 'Thus, in effect,' says Peter McDonald, 'men have traded off economic power in the relationship against access to additional family income. Again, attitudinal surveys confirm that most men are happy to make this trade-off.'

No one could deny that progress of women in the workforce has not had an effect on the family. Today, 67 per cent of all women aged twenty-five to fifty-four are in the workforce. This is a staggering figure that surely has tremendous significance for Australia as a society. Where does this leave us? It is hard to say, but each new generation since the sixties has seen more females join the labour force. Economically too, it is difficult, if not impossible, to see families getting ahead, even in these times of low inflation, when only one partner is working.

Peter McDonald has observed:

The entry of women into paid employment is irreversible, at least in the foreseeable future. Each successive generation of women over the past sixty years has had a higher level of attachment to the paid labour force than the previous generations. While the participation of women in the labour force has increased, the participation of men has decreased. In the not too distant future, women who do not have very young children will have similar if not higher participation rates than men. Women also will be able to command higher wages than their husbands will. This situation will fundamentally change the ways in which families operate.

But has this evolution been to our benefit, economically, emotionally or morally? Is it any accident that the eighties 'Me Generation's' acquisitiveness presided over some of the periods of highest inflation in Australia's history? Does having two incomes make us better or worse off? Does our extra disposable income merely drive up prices, say, for houses? Ultimately, has it merely accentuated the gap between rich and poor?

Social historian, Anne Henderson, who is deputy director of the Sydney Institute, made another observation – which is income related – in October 1997. She wrote in the *Australian*:

There is increasing evidence that young people may be effectively forced into close relationships with their families because they cannot afford to leave home. While it's true that young Australians of the 1990s are better educated than their parents, it's also true that, unlike their parents, they have fewer chances of finding jobs that match their qualifications, investing in property or starting a business. They are economically handicapped as their parents never were, at a time of their lives when they should be contributing to the economy and setting up independently of their parents.

Henderson warns of a new phenomenon entering the family's experience.

Established nests may be empty, but the chicks are still hungry and young nests are not so easily built. Baby boomer parents, who keep in touch with their children, will have to subsidise them as adults or stand by and watch as many fall into poverty traps.

While young people may draw strength and morale from the family, I'm sure that nowhere in their wildest dreams did they ever think that perhaps they would be dependent on their parents well into adulthood – and neither did their parents!

More than ever before, there will be increased pressure on families to communicate better than they have in the past. There is such a heartbreaking need for families to learn to talk properly to each other. Playwright Nick Enright told the *Good Weekend* in 1994 that not being able to express our feelings is an Australian disease. 'There is a stoic repression of emotion, of keeping distance from our feelings as if we are embarrassed by them.' Enright's observation is spot on. I am sure that it's this lack of communication in families – and the bottling up of our fears and frustrations, and venting them on others because we can't express out loud what worries us – that causes the family unit harm.

It's our inability to express honestly the way we feel that hinders us in finding solutions to family problems. No one, whoever we are and whatever family we are in, likes to admit that perhaps we have failed in some area, or that we are resentful that our expectations have not become reality. It is so much easier to pretend that everyone else's family is less than perfect, while our own is fine – maybe there's the occasional problem but it's nothing serious.

If families have changed because of numerous external as well as internal influences, perhaps it's time to officially rethink the role of marriage and stop making men and women feel that they are incomplete without a partner. Today's women no longer need marriage to achieve social status and esteem, but there's still a belief – or perhaps it's a hope – that marriage will last for forever and a feeling of mortification when a marriage fails. I wonder if these days we ask too much of marriage. Perhaps it isn't in the human make-up to marry at twenty-something, or even in our thirties, and still be married to the same person at death, especially as we are all living longer and a marriage could last fifty or sixty years. Maybe this is why so many couples are choosing to live together without marriage.

There is something requiring urgent reassessment and that is the need for a radical rethink about motherhood. It is a high calling, yet in mid 2000, Sydney newspaper columnist, Sue Williams, declared: 'Why would any sensible woman today decide to have kids? There's the cost, the pain and then the total trashing of a woman's career, ambitions and life hopes in the face of her parental duties.'

What absolute codswallop! If our mothers had espoused this line of thought many of us wouldn't be here today. What worries me most though is that young impressionable women read such diatribe and subconsciously absorb the idea that becoming a mother is to be avoided at all costs. How have we allowed something as precious as having a child to become so denigrated, and when did our priorities become so muddled? What bigger challenge could a woman want than to create a life and then have the responsibility of moulding and shaping it so that the child becomes a worthwhile human being?'

But motherhood has been so devalued as a profession – its denigration began in the seventies – that many women, I think, feel they have to deny enjoying it. Not long ago a group of mothers told me they had to find something else to do apart from running a family so that they wouldn't go crazy. Interestingly, they all used the same expression 'keep my sanity'. Since when did the raising of children become a question of sanity?

A change in attitude is crucial. Australian women are now having fewer children than ever before in our country's history: the national fertility rate has fallen to 1.8 births per woman and the Australian Bureau of Statistics says that 28 per cent of women will have no children at all. Unless we encourage females to have children, there won't be enough people to carry out the essential work and jobs required for Australia's continuing prosperity, especially given our fast-ageing population.

Attitudes may have changed about child-bearing (and raising children today is certainly not easy), but I think a great many women who decide against having children will regret it later in life. It's hard to explain to a woman who is thirty-something how your thinking changes by the time you are fifty-something. There is a gaining of some kind of wisdom that gives an insight into why we do the things we do. At fifty-something you know only too well the things you haven't done and you are more realistic about what else you might be able to do. While I don't live my life through my children, they certainly give me the most enormous pleasure. I consider them my two greatest achievements. I not only enjoy their company but also their attitudes and expectations of life. I do wonder what their children – my grandchildren – will be like. I am keen to make their acquaintance but in my children's own good time, not mine.

The International Year of the Family in 1994 did not achieve much for Australian families, but, as convener of Australia's First National Family Summit at Parliament House Canberra in 1992, I was able to bring together people working in many areas of family welfare and care. We met as a committed group of people who acknowledged that many Australian families needed help. My interest in the family has been a long-term one, but the idea of having a summit first came to me in 1990. In my editorial for that year's June issue of *ITA*, I wrote about the sad state of Australia's children. With poverty among children being such an enormous problem, I wanted more than anything to know why so many of our children felt more at home on the streets than they did in their homes. What was going on? Why did our children prefer to call the streets of our cities home?

Thirty-seven per cent of people seeking beds in refuges for the homeless were under the age of sixteen. No one could tell me why, although I didn't have to be a genius to guess. In many cases, these were the kids whose mothers sometimes had three or four children by different de factos. These were the kids whose mothers and fathers were unemployed, who drank, who came from broken, violent homes themselves. These were the children who had mothers and fathers who had never known love and did not know how to give love to their children. Children of well-to-do parents often encountered the same set of problems. Money might make life easier, but being a good parent doesn't automatically come with a fat income. Alcohol consumption could not be ignored as a factor in making kids prefer life on the streets. It is a widespread problem and doesn't recognise differing economic situations either.

When I asked the *ITA* readers whether they would support a National Family Summit, I did so because I knew they shared my concern. But no one had any answers, even though families were falling apart at the seams. The response was overwhelmingly positive, but the readers urged me to have the courage to lead the way. Never one to retreat from a challenge I contacted State Governments and Oppositions and the Federal Government and Opposition. We had crucial input from the Australian Institute of Family Studies, Sydney City Mission and the Catholic Family Welfare Bureau in Melbourne. Everyone I dealt with agreed that there was a need for a fresh approach to issues facing Australian families.

I was often asked if I had a hidden agenda for organising the Summit. I did not. I simply do not think we can leave it only to governments to solve the problems of our families. I fervently believe in the family because I believe its survival is in the best interests of the human race. I'm also of the unshakeable view that adults have a responsibility and commitment to children, that transcends any other interests they might have.

Both the Prime Minister Paul Keating and Federal Opposition Leader John Hewson delivered papers at the Summit, which was opportune for them both as it was very close to the 1993 federal election. What they had to say sounded good at the time, but once the election had passed it was clear that their comments were intended to win government rather than do anything positive for children and the family. (And politicians wonder why voters are becoming increasingly cynical.) Keating's paper touched on several interesting issues.

The second issue I wish to argue for is the rec-
onciling of our work and family lives – for policies
and arrangements on how to make the various
aspects of our lives fit more harmoniously together,
so that our lives can become less stressful and, in
particular, so that women's lives can become less
stressful. It is women who, these days, are more
often the ones who shoulder the 'double burden' of
managing the timetables of family members and
who run family finances in addition to their paid
job outside the home.

It is no wonder they are just dead tired all the
time. We should be looking for ways to make it easier
for them, be they at home all day with kids or in the
paid workforce.

But with a wife not in the workforce – Annita Keating
stayed home and raised the four Keating kids, and good luck
to her – I suspect Keating's words came from the pen of one
of his advisers, Dr Anne Summers, the former head of the
Office of the Status of Women. Only another woman could
know how tired working women always are. Still, I guess it
doesn't matter how men find out about such things as long
as they absorb the lesson.

At the Summit, we began to digest the enormity of the
problem facing Australian families. Dr Don Edgar delivered
a paper indicating that 430 000 Australian children were
growing up with an unemployed parent and over 611 000

Australian families had either the wife or husband, or both, out of work. Though I had been speaking about the subject for years, it was obvious from papers delivered at the Summit that little progress had been made in making the workplace more 'family-friendly'. Don Edgar also warned that demands on working people were about to become even greater because the baby boom generation is hastening toward retirement. He predicted that eldercare would become a big issue beyond 2005.

Delegates came up with a number of recommendations seeking Government response, and also statements of principle that identify family and community needs. They were included in a special book in which the full text of all the speakers was also published. The Summit concluded with a call for:

- the establishment of a Ministry for Family Support and Children
- a comprehensive and urgent response to the issues of balancing work and family responsibilities, and to the elimination of violence and sexual abuse
- a requirement that all proposals and submissions on legislation contain a family impact statement
- recognition of the role of the family to nurture and care for young people
- more and better distributed research on family issues

- further community involvement in the development of family support services
- the elimination of anomalies in the social service and community service areas
- the outcomes of the Summit to be used as a starting point for national community consultation in the lead-up to the United Nations International Year of the Family.

The Summit endorsed the following principles:

- all families need support
- a just society provides rights for the individual, and the family sustains many of these rights
- the family's strength is fundamental and necessary to the continuance of a stable society
- every family in our society must have the basics for living
- the need to encourage parents and parenting
- the need to involve men in parenting, family relationships and conflict resolution
- the requirement to recognise the real worth of unpaid home caring of children
- unified community rejection of violence
- the removal of barriers that hinder access to services, for example, language
- realisation that social and emotional factors do influence physical health

- the need to address the basic issue of public versus private domain
- greater access to respite care for families with disabled children
- further research and resources directed towards refugees, victims of torture, etc.

Copies of the National Family Summit recommendations and principles were sent to Prime Minister Keating and others in his Government. Nothing was done, even though Keating told the Summit that he looked forward to hearing from us. The Government's response was a big disappointment for all of us who had met in Canberra for this important event.

Given my involvement with the Summit, I might have expected a role within Australia's participation in the International Year of the Family. I hope that doesn't sound like a hidden agenda! As I said, I didn't have one – it's just that I would have liked to make a further contribution to the needs of Australian families in the Year of the Family. But it was yet another 'punishment' for indicating that I would accept John Hewson's offer of a job in the Kitchen Cabinet. I was surprised at the amount of hostility I encountered from Labor supporters, some of whom I considered friends and haven't heard from since, and also some politicians, after Hewson announced my potential appointment. And that's all it was – something that might have happened if circumstances had turned out differently.

On the other hand, when I agreed to chair the National Advisory Committee on AIDS in the eighties when Labor was in office, on many occasions I helped the Government through very difficult and sensitive times. Not one of my Liberal friends, nor any Liberal politician that I knew of, criticised me for accepting the NACAIDS chairmanship. They knew that fighting AIDS was above party politics. It's tragic that Labor didn't feel the same about the family, especially as they had contributed $50 000 to defray costs for the Summit. Without Government support, we would not have been able to put it on or gather the experts from all over Australia and overseas to achieve the excellent results we did. They definitely failed to maximise their investment.

I had thought that the Keating Government was genuine in its concerns about the family – he certainly gave the impression that he was a committed family man. But given his Government's poor response to the Year of the Family, perhaps all we can conclude is that the problems facing the family were so vast and complex that the Government con-signed them to the too-hard basket. The 1994 Year of the Family could have been a significant year for Australia and its families, especially with the work that had been done at the Summit, but the Government wasn't up to the job.

In May 1994, the Federal Liberal Party convened a con-ference at Parliament House, Canberra, to coincide with International Family Day and asked me to speak. I floated an idea at that conference which I still think is worthy of thought. I referred to a 1993 United Nations Report, which said the job of parenting is being devalued and with it the quality of children's lives and society's future. What the report didn't say, however, is that some people don't know how to parent. It must be the only job we learn on the run – but in the nineties, something else happened. Parents handed over many of their rights to governments. I suggested to the conference delegates that perhaps that was why we have so many troubled children.

In a compassionate, civilised society there are people who are advantaged and those who, for any number of reasons, are disadvantaged. The playing field for all children is not level. This is recognised by governments, irrespective of the party political system. It is because the playing field is not level that the Government provides access to almost free education and an almost free health system. (I can't be the only person in Australia wondering how much longer the latter will last.) In providing these two vital elements in society – our education and our health – the Government has largely taken over responsibility for them. Once responsibility has been removed from parents, relinquishing it becomes a right.

Is it the parents' duty to teach children to accept responsibility for their own actions? Should parents teach children kindness, compassion, moral values, the rewards of hard work, and duty? Or is that the function of the education system? Should schools take over the role of teaching children about hygiene, nutrition, stranger danger, sexuality, the dangers of drug abuse and AIDS? What, we should perhaps ask, have these things to do with education? Are they not a responsibility of parenting? Where should we draw the line? If parents consider education a right, and most thinking people believe it is, then does this right end when young people complete their education and enter the workforce? Or do they look for continuing support from the Government as a right, removing all responsibility for family from the parents?

My friend Barbara Holborow, a former children's magistrate in Sydney's Campsie Care Court, tells me that the single outstanding and destructive social phenomenon she saw at her court was 'people who no longer take responsibility for their lives. They expect to be looked after by the system and when they are required to make decisions, or take responsibility for their own lives, or their children's lives, they cannot cope'.

When she told me this, the penny dropped. Being looked after has come to be considered as a right by a great many Australians. We have crippled people by removing their sense of responsibility. At the same time, we have separated love from responsibility. Taking responsibility for one's family is really an act of love. If responsibility for the care of vulnerable young children and young adults was accepted in society as an act of love, I believe we would not have the great numbers of unhappy, unwanted and troubled children on our streets.

Can the family survive? Well, surely there will always be families as long as there are people? But, as sociologist Peter

McDonald notes: 'Mere survival should not be the aim. The aim should be to enhance the wellbeing of all Australians, but there needs to be recognition that the individual's wellbeing is often best served by providing support through the family. The family is an integral part of the social fabric.'

As I first wrote in the seventies: 'We can only hope that the family will survive because in an increasingly uncivilised world, it's the only civilised thing that we have.' All these years later, I still think so.

12

WOMEN TODAY

Women are not bastards enough to be successful. They are too honest.

JOHN SINGLETON

There has been the odd occasion when I have tried to think like a man, but only in an attempt to understand the opposite sex better, hoping to find an answer as to why, in my endeavours to get to the top in corporate Australia, men have not always made me feel welcome. But the male mind is a complicated one and to this day I've not been able to fathom what makes it tick. Then one liberating moment some years ago, I decided it wasn't important. I had no intention of abandoning my female traits and way of doing things in order to be considered successful by male standards. Success after all is a personal thing – it is knowing that we have done our very best at all times. It is all to do with getting up in the morning and seeing yourself in the mirror and liking the person you see there.

I thought long and hard about the 'pronouncement' John Singleton made late in the eighties: women were too honest to be successful! He probably didn't realise just how profound a statement it was. At the time I dismissed it as just another one of John's throwaway lines, something for which he is well known. Looking back, I wonder now if he was offering women a unique insight into the workings of the corporate Australian male mind. Is this the kind of thinking that produced the business heroes of the eighties who later turned out to be a bunch of crooks? The men like Alan Bond, Christopher Skase, George Herscu, Laurie Connell and others of their ilk – completely discredited and definitely dishonest.

It has been a big disillusionment to many Australians (particularly corporate men) to discover how shallow and corrupt so many of our former heroes are. Does John Singleton reflect the views of all men when he suggests honesty is not a requirement for success? How could integrity seriously be considered an impediment to women's advancement? Is that why we haven't been welcomed into corporate life at the top? Is duplicity more prevalent in business than we realise? Is it one thing to know and another to be caught? Is it any wonder that a great many women have rejected the male model of achievement?

These days women are feeling confident enough about where they're going to be able to re-evaluate their position. The workplace has been transformed; family life has been altered permanently (but not necessarily for the better); and there are more women in Government than ever before. Women are better educated today than in the past and are fast becoming the privileged 'overclass' who will supersede men in the years beyond 2000.

There are predictions of the coming of 'The Female Age' and with it, according to the British futures think tank Demos, 'a crisis in masculinity'. Demos surveyed more than 3000 women in the late nineties and says that in the next decade men could become 'shadows of their former selves as women become more confident and dominate the workplace. As women develop a taste for power and success, special measures to help men find work may be needed'. By 2010, three in five women in Britain will earn more than their partners and women will own 50 per cent of small businesses. The same thing is happening in Australia. More than 30 per cent of all small business proprietors are women. Women are establishing their own businesses at approximately twice the rate of men.

Businessmen may be surprised at how far women have gone, but it will come as no surprise to many women. Frustrated in their careers, blocked by men in advancing to top management positions in corporations, forced to play the game the way men have always played it, women have become fed up. Why stay in a hostile male environment where they were, and often still are, made to feel unwelcome? Who needs it?

Press clippings from the early and mid nineties about the resistance toward women in management from the old guard of the men's club are a startling reminder of just how tough it has been for women. Bob Joss, the CEO of Westpac, told me shortly after he arrived in Australia in 1993 that the Australian boardroom scene shocked him. 'It's so male and white,' he said. He was used to seeing a few women and African–Americans in the boardrooms of the United States. 'Welcome to Australia, Bob,' I said.

Despite Joss's best efforts to make women at home at Westpac, senior male staff railroaded his schemes. In the six months prior to January 1997, the bank lost six of its top women executives. The *Financial Review* announced the news with the headline: 'Macho Bank Culture Drives Top Women from Westpac.' One of the departing women executives, Pam Steele, who was Chief Manager, Business Operations, said the commitment made by Bob Joss to develop female executives was being undermined by the aggressive and macho behaviour of some key individuals at senior levels. 'The prevailing culture at Westpac,' she said, 'is an old style command and control culture. Westpac hasn't moved on to a supportive, true team-based feminine and empowering culture.'

This situation is not only true of Westpac. Not long after the *Financial Review* article, the *Australian* published another article highlighting further the problems women face in seeking careers in banking. 'Bank Women Resigned to Frustration' recounted the sorry tale of women senior managers in the ANZ Bank: 'More than fifty-six female managers have left the ANZ Bank in a little over eighteen months, a confidential consultant's report to the bank has revealed, in what appears to be senior women's wide-spread frustration with the bank's glass ceiling.' The report indicated: 'While men left the bank for opportunities elsewhere and salary dissatisfaction, women resigned because of a lack of mentors and role models and a belief that their skills were not valued.'

Yet some of our most talented women are still prepared to battle on. What heroes they are! My Chief Executive Woman colleague Helen Lynch, arguably one of Australia's most successful corporate women, gave some useful advice to all ambitious women in an interview with *Management Magazine* in 1995:

> Women fall short of their goals because they underestimate men's needs to maintain rather than share the power. You have to have high expectations of your own ability to be able to smash through the power structure at various levels, because the glass ceiling doesn't only exist at the top of an organisation. Women need to hold their career destiny in their hands with a view of moving from organisation to organisation. Feel the power in you rather than the power within the organisation.

Helen, the former Westpac Chief General Manager of Corporate Affairs, who was appointed to the board as a non-executive director in October 1997 (the second woman to be appointed a director of Westpac), says she doesn't think there has ever been a better time for women to make their mark. She says we are fast approaching the time when finally there won't be enough experienced, white Anglo-Saxon men to carry out all of the new-style executive positions that the economy will generate. Women therefore are poised to get there on their merits.

In their book, *Megatrends for Women*, Patricia Aburdene and John Naisbitt declare: 'Whether you are female or male, the ways that women are changing the world will influence your education, career, marriage, recreation, next business venture, investments, election or advertising campaign. If you are a woman, you need to know this is not the time to hold back. It is the time to go for it.'

I agree with that sentiment, but I also firmly believe that the time is ripe for women to go for it 'their way'. Many women have spent a major part of their professional lives trying to live up to men's expectations of what it means to be successful, trying to contribute while sitting alongside them in positions of power (but never frightening them, of course). Looking at the male track record, why shouldn't we now question the male way of doing things? Look at the wars, the damage to the environment, the poverty – not only in the Third World, but also in Australia. Why are Aborigines still so disadvantaged after more than 200 years of white settlement?

It has become clear to women, especially the pioneering females of my generation, that honesty has a lot going for it and that as far as we're concerned, integrity is important for job satisfaction. By the way, make no mistake about it, my generation of women have been pioneers. We have led the way in getting economic and emotional independence for the women who have come after us. We had no role models. Our mothers accepted the post-war assumption that women's place was in the home. What's more, they grew up in one of the most politically stable and economically prosperous periods of Australian history.

Some 21st-century women are saying they want more – not more of what men have, rather more the right to really do their own thing. In trying to break through the glass ceiling many women have lost respect for their male colleagues. Once respect has gone, it follows that emulating men and their way of doing things goes too. Many women have paused to take stock of the situation and are going through a period of reflection, considering their options. They know they have ability and realise there's no longer any need for women to prove to men, or to themselves, that they have what it takes to be successful in business. Most women don't equate power with success to the extent that men do because most women do not see power as the ultimate goal. Today's woman has other priorities. She wants work that gives satisfaction, pleasure, happiness and time to enjoy living and many, like me, want time to smell the roses.

Susan Oliver, the former managing director of the Australian Commission for the Future, told the *Good Weekend* in March 1996: 'Women used to think that big business would adjust to their presence; it hasn't. I don't think they're going to change the large corporations, they're going to spin out of them and invent new businesses.' Oliver says that women are reinventing the way work is organised. 'It is not swimming upstream any more; it's changing the nature of the stream.'

In the same article, Charles Brass, the Chairman of the Future of Work Foundation, agreed that women are changing their professional goals, losing interest in clawing their way to the top of the corporate pyramid. 'Most of them are smart enough to know what a lousy game it is and they don't really want to play it.' As food for thought Brass added: 'I might say I know a lot of senior executive women and they fall into two categories, those who are honorary men and those who hate what they're doing.'

This feeling that it's no longer important to stay at the barricades accelerated stronger through the nineties. We wrote about it in *ITA* as early as 1989. Hugh Mackay told us that many women were seeing their jobs as a shackle rather than a passport, and that women who were at work were less likely to be trying to prove something about their status as women and more likely to be relaxing into the satisfaction of the job itself.

> Rather than being obsessed with 'beating men at their own game' many business and professional women have emerged from the battleground of the seventies and eighties with renewed self-respect and a deter-mination to do their own work in their own way – whether that happens to be the same or different from the way men do it.

Melbourne's Phil Ruthven, who runs Ibis Business Information, says the future of work advantages women because the 21st century will see the ascendancy of the franchise over the corporation and the managerial style of women is better suited to working with small groups of people. 'Women know how to get people to work as a team, probably because they've been making families and tribes work for the last 80 000 years. That's the approach that will work in the new age.'

Ruthven's predictions are good news indeed, yet sometimes when I look at all the data hitting my desk about the progress of women, I get a little confused. On the one hand we have Britain's Demos telling us that the Female Age is coming but on the other we have, according to the *Financial Review*'s Sheryle Bagwell, Australia's executive recruiters and management organisations telling us women are not succeeding because they lack ambition and drive, won't take risks, and generally hide their light under a bushel. The more than 250 000 women running their own businesses in Australia wouldn't recognise themselves in that kind of description.

Women may not brag about their ambition, but surely their success in small business illustrates that they are prepared to take a gamble and certainly do not lack drive. It's almost as if those executive recruiters and management people Bagwell writes about are living on another planet. Or have they made the mistake of assessing women by the male standard? The 21st century fact of the matter is that women are so busy taking risks that they are prepared to forego the business world that men inhabit to forge one of their own. How much more daring do women have to get? When will we stop being judged by male standards and told that to be successful we must emulate the male way of doing things?

Surprisingly, it is often women who tell other women this. I was somewhat taken aback in December 1997 when Sandra Yates, during her term as president of Chief Executive Women (a position I held from 1992 to 1994), suggested that dress and demeanour were among the last remaining things standing between women and the boardroom.

Studying successful men – most of whom dress, talk and act the same – provided clues to the best ways into boys' clubs, she advised. Basic rules included always looking 'professional, sober and conservative and always sounding prepared and pleasant'. Sandra suggested that jewellery should be discreet, just gold and pearls. Silver and gemstones should be left at home. Glasses should be discreet and preferably have non-reflective lenses. No coloured eye shadow ever. And any make-up should be very, very discreet. Hair should be neat, unobtrusive and capable of movement. Stiletto heels should never be seen in the office, and neither should anything overtly trendy.

She also said that successful businesswomen had to learn to 'speak bloke' and phrase things like men do. A properly modulated voice (the deeper the better – take singing lessons if you have to, said Sandra) is almost as important as professional qualifications for women aspiring to be business leaders.

But having said that, Sandra went on to tell a Sydney management conference that 'women should forget notions of changing stupid unwritten rules of the male business culture. Work with men,' she said. 'Don't frighten the horses – you can change the world later.'

There is no shortage of women prepared to tell other women that we must behave like one of the blokes if we want to be successful. Sometimes it takes my breath away. I remember the time Jill Ker Conway, the Australian academic and author, addressed a Chief Executive Women lunch in 1995 and said that businesswomen should study the football results on the weekends so that we would have something to talk to our male colleagues about on Monday. She repeated this advice in a media interview not long after she became Chair of Lend Lease Corporation Ltd in Novermber 2000. As one of the first women ever to chair a public company in Australia brushing up on her sporting knowledge seems to have been a real plus, career-wise. But while it's one thing to know a bit about football, surely women don't also have to dress like men to get ahead? Sometimes I look at young middle-management females in the CBD areas of Melbourne and Sydney dressed in black, grey and brown suits in which they look almost as nondescript as men and think how drab and ugly they look. What's wrong with a touch of femininity in the workplace?

A good deal it seems – even in the 21st century and

particularly if your chosen field is politics. In January 2001 I talked to five women politicians (Senator Jocelyn Newman, former Democrat leader Meg Lees, Tourism and Sports Minister Jackie Kelly, Labor MP Cheryl Kernot and New South Wales Liberal leader Kerry Chikarovski) in a round-table discussion for *The Australian Women's Weekly* on the state of politics and how it affects their personal lives. All of them told of the bullyboy tactics of their fellow male politicians.

'I think they sit down and have a little strategy session and work out where the weaknesses are . . . then they think, let's see if we can get the women to react in a particular way,' Cheryl said.

'Cheryl is right about strategies,' Meg added. 'You overhear a few things occasionally and there is the "Oh look what's she's wearing today" and a bit of an arm nudge.'

Both Meg and Jocelyn revealed that they had 'copped the treatment for a couple of years' in the Senate. 'Just the two of us,' Jocelyn said. When I asked her to eleborate she demurred. 'It was just boys' games'. But on a couple of occasions Meg has had to approach the President of the Senate to put an end to what she described as 'the very sexual innuendo type of remarks – which can be very nasty – that go on at our end of the chamber during Question Time'.

And Kerry reminded us of the State Labor MP who yelled to her in the New South Wales Parliament in 2000: 'Go get yourself a facelift.' I still find it hard to believe that an elected representative, whose electorate presumably includes women, could behave this way. If this particular moron were in my electorate, I'd be campaigning to have him removed. But is it any wonder women are reluctant to go into politics? It must be the meanest, nastiest boys' club in Australia.

According to Jocelyn, knowledge of sport is as useful in politics as it is in the boardroom – the first item discussed in Cabinet on Monday mornings is the football or cricket results. Jackie, married and with a small child, has somehow found the time to take golf lessons because she says 'heaps of deals are done at the golf course, in the corporate boxes at the footy and the cricket. At the end of the day, if you are doing business with someone and you've seen them bar-racking for sports, you know what they think is fair play, and how they think socially.' Maybe – but I reckon I'd be very wary of doing business with anyone who followed cricket with its corrupt practices!

Westpac introduced golf lessons for their women man-agement personal in 1997, so that they would be able to network and discuss business on the golf course the way men have done for years. I wonder if Westpac will advise their male management personnel that an early morning visit to the hairdressers is an ideal way to network, as many of our top businesswomen have discovered!

Women have to resist these efforts to make them more like men. That would be the ultimate sellout of our woman-hood. I do not believe we have to sacrifice any of our fem-inine attributes to be successful in our careers. It has never occurred to me to attempt to 'speak bloke' as Sandra suggests – and I'm certainly not about to start now.

I agree with the advice Imelda Roche gave for aspiring women leaders in an interview in the *Australian* in February 2001. She was president of Chief Executive Women in the early nineties. (I succeeded her.) The former boss of the multi-million Nutri-Metics cosmetics empire said: 'Never behave in business as if you are pseudo-men. Men relate better to women who do not pretend to be men. It is important to make men feel comfortable to work with you. While you can be assertive you should not be aggressive – follow your instincts.'

Some may deny that women are becoming more like men, but staggering research from Britain has far-reaching implications. The *Good Weekend* reported in March 1996 that, after a year-long study described as one of the most thorough analyses of a generation's attitudes taken in the United Kingdom, Demos released a report suggesting that girls are becoming more like boys, and vice versa.

> Younger men are becoming much more attached to what might be seen as soft and caring, feminine values. This includes changed attitudes to parenting where the younger men want more involvement, to more interest in caring type jobs, intimacy, emotional honesty and so on. On the other hand, we're seeing the masculisation of young women, where they're becoming more attached to the sorts of values that

have traditionally been seen as masculine values. Things like risk-taking, success and hedonism.

The Demos researchers say they were surprised at the significant 'rise in attachment to violence among young women, with 13 per cent of eighteen-to-twenty-four-year-old women agreeing with the proposition that "it is accept-able to use physical violence to get something you want"'. The report's authors said they expected female violence to be a major issue in the years ahead.

Australian evidence suggests that women are already beginning to exhibit male traits behind the wheels of their cars. In December 1997 the Australian Associated Motor Insurers Limited (AAMI) released findings of a study carried out for them by Brian Sweeney, which showed young women drivers were not far behind their male counterparts in aggressive driving habits, and in displaying the sort of aggressive driving behaviour normally displayed by male drivers, such as verbally abusing other motorists and chasing and cutting off other drivers.

When the early women's liberationists said, 'Tell your daughters, girls can do anything,' I doubt it occurred to any of them that those girls might one day take on the antagonistic traits of some young men. It is a horrifying development and I'm sure it is also influenced by the amount of violence on TV, films and videos. Girls watch as much of this stuff as boys do. We know it affects boys' behaviour. Obviously it must influence girls' conduct, too.

I don't think the early feminists gave much thought, either, to the effects on women's health of combining work and home duties, yet evidence again suggests that this is another area where we are becoming more like men. Since 1989 COMCARE, which handles workers' compensation claims for Commonwealth employees, has accepted more than double occupational stress claims for women than men – in 1996 the figures were 4256 claims for women as opposed to 2803 claims from men. What's more, throughout the nineties greater numbers of women reported suffering from traditional male conditions such as heart attacks, high blood pressure, ulcers, cirrhosis of the liver and executive burnout. It's hardly surprising. Figures show that Australian women in senior management are working, on average, fifty-one to sixty-five hours a week, with an additional two hours devoted to professional development studies. According to the Australian Bureau of Statistics, the number of women who consume more than two drinks a day has quadrupled in some States. American studies show that female managers smoke more than their male counterparts, and that 40 per cent of senior female executives use tranquillisers, anti-depressants or sleeping pills to relieve tension.

I have no desire to throw a spanner in the works, but this is a matter women must take seriously. We mustn't ignore the warnings of recent years. For instance, in 1995, Dr Peter Birrell, a psychologist and sleep expert at the University of New South Wales, reported that adult women need thirty to forty-five minutes more sleep at night than men. Why? Because women's biology is 'intrinsically more complex' than men's. As all working women – especially those with children – know, feeling exhausted most of the time is something we take for granted. Dr Birrell says:

> The average man would collapse if faced with the demands that the average woman takes in her stride. Until menopause women live on a 'hormonal roller coaster' and the biochemistry of their brains is more changeable than men's. The biological demand for sleep increases when women are pregnant, breast-feeding or are premenstrual. Such women need ten hours sleep at night.

Apparently we burn up more energy meeting these biological needs and require top-up sleep to make sure our bodies recoup and repair. Yet as all women know, we take shortcuts to meet the demands on us. The female sleep deficit crisis is part of a worldwide trend towards less sleep. The warnings are clear: unless we are careful, our health could be at risk. Diaries and records from the eighteenth and nineteenth century show people used to sleep about nine and a half hours a night. By the 1950s this had dropped to between seven and a half and eight hours. In the nineties many of us got by on four or five hours. We are suffering from an epidemic of fatigue and women are the worst affected.

Hugh Mackay raised the issue of women's tiredness in

Reinventing Australia, but few seemed to heed what he said.

To understand the real impact of the redefinition of women's role in Australian society at the end of the twentieth century, therefore, we have to devote our primary attention to the phenomenon of the working mother. What is it like to be a woman who has decided to combine a job that her mother thought was a full-time job with another job outside the home?

First they have to deal with the problem of daily exhaustion. They see their lives as a constant battle against fatigue. The long-term effects of this kind of sustained fatigue are easy to imagine. Women who feel as if they are constantly over-tired are almost bound to find themselves constantly on the edge of crankiness and irritability.

Mackay had already made note of some of these things in an article he wrote for the first issue of *ITA* in February 1989:

But, above all, women have paid the price in sheer exhaustion. Trying to reconcile two sets of apparently irreconcilable values (the contemporary liberationist values, and the traditional wife-and-mother, home-and-family values) has led many of them to end up leading a double life: going to work all day and coming home tired (like anyone else who goes to work all day) and then starting the second day's work of running the house and trying to act like a traditional mother. Is it any wonder that such women feel permanently tired?

I can vouch for that constant tired feeling, especially when my children were small. There were days when I would get out of bed in the morning and think to myself, thank heavens, in only fourteen or fifteen hours, I can get back into bed again. When I was running *ITA* I often got by with only five hours sleep a night. When I was Publisher of *The Australian Women's Weekly* and had to go to a function in the evening after a long day at the office, I would sometimes take No Doze tablets to stay awake.

Dr Bruce Shadbolt from the Public Health Division of the Federal Department of Health and Community Care, produced a paper in 1996, 'Health Consequences of Social-Role Careers for Women: A Life-Course Perspective'. I discussed his findings with him on my afternoon radio show on Sydney's 2GB. In essence, he found that combining work, marriage, and motherhood may not be good for some women's health. Results suggested that women who spend five to ten years of their twenties employed while rearing young children tend to have the largest relative risk of developing serious chronic disease.

As Dr Shadbolt points out, the association between social status and health for women is complex. But there is mounting evidence that socioeconomic and social role indicators are significantly associated with the physical and mental health of women. While there is a need for much more research on the effects of work and social combinations, Dr Shadbolt suggests that women's health policies should consider 'mechanisms for creating opportunities for women who are starting a family – to have choices about when they join and leave the labour market'.

Another mid-nineties Federal Government commissioned report on women's health said that the most frequently reported illnesses for young women were headaches and, again, tiredness. The report was drawn from the first Australian longitudinal 'Study on Women's Health' currently being conducted by the Universities of Newcastle and Queensland. It will track the health of 40 000 Australian women over the next two decades, providing us with invaluable and previously unavailable information about the health needs and problems of women of all ages. Such information is urgently needed.

The question that often comes to my mind is: are women happy? Some are of course, but others are too busy to even stop to think about such things. My gut instinct tells me that huge numbers of women aren't as satisfied with their lot as they thought they would be. It's hard though to get women to concede that particular truth because they are so skilled at masking their feelings. It is still the way women are raised.

When *Fortune* magazine commissioned a survey in 1995 of 300 American female executives and managers aged from thirty-five to forty-nine, the results took some people by surprise. The survey revealed a high level of frustration among these women. 'All but 13 per cent said they had made, or were seriously considering making, a major change in their lives. Almost a third said they frequently felt depressed. More than 40 per cent said they felt trapped.' No doubt a great many men 'stuck' in their careers understand those feelings.

I am sure that women's unhappiness, or perhaps discontentment is a better way to describe it, has much to do with the constant need to juggle work and family commitments. Even if they wished to give up work, all women know it is not politically correct to say they'd rather be wives and mothers at home and not in the paid workforce at all. We can't ignore the fact either that many women have to work these days whether they want to or not, because we have created a two-income system of living. The economy would collapse if women were to leave the workforce in large numbers.

At the same time we have also created a 'more we have the better we like it' society – two cars not one, two bathrooms, two TVs, a regular oven plus a microwave, a kitchen sink and a dishwasher. I adore mod cons too – but I'm aware that when I was growing up with my parents and three brothers we managed to live well enough with only one bathroom and one TV.

At different times of my life, during the years when I was married, I suggested to my respective husbands that I thought I'd like to stop work and look after the kids and run the home. They both told me I'd be bored. I wasn't sure but they were and, caught up in the propaganda that the only good woman was a working one, I went along with it.

Don't get me wrong: I did and still do enjoy my work and I've unquestionably been on a remarkable journey since I signed on as a copygirl at *The Australian Women's Weekly* when I was fifteen. But I know so much more now and I am aware of how life speeds along.

My fellow women travellers and I have blazed new trails and scaled heights that many believed women had no right to attempt. We have proven once and for all that we are intelligent, skilful and talented people. But then we always were. By going out into the workforce and knocking on the doors of top management and the boardroom we have simply made our skills more public than they were. Previously our talents were reserved for the home: providing comfort for the family, making life easier for our husbands, cooking nutritious meals, being there for the children when they needed a mother's love and education. No one, surely, can dispute that women are the civilising influence in life; and nowhere is this more important, and perhaps more than ever needed in the 21st century, than in the home.

Whether we care to admit it or not, I believe children are worse off for both parents working. When women embraced liberation in the seventies they did not do so with the intention of harming children or their families. But no matter how good the childcare, my feeling is that nothing replaces a mother. I am convinced that there would be fewer children living on the streets, abusing alcohol and other drugs, if fewer mothers were in the workforce. I am not a lone voice crying in the wilderness about this. An Australian Institute of Family Studies survey published in December 1997 showed that 60 per cent of Australians felt a family suffered if mothers worked full-time.

Raising children requires time and patience, something that many working women don't have a lot of, because of the demands of going out to work. There has been much discussion in recent times about the increasing illiteracy problems of young Australians – no one wants to admit that perhaps it has something to do with the fact that many mothers no longer read to their children. How could they? When they get home after a hard day's work, they are often too tired and have too many other things to do around the home to find the time to read a short story to their children before bedtime.

I said something to this effect on the *John Mangos Show* on Channel 7 in 1995 and the phones rang hot with angry women saying 'it's all right for her to say that, she has raised her children'.

Well, to those women I say it is not only all right for me to say such things – it is imperative. I am not accusing women of any deliberate wrongdoing, but I am sounding a warning bell. I am sure other women hear it too and I want to encourage them to listen to it and if necessary change their lives. I believe a lot of women have made a mistake in underestimating their importance in the lives of their children. Many of us have allowed our role to be downsized and the time has come to change all that. I know well the argument of 'giving the kids quality time rather than quantity' because I've used the quality time argument when it suited me. I now have serious doubts about quality time – I think kids need quantity time and plenty of it. And if I can't say that without women heaping abuse on me, then we have learned very little during the revolution.

Assessing our priorities, coping with all the changes and battling for sexual equality has come at a price. Many women are now asking whether it has been worthwhile. Do we want the boardroom after all? Do we want to continue to act like men? There's an old joke that's been doing the rounds for years: women will only be truly equal when there are as many incompetent women running businesses as there are men. Is that really what we want? Do we want to continue to sacrifice our quality of life? Do we want to bring our work home with us, or work back at nights until eight or nine, or get into the office at seven in the morning in order to prove we have what it takes to be successful? Do we want to give up time with the people we love, and not have enough time to enjoy our kids and be there for them when they need us?

With the advent of 'The Female Age' women will have the opportunity to show that there are other ways of running businesses and governments, of combining marriage, motherhood and work, and of caring for the poor and underprivileged, too. We are now in an important period of evaluation.

I believe the time is right to begin another journey where we use all our experiences of the past fifty years to shape ourselves a future in which we can think, look, work, live and talk like women, cherishing our differences and using them for the benefit of humankind.

Most men have no idea of the distance women have come, their blinkered attitude to us having made them blind to the advances that have been made. Today, men need women, both professionally and personally, more than women need men. Some women are even questioning whether we need men at all. Sperm can be stored these days and called upon when women feel the need to create another human life. In 1997, an English woman was given the right to use the stored sperm of her dead husband. Now that the precedent has been set, we can expect other cases. Women will be able to organise their pregnancies with precision!

Family concerns will continue to influence women and the way they work in the 21st century. With more women running their own businesses this should be easier. Women understand, or they should, the dilemmas working mothers – and fathers – face when a child is unwell or wants you at school for Sports Day. Those women who remain in the corporate battleground will insist on better family-friendly policies. Men will want them too. There has been a growing awareness among men, younger men in particular, that their fathers missed out on many of the joys of parenting because of their career demands. They don't intend to make the same mistakes. I hope they don't but, as women know, wishing things were better doesn't make them happen. You have to be prepared to fight for the things you believe in.

There are other significant changes happening in the workforce. Besides the fact that there has been tremendous growth in home-based businesses, especially for female entrepreneurs, many large corporations are moving toward telecommuting, particularly in communications and consulting-based industries. Employees work from home and 'telecommute' to the office. This can be as simple as having a fax, email capability, and home-style PC. This surely will allow women to more easily combine their work life with their family life. Childcare demands should decrease as in the future women will be able to care for their children themselves at home, and work at the same time. The key to family-friendly policy in corporate life is to encourage this type of approach.

Women today have tremendous opportunities, especially those whose children are beginning to leave home. They are starting to develop whole new lives, with virtually nothing standing in their way. I believe, however, that there is one area we need to work on. Women need to be more generous in the way we view each other's choices.

But then women are always toughest on other women. That's something else that I wonder about. Why are we so judgmental? We tell each other that it's okay to make choices about our lives and then immediately criticise another woman's decision. Shere Hite writes about the rivalries that exist between women in her book *How Women See Women*, published in the late nineties.

In twenty-five years we have changed our relation-ships with men and have changed ourselves, but we have not changed sufficiently the ways women deal with other women.

When a woman walks into a room at a business meeting or a party, another woman watching her may automatically think to herself: 'Is she prettier than me? Younger, better dressed?'

What if a woman thought instead: 'Here comes a woman. Will she be a good addition to my life? How would I like to relate to her?'

Hite gives some food for thought. She goes on to pose another thought-provoking question: 'Why do men create male loyalty systems that work (political parties, sports teams), whereas women do not?'

Perhaps it is because, as Jill Ker Conway also suggested at that incredible Chief Executive Women's lunch, women don't play football or enough team sports.

God help us!

But after One Nation's success in influencing the out-comes of the State elections of West Australia and Queens-land in early 2001, Pauline Hanson provided a perfect case of female double standards. The *Weekend Australian* of Feb-ruary 17/18 asked its readers if Pauline was 'Dressed to kill

or to distract?' Why isn't clear, but when will women journalists persuade their male colleagues to desist from treating
women in this pathetic way? The New South Wales Labor
upper-house president Dr Meredith Burgman (whose Labor
colleagues are probably still grateful to Ms Hanson for the
part she played in their respective State victories) commented on what she believed was the 'totally inappropriate
party dress' Ms Hanson wore to the WA tallyroom on the
night of the election, claiming that it was ' part of her weap-
onry'. Even the Women's Electoral Lobby's Victorian con-
venor Lisa Solomon couldn't resist passing judgment: 'I
would suggest that perhaps Pauline Hanson uses her gender
to appeal to a certain type of voter.' Whether we agree with
Pauline Hanson's policies or not, she doesn't deserve this
kind of scrutiny about her appearance. No woman does.

Advances in technology have changed women's lives in
many ways in the home as well as the workforce and it
occurs to me that the Internet offers women the voice long
denied them and the opportunity to create a loyalty system
that would benefit women everywhere. It offers unlimited
power, the chance to share experiences and to have a real
say in the world's future.

With it, we could form an international women's communications network with enormous influence that would
allow us to share our problems and solutions as well as work
out strategies for tackling government lack of interest in
causes that affect our wellbeing. There are so many ways we
could use our combined might – such as raising awareness

of the discrimination against women in all countries of the world (as well as Australia), of the brutality against women, the incidence of rape, sexual harassment and discrimination in the workforce. Imagine, too, the lobbying that could be done to get even more women into parliament!

And perhaps even more importantly, if the earth is to have a future of any real worth, women could play a significant role in the control and management of the world's environment. We would do a far better job of keeping our planet more viable than men appear to be doing. What the environment needs is not male muscle but women's mental agility and our rational and logical approach to an issue that is critical to us: a safe and rewarding environment for our children. Women's child-bearing and nurturing roles, used as excuses against our corporate rise, equip us superbly for caring for the environment. We have only to look at the way men in power are endangering the world, making its survival hazardous. Women are the logical custodians of the environment, its protectors and enhancers.

A united women's voice would be a striking breakthrough in Australia, with the potential to free women's lives and careers from the dominance of male decision making. Not enough of us appreciate our best attributes – our determination, our compassion, our dedication, our honesty, our humour. Think how much more women could achieve if they worked together on a grander scale than they have been.

The Internet offers women unlimited opportunity. So my

advice is to keep up with technology – if you're a woman without a computer, beg, borrow or buy one without delay. Take a course so you know how to use it properly. Don't be left behind!

13

AUSTRALIA: WHERE TO NOW?

I think there is an enormous chance for Australian leadership.
I think we have everything but the courage to do it.

JIM WOLFENSOHN, PRESIDENT OF THE WORLD BANK, 1997

Wherever I look, Australia's future is not as bright as it should be. It may be too late for us to ever be the Lucky Country again, but it seems we are not a clever country either, certainly not smart or efficient enough to compete effectively against other countries. At the same time, we've sold off precious assets to foreign investors; our manufacturing industry is just about non-existent, and every Tom, Dick and Harry can import his goods into Australia at the expense of our own producers. Perhaps, even more worrying, we are not endowed with men and women with leadership qualities. We are a nation in urgent need of leaders with vision who can inspire us to move forward into the new millennium.

In my book, *Early Edition: My First Forty Years*, which I

wrote in 1985, I said that Australia was a nation that appeared to have missed the boat and quoted Lee Kuan Yew, the then Prime Minister of Singapore. Lee told Prime Minister Bob Hawke in 1984 that Australian industry would have to adapt to changing markets if it were to survive. Mr Lee asked: 'Is Australia willing to say: "Let's go at the pace of the rest of the world?" If, either because of labour practices or lack of entrepreneurship, you don't move ahead into new technology and shed your down-market products, then inevitably we in ASEAN find ourselves more locked in with those that give us that pull.'

Did Australia hear Prime Minister Lee's warnings? It doesn't seem so. The 1995 Karpin Report for the Keating Government found that 'Australia needs a more highly developed entrepreneurial spirit and much better managers if it is to flourish' in what it describes as the 'Asian-Pacific Century'. The Karpin Report identified large skill gaps in all levels of business. It said that the 'majority of Australia's managers do not have the education or skill levels of those of the major trading nations, nor are most of our education and training institutions world class services'. It seems we can never get education right. We fail our kids and then we fail our possible future leaders.

We are missing opportunities because of ignorance and bad management and as a result we are not ready to meet the business challenges that lie ahead. The biggest task Australia faces is to create a positive enterprise culture. It involves a change in the values inbred in our education system, our workforce, and our firms. I'm not sure we're up to it.

Not long after the Karpin Report was released, the former Chief Executive of Telstra, Frank Blount, said that Australia faced a period of unprecedented change and that its traditional tools for managing such change were ineffective and counterproductive. Blount, an American who has since retired from Telstra, now sits on the boards of some of our major companies, including BHP and the National Australia Bank. He was typical of the new kind of CEO of those years – recruited from overseas because Australian organisations are unable to find men and women here with the right kinds of skills. Blount said he believed that Australia needs leaders rather than traditional managers and that Australia has to forge ahead rather than focus on catching up with its dynamic economic neighbours. Sydney publisher Barbara Cail (who was also a member of the Karpin committee) expressed the views of most women on the matter in an article she wrote in the *Australian* in September 1997. 'It's no mystery why Australian management is regarded as inferior to private sector leadership overseas. Half the talent is blackballed.'

When Australian-born Jim Wolfensohn, who is President of the World Bank, was given an honorary doctorate in economics at Sydney University in September 1997, he spoke of the need for Australia to have courageous leadership and how he hoped our leaders had that courage. From what he said, he seemed to be indicating that he doubted this was the case.

I worry in terms of Australia's leadership, about whether we really adopt the fact that the world has changed, that Asia is the fastest-growing area of the world, that we have the greatest opportunity being on the doorstep of Asia, and that if we miss this chance, it's not you who miss the chance, it's your kids who will miss the chance. And that's where leadership comes in.

We do have a tendency to live in the past in Australia, and there's plenty of research to confirm this. There are so many Australians who would like the country to return to the way it was, to what are sometimes called the 'good old days'. But we can't, and it's no use wishing we could. The 'good old days', if indeed that's what they were, are gone forever.

Not only did we not heed Lee Kuan Yew's warning; we also seem to be taking our time absorbing the messages of the Karpin Report. Its criticisms and recommendations have brought about some academic changes. Prior to the Karpin Report students doing MBA courses at Australian management schools were given American company case studies, but none involving Australian companies. Incredible as it may seem, we were producing graduates who were experts at solving the problems of American companies but not Australian ones. This has now been rectified.

But the implementation of the Karpin proposals – recommending that Australian business smartens up its skills in areas where improvement is urgently needed – has been slow. Why, given our track record, should that be surprising? It seems business just doesn't want to listen. The Australian Business Council's round table report on e-business released in February 2001 warned: 'A large fraction of Australia's biggest and best companies run the risk of quickly losing ground by not moving forward fast enough to create the ongoing systematic capability to innovate.'

As the *Australian*'s economic columnist Robert Gottliebsen wrote:

Unfortunately, Australian share analysts, who manage the superannuation savings of the nation, have little understanding of these issues and concentrate almost entirely on the next year's profits. This increases the risks to Australian superannuation fund members. The big investment return of the next decade will go to shareholders in companies that reduce their costs using the new systems and make sure that a substantial portion of the benefit goes to the bottom line. Simultaneously they will have to innovate and create new products using the new technologies.

... most of Australia's productivity growth [in recent times] has come from micro-economic reform; tax and tariff reform; industrial relations reform; and opening the economy to international trade and investment. In the United States, by contrast, almost half of recent productivity growth has been driven by information technology. That shows the enormous potential Australian companies have to lower their costs and to increase their profits.

The question is whether Australia CEOs are up to the task. Gottliebsen believes a great many of them are not.

Australian management not only lacks skills but also leaders. We rarely hear from our captains of industry – those men (mainly) who run corporate Australia – when important community and business issues are in the news. There are few that are prepared to raise their heads above the crowd and yet they are supposed to be our leaders. The captains of industry must take some of the blame for Australia's poor performance.

They might deny they're wimps, but evidence suggests otherwise. Towards the end of the nineties, Roy Morgan Research conducted a special poll for the *Financial Review* which showed that a substantial number of business and professional people believed that the Howard Government was squandering its opportunity to pursue economic reform and was moving too slowly. The *Financial Review* asked company executives for their opinion on the Howard Government also – with the exception of stockbroker, René Rivkin, all of those who only had something critical to say about the Government preferred to remain anonymous!

Not only do Australians not speak out; we don't think big, either. In 1988, Dr Alan Reynolds, a prominent American economist and adviser to the United States

Government, criticised Australia for thinking small. He accused us of being over-governed (which we are), under-populated, and unwilling to compete internationally. He felt Australians were their own worst enemies, having bucketloads of potential but lacking the determination to use it.

How many times have we seen Australian inventions go offshore for development because their inventors couldn't find the necessary capital to develop them here? Year after year some of our best and brightest men and women leave Australia because our governments and businesses lack initiative and the big picture vision. The odds are stacked against expansive thinkers. Young entrepreneurs are discouraged from thinking big, because Australia is a big country that thinks small.

The Australian system, from government to public service, is excellent at keeping us down, making sure we don't excel or get too big for our boots. The tall poppy syndrome is alive and well and is designed to keep the few go-getters down. Any Australian who does make it eventually moves overseas out of frustration at the bureaucracy and red tape stacked against him or her. Then they are branded traitors with the same bloody-mindedness that forced them to look elsewhere in the first place.

Like the rest of the world, Australia has been caught up in a period of unprecedented change and because we lack leaders, not only in politics but also in business, nothing has prepared us for where we are today. Nothing is the way we expected it to be. We have been caught up in the most tumultuous change and it has terrified us. Those who are supposed to lead us have been caught up in it too and probably have the same kind of fears as the rest of us.

In spite of the financial crisis experienced in several Asian economies in late 1997 and early 1998, the 21st century will be the Asian–Pacific century (just like the 19th century was England's and the 20th century America's) – and it has begun. Australia has run out of time. We must get our act together. If we don't – as Jim Wolfensohn stresses – we will miss out on benefiting from Asian markets, which in twenty-five years will account for almost 40 per cent of the world's output. There is little evidence to suggest that the Federal Government has a vision for Australia and if it has, Prime Minister Howard and his Cabinet ministers haven't explained it very well. Consequently, as a nation we are not sure in what direction we are, or ought to be, heading. Australians are crying out for leadership. Trying to find solutions to our problems inevitably leads us back to one inescapable fact – we're a nation desperately short of leaders.

Some people believe leadership and management are one and the same thing. They're wrong. Management is about operational control using systems and procedures, while observing the status quo at all times. Leadership is about getting things started, challenging the process, facilitating change and shaking up organisations. Leaders must have a vision and the ability to inspire others. Leaders are people with passion. As Jim Wolfensohn said: 'You cannot lead without involvement. You have to get involved.' Wolfensohn is right.

These days, more than ever before, people want to be involved. They believe they are entitled to their say. Nowhere is this more evident than the workplace, where we now employ teams rather than staff. Every member of the team wants to have his or her say – in other words, they want to feel involved.

As Wolfensohn said:

There is no chance for Australian leadership unless there's involvement, unless there's belief, unless there's a real desire to say we're going to change, we're strong enough, and we're tough enough and we're self-confident enough to be Australian and to be open to outside influences. Then we can lead.

It takes guts to be a leader though. Perhaps Australian men and women are afraid to lead because they are obsessed with opinion polls or their own popularity? As Lee Kuan Yew says in his 1997 autobiography: 'It is better for a leader to be feared than loved'. He said he saw his job as Singapore's Prime Minister as one in which he had to persuade his flock – 'my people' – of the right way to go.

Along with their need for leadership, I believe Australians are yearning for a resurgence of patriotism but, as usual, they are waiting to be shown the way. No leader has made Australians feel patriotic since the early days of Gough

Whitlam's Prime Ministership in the seventies. Sydney's 2000 Olympic Games saw an emergence of patriotism – at least for the two weeks the Games were on – but it seems to have disappeared almost as quickly as it came. I get the feeling Australians feel something is missing from their lives. It probably has something to do with that involvement Jim Wolfensohn talked about and the fact that Australians don't feel in charge of their own destiny.

Patriotism has never been a crucial part of our social fabric. So many Australians have no conscious awareness of our nation's history or heritage, even though in 2001 we are celebrating 100 years of Federation. There is a careless public ignorance among the great majority of Australians about the people and events that have shaped this country since the First Fleet arrived here in 1788. If we don't under-stand much about the modern history of Australia, it is hardly surprising that we seem, as a nation, to be very short on patriotism, national pride and an acute sense of our identity.

If only we could find it in ourselves to emulate Americans who are able to make simple demonstrations of patriotism without embarrassment. It's the uncomplicated ability of most Americans to express a respect for their flag, their anthem and all that they represent that has a great deal to do with their self-confidence, self-assurance and national self-esteem. Australians cannot claim the same qualities. We are apathetic about our flag, still can't agree whether or not the words of our national anthem should be changed, are easily embarrassed by any show of patriotism outside the sporting arena, and indifferent towards our heritage.

Although, as journalist Bill Peach once said, when we fly away from home there is a strange rebirth. We suddenly discover a sense of nationalism and we fiercely defend our country. And after the umpteenth chorus of 'Waltzing Matilda' some of us even become sentimental.

I've often thought that Australians are inclined to accept their inheritance without much thought for the human endeavours that have shaped our country over the last two centuries. There is not a high regard for Australian history. Many among the present generations of adults were brought up under a system which placed much more emphasis on the Kings and Queens of England than it did on the men and women who led and helped to pioneer Australia.

I am sure there are some Australians who are surprised to discover that Captain Bligh of *Mutiny on the Bounty* fame is the same man as William Bligh, the fourth Governor of New South Wales. Americans, on the other hand, have a much closer understanding of their national history – despite what Hollywood has sometimes done to historical facts. The teaching of American history in their schools is intensive and comprehensive, and by the time their children have finished school, there's not much they don't know about the origins and development of their own country.

If Australians are ignorant about Australia's past it might explain in part why they are nervous about the future. The lessons of the past are always helpful in determining future directions. There are many things we need to consider as we move into the 21st century, but I believe the three most important issues are education, employment and longevity.

Instant communication will change the way we educate people. Technology means young men and women of today will become the first generation to have education accessible to them on demand. When they tap a few instructions into their computer, information will be immediately supplied to them, indexed and coded, so they can easily find the pertinent extracts they are looking for.

What's more, information will be available twenty-four hours a day. Computer terminals will not only be found in the office, but at home, in schools and at universities. Knowledge will be power in the new century and learning will be something that will continue throughout a lifetime. It will be a century of continuous development.

Australian literacy standards would suggest that we are falling behind in education. In 1997, the Federal Government told State education ministers and departments that they needed to lift their standards because education was failing Australian children. Federal Education Minister David Kemp released findings of a national survey in September 1997 which showed that one-third of Year 3 and Year 5 students cannot read or write properly. If our own Federal Government says Australia is not educating its children well enough, can we assume that these students are not being provided with the right kind of skills for success in the 21st century? Whatever they're learning now will influence their attitude to learning for the rest of their lives. It seems that many of our boys and girls have already been turned off learning and once this happens it is difficult to get them turned on.

All does not appear to be well at Australian universities either. In recent years learning seems to have become a secondary issue, with more time — or so it seems — spent on debates with governments about payrises for everybody working in the university system. As well, not long after the Howard Government came into office bitter battles between it and students broke out over the contentious issue of whether or not students should be expected to pay more for their university degrees.

While I can understand people's feelings and need for payrises and also objections to fee increases, Australia cannot afford to have its universities lose their focus on the main issue. We have to be certain that they are properly equipping young Australians for the 21st century.

But it may be too late for some of them. As Shadow Education Minister Michael Lee pointed out in January 2001, following the release of John Howard's innovation package 'Backing Australia's Ability', the Federal Government 'hit the pause button on education, research and development five years ago. Now with an election looming Howard is trying to catch up. But we've lost five years, and those five years are lost forever.' Lee said that since 1996 the Prime Minister had 'taken $5 billion out of universities, research and development. The Government's big claim now is that they are now going to put back around $2.9 billion. But even if you accept their figures, they have still short-changed innovation in this country, and we are all paying the price.'

Michael Lee may well be right. It's probable that we might see the prediction (often made in the last ten years or so) come true – Australians who want a good university education will have to go to an overseas university to get it. The prerequisites for a successful business career might well be an intimate knowledge of two or three Asian languages – and possibly a passion for sushi!

In England, educationalists, among them Exeter University's Vice Chancellor Sir Geoffrey Holland, warn that: 'Universities need to become places of learning, not teaching.' As he points out schools, colleges and universities are workplaces that have not changed much in decades.

> The world people are going to own and live in is not a world in which people sit neatly and tidily and change every hour from one subject to another. It is not a world of bits and pieces; it is not a world of didacticism; it is not a world of certain answers; and it is not a world of prearranged sets of circumstances.
>
> It is a world where the individual has to learn and make her or his way for herself or himself and therefore where the teacher has to become the supporter of the learner, which requires a fundamental reversal of the traditional role of the teacher.

Our teachers, both in schools and universities, have their

fair share of knockers and I don't wish to join the brigade – but what if teachers have turned off too? What will switch them on again? Redefining teaching is an urgent priority, but without effective leadership it won't happen.

Australia also urgently needs to examine the future of work and understand that, like education, it requires immediate attention. In the new millenium, wealth creation will not necessarily mean job creation. People who are unemployed must be told that they may never be employed again because not only are there not enough jobs but they don't have the right skills. In the future it will not be acceptable to produce people without the right skills – no one must ever again be left behind in the education system. No one can be permitted to get through the system without knowing how to read, for instance.

In September 1997, journalist Geoff Kitney predicted that the future for the Australian workforce looked gloomy. 'The world,' he said, 'will not be a free-market utopia, with opportunities for all as promised by Prime Minister Howard, but a universal Brazil – a place where the wealthy, working elite will live in fortressed enclaves and the poor, non-working masses struggle for survival outside. More resources will go to providing prisons, than schools.'

Kitney who opened the *Sydney Morning Herald*'s news bureau in Germany in 1997, wrote of a future world in which only 20 per cent of the world's working population would be needed in the workforce. The other 80 per cent, he said, would be denied productive, satisfying lives. Instead they will live on the fringe, surviving on what the productive population is prepared to pass on to them.

Australia vigorously supports free trade and globalisation. But increasing numbers of people, including me, believe the latter is not in the world's best interests.

The 1999 *United Nations Human Development Report* said that globalisation lacks a moral dimension and that there is an urgent need to bring human development and social protection into the equation. It is wrong, says the report, to accept the lie that globalisation is a force of nature rather than something directly affected by decisions made at local, national and international levels.

But there seems to be an assumption that technology is rushing us forward to some brave new world that we will have to accept, warts and all. But I think such thinking is naive – what's really driving the world forward is 'market profitability and economic efficiency'. At least that's how the economists describe it.

Others call it greed. These days companies are pre-occupied with achieving profits at the expense of people. Chief Executives pay themselves millions of dollars per year yet think nothing of tossing once-valued employees on to the unemployment scrap heap, blaming the demand of competing in world markets as the excuse for 'down-sizing'.

The hidden price of globalisation is a world where people have become expendable. At the end of World War II full employment was a world priority. But as so many Australian workers have discovered, this is no longer the case.

Multinational employers give work once done by Australians to people in other countries.

Globalisation means that increasingly Australian workers will have to compete with workers of the Third World for jobs. Work will go wherever it can be done for the cheapest price. The need for people to be employed – for their own good – is no longer a consideration.

'Globalisation' is a word suggesting one world – communicating, trading and working together for the common good. In reality it means that large companies will continue to swallow up little ones and that, when it suits them, major nations like the USA will tell countries like Australia to get lost. Developed nations will dominate the developing nations because they control important organisations such as the World Trade Organisation, the International Monetary Fund and the World Bank.

Surely this relentless obsession with economic goals will ultimately jeopardise world stability? Effective globalisation requires new rules to protect the workplace, the environment, education and, most importantly, people. I believe a world apathetic about the global destiny of the human race is indifferent to its future and that, if we allow people to be regarded as non-essential, then the world will be a dangerous place in which to live.

Imagine the adjustments that we will have to make in Australia. If we can no longer take it for granted that we will have jobs – for which we are paid – for what was once regarded as a working lifetime, how will this affect our prospects for a happy, fulfilled life? What will happen to the work ethic which has been so fundamental to our existence so far? How do we prepare our children for a workless world?

After all, up until now it has been accepted that we would spend the greater proportion of our lives working. We define not only ourselves but also others by the work they do. Work allows us to organise our lives. It determines (because we are paid for our efforts) how we spend our leisure time as well as the way we shop and eat. It is impossible for most of us to contemplate a future without work, and yet on present indicators that's what lies ahead. How will people buy their homes, educate, clothe and feed their children or prepare themselves for old age – that in the future will be even longer than it is today – without an income?

Obviously we will have to redefine work and accept that some will have work to do – often too much, and often under too much pressure – while others will have no work at all. Work may have to be something for which we are not paid but something we do to give ourselves a sense of purpose and a reason for getting up in the morning. Voluntary work may be the answer. Further education to keep the mind occupied may be another.

Hobbies will become more important; so will things like playing a musical instrument. Women may even discover once more the satisfaction of making their own clothes, of knitting jumpers, and even the joys of preparing a home-cooked meal. With unemployment set to become a way of life, who'll need fast foods and quick takeaways? People will have plenty of time to cook the most complicated of dishes.

In *The End of Work*, Jerry Rifkin argues that the march of technology is unstoppable. Technology, he says, has already taken the manufacturing sector to the brink of an era where new products can be designed and introduced with little intervention (by a human). A similar, if less noticed, revolution has taken place in agriculture which in all industrial societies now employs only a fraction of the people it did half a century ago and which has more potential to dispense with human labour.

Nothing much has been said either about the fact that our workforce, once predominantly male, has been replaced by one in which women are rapidly approaching half the total. As well, many workers today are in service occupations, yet it is generally recognised that service is an area in which Australians need to improve. I can never understand why Australian workers have such difficulty in delivering service. It's not that hard really. Everyone knows what good service is – we all know when we have received it and when we haven't. It should not be all that difficult to deliver it.

Australia is also part of a world that is rapidly ageing. This is now a major global problem and yet many Australians haven't given any thought to the implications that an ageing society will mean to the way we live. I doubt that many businesses have either, even though the longer lifespans of human beings are going to have ramifications for every aspect of our lives such as education, building and housing, employment, travel, and welfare and care services. Once more, business opportunities are being overlooked.

Clever entrepreneurs, though, will see enormous opportunities in the ageing population, particularly as older people will have tremendous spending power in the years ahead and will control significant portions of the nation's disposable wealth. Currently, the over forties control 80 per cent of Australia's assets and have $70 billion a year to spend. Today, more than 79 per cent of fifty- to sixty-four-year-olds have finished paying off their homes and most no longer have children at home. Anti-ageing will become a real 'seller' in the years ahead. We're already seeing this with the development of anti-wrinkle creams and a bigger interest by women and men in cosmetic surgery.

Let's hope we won't emulate Americans too much in this area. I look at Americans, both men and women, who in their impossible attempts to stay young forever have their faces and bodies nipped, tucked and lifted, and wonder who they're trying to fool? They look so unreal, so unlike the person they once were, with all of their life's experiences taken from their faces by the surgeon's knife. They are left with blank faces, taut skin and wide eyes. It's a horrible look.

But Americans are not the only ones who try to hide ageing. Cosmetic surgery is a growth area in Australia, too, with some 50 000 cosmetic surgical procedures carried out annually. Even men are lining up for nips and tucks! One well-known Australian woman has had so many facelifts that her mouth seems to have moved position. She may think she looks young, but she walks like the older woman she is. Surgeons haven't quite worked out yet how to change the way we are inside our bodies, but I'm sure they're working on it!

By 2000 one in every five Australians was over sixty; by the year 2010 the number of people over sixty-five will out-number the people under sixteen; and by the year 2020 there will be more 'retired' people than ever before in our history. The only consolation, I suppose, is that we are not the only country going 'grey'. The world's elderly population is increas-ing by 800 000 every month and by 2025, 14 per cent of the world's population – 1.2 billion – will be over sixty.

Ageing is no longer an issue that we can confront when we are elderly. It is something that needs to concern us not only in old age – or Third Age as it is frequently called – but also in our youth and middle age. How will Australia provide the necessary support for this ageing pop-ulation? Are we preparing people well enough? There has to be a massive shift in the way we think about age. Many senior citizens are portrayed as elderly or frail – sometimes even useless – yet the reality is quite different. Most older people are busy and active and doing all sorts of exciting things with their lives, which those of us who are young don't have time for but wish we did! I'm often perplexed to see people over thirty-five, especially sports people and, for some reason actresses, described as 'veterans'. The Sydney *Daily Telegraph* a couple of years ago reported on the death of an 'elderly' man of sixty-one. Elderly at sixty-one? Good grief! These days, people are not elderly at sixty-something.

I got something of a shock when I turned fifty and received a copy of *The Australian Senior* newspaper with a note from the Editor saying, 'Now that you're one of us ...' I rang the Editor and said he had it all wrong. I didn't think I qualified at fifty to be considered a Senior Citizen and if I were, then what did that make my father who was then eighty-five?

We need to redefine age. Anything up to sixty is young (people under thirty-five could be described as very young); sixty to eighty is middle age; eighty is old; and ninety and over is elderly. Five hundred years ago people didn't expect to live much beyond their twenties; now men live into their late seventies and women into their eighties. The American TV show, *Today*, no longer congratulates people on reaching 100. That is too commonplace. Men and women only get a telegram when they reach 105.

To me, ageing is like leaves gently falling off the trees in autumn – quite beautiful really, if seen through open eyes. There is nothing anyone can do to prevent it happening, so you have to let go and enjoy it. Ageing is not an illness but a normal life experience. There is an old saying that 'youth is wasted on the young'. They have the vim and vigour to do everything, but not the wisdom to go along with it.

Perhaps that is God's joke on us – that older people have the wisdom but lack the vitality. But life does not end or become less worthwhile if we lose a leaf or two – who would want to miss autumn anyway?

When I was a younger woman the man I loved left a bunch of flowers on my doorstep with a card that said: 'Grow old with me, the best is yet to be.' I knew what he meant, not just because I loved him, but because he was talking about the time, wisdom and experience we would be able to share and enjoy in the years ahead. It seemed like an invitation to paradise – but unfortunately it did not eventuate.

People living longer offers all kinds of opportunities for creative living. It will require a very different outlook and a change in the way we care for older people, as well as in the services offered to them. With all the changes we have been through, and all the ones yet to come, it is important for Australians not to fear old age. But for us to achieve all this successfully, we will of course require strong leadership.

I became aware of some of the more pressing issues related to ageing when I chaired the New South Wales Seniors Media Network Council in 1994–95. It was set up by the New South Wales Liberal Government to improve the image of older people in the media. In 1997 I became a member of the Conference on Older Australians, a Federal Liberal Government initiative, to advise it on a range of issues including health, education and community service, and to offer ideas on how Australians might best celebrate the International Year of Older Persons in 1999.

All our plans on how we will care for our older citizens are based on the premise that most Australians will go on working full-time. Given what I've written on the future of work, this seems highly unlikely. It seems to me that if Australia is doing any planning for the future it might be doing so with the wrong information. Surely caring for older people will be less of a problem because if fewer people are in the workforce, caring for elderly parents will give people something to do. It might even put some meaning back into family life.

In her book *The Fountain of Age*, America's Betty Friedan says we must stop describing age as a problem because the more we do the worse the problem will get. She has a point – but however much we wish to call it something else, the number of people ageing will be a problem for governments which will need to make sure older people are cared for if they are unable to care for themselves. Governments will also be called upon to provide treatment for the diseases of old age, which will increase at the same time. Estimates are that in the next few years something in the order of $25 billion will be added to the national spending in terms of pensions and health care.

Is it little wonder that Australians are now being urged to save as much as they possibly can for their old age? Many financial advisers say that 15 per cent of income should be saved throughout one's entire working life for that person to be comfortable in retirement. Well, that will take another big shift in thinking because the fact is Australians aren't very good at saving, and the baby boomers have been very ordinary savers – the lowest in our history.

This is just one of the reasons we are a nation in increasing debt, with current statistics indicating that as a nation we owe more than $300 billion to creditors overseas. We are set to become tenants in our own land, and few seem alarmed that each and every Australian is in debt to the tune of almost $16 000. We have lived beyond our means for years and are saddling our children with the legacy of our greed and our over-inflated lifestyles. How can our children look forward to the future when we have left them such an inheritance?

Prime Minister John Howard, when asked after winning the Federal election in 1996 what he wanted for Australians beyond the year 2000, replied that he hoped we would feel 'comfortable', but maybe we're just too comfortable for our own good. Maybe Australians can't afford to be comfortable. Paul Keating never made Australians feel comfortable. He was always giving us a prod. He warned us that we would become a Banana Republic. And before the 1996 election, when small business was venting its anger at Government indifference to the difficulties it was still facing because of the lingering effects of the recession, he told them: 'This is as good as it gets.' Keating used to get people mad. Maybe in retrospect this wasn't such a bad thing after all.

Former Whitlam Government minister and Chief Judge

of the New South Wales Land and Environment Court, the late Jim McClelland, once described Paul Keating as 'the ablest man in Parliament, but like many men of humble origins, his orientation is more and more towards the big end of town. He wants to join the big battalion'.

Towards the end of his Prime Ministership, Keating began to develop signs of wanting to be a statesman rather than a politician. He had moved a long way from Bankstown and had, seemingly, forgotten his roots. Yet at the beginning of his Prime Ministership it was clear that Keating had the vision – as Treasurer, he wanted to change Australia's tax system (but was outmanoeuvred by Hawke who wanted to remain a popular Prime Minister); he deregulated the financial market and let the overseas banks in – but somewhere along the way he ran out of ideas. I think it happened in 1993 when Keating expected to lose the election. Everyone told him he would and he believed them. When he was returned to power he took his focus off the main issues like rising unemployment and the needs of small business.

Keating is one of Australia's tragedies – he could have been one of our great leaders. He knew we had a role to play in Asia, a role that has become more apparent in the upheavals of the Asian economies in early 1998, when it transpired that Australia was more financially viable than many of its Asian neighbours, notably South Korea, Indonesia, the Philippines, Malaysia and Thailand. Keating also had the ability to inspire the nation to come with him to the Promised Land of the 21st century. Keating did have the courage to lead and perhaps was the only true leader we've had in Canberra since Sir Robert Menzies. We will have to wait for the history books to be written to see if my judgment is correct. When John Howard succeeded Keating, his Government inherited a potential $10 billion deficit. However, by the end of his first term, Howard was able to announce an actual budget surplus of $1.6 billion. Australians welcomed the return of economic stability and the consensus was that Prime Minister Howard was a good economic manager. But like so many politicians who have been in office for a number of years, he now seems to have forgotten that flexibility can be an asset in politics. Howard has always been intransigent – some might even say pig-headed – about changing his mind, even when faced with mounting public concern.

Howard was well aware of the need to win the support of small business in 1996, given that this group had been infuriated by Keating's indifference to their financial problems during and after the recession. But by 2001 Howard seemed to have forgotten the need of keeping small business on side and turned a deaf ear, at first, to their howls of protest about the time-consuming nature of the Government's Business Activity Statement (BAS) introduced with the GST as part of Australia's national tax reform. The Government's ignorance of the demands on small business owners was obvious, and its advice that anyone having difficulties in filling in the BAS should consult the Tax Office's 148-page instruction booklet was useless – no one running a small business has time to read 148 pages of information written in hard-to-understand bureaucratic mumbo-jumbo.

Australians knew the country needed tax reform, but they didn't expect it to be rammed down their throats with a we-know-what's-best-for-you approach. Anyone introducing change needs to understand the implications on those obliged to accept it; community sensitivities cannot be ignored. If One Nation's Pauline Hanson hadn't re-emerged as a political threat in early 2001, small business might still be stuck with the quarterly BAS. But with Pauline's influence on the outcomes of the Western Australian and Queensland elections that year and the devastation of the Liberal Party in both States, Howard got the message, but perhaps not soon enough.

Pauline Hanson breaks every rule in the politically correct handbook and is in marked contrast to the political correctness that virtually silenced us as a nation during Keating's time at the helm. It is still difficult to have a reasoned debate in Australia about so many matters. From Aborigines to immigration, any discussion that touches on a taboo issue is branded as racism. Indeed, 'racist' and 'racism' are probably the two most abused words in our language.

As early as 1988 I flagged my concern about our national silence when as Editor-in-Chief of Sydney's *Sun-Herald* I wrote:

Immigration must be the great unspoken issue in Australia. It's like death; no one knows how to speak about it without causing offence.

It should be possible to talk about the issue without being proclaimed a racist. If we can't, how can we be a truly multicultural society? Who decreed multiculturalism as our future anyway? Were the people who live here asked? Is it too late to turn the clock back? Do we want to? Should we have a referendum on the issue? I think we should.

A poll released last week [14 February 1988] revealed that more than two-thirds of voters want a cut in immigration levels and a quarter want no immigrants at all this year.

[I concluded] There are problems with multiculturalism and it's about time our politicians had the guts to mention some of them. For example, there are many practices, rituals and attitudes I find unacceptable and wouldn't want to see introduced into Australia, like the custom of some Middle-Eastern and African countries of female circumcision.

I don't object to specific groups of people, linked to their country of birth, congregating in a specific area [in our suburbs], but I can also accept that the original inhabitants of the area could object because they may be made to feel like aliens in their own country.

Some people would consider me a racist for having said that, but I fail to see why. To my mind, it is more basic that Australians, firstly, be permitted to debate sensitive issues and, secondly, have the will to do so. When we shut people up, negative feelings are only sent deeper into the pit of the stomach where they become bitter like bile and ultimately turn to hate. The *Sun-Herald* received 12 000 letters in response to my column, most of them in support of a referendum on the issue of immigration. We sent them to Prime Minister Hawke's office as we told the readers we would and never heard another word about them.

But in spite of continuing reservations in some quarters about who should and should not be allowed to immigrate here, I think most Australians are proud of the fact that we have built one of the finest, free, democratic societies that the world has ever known and just knowing that should give us a sense of great pride. It is the reason why so many from distant lands want to live here. Last time I checked we had immigrants from 170 countries calling Australia home and bringing to our island continent their cultures, knowledge and skills, all of which have been to our nation's gain. Surely there must have been something good about Australia and its culture which others saw and later appreciated.

Our Aborigines are one of the world's oldest peoples; and now, with all the many other people who make up our population, we are a fascinating, complex society – a unique mixture of old and new. Other nations look at the way we get on with each other and marvel at how we've done it. When all is said and done Australia is one of the best integrated multicultural societies in the world. I sometimes think its success has taken us by surprise.

As far as Aborigines are concerned, I believe the nation owes them an apology and that John Howard has failed to lead on this issue. The Government quite rightly has given millions of dollars to improve Aboriginal health, education and general wellbeing, but money can't give Aborigines back their sense of pride that has been destroyed ever since the first settlers arrived here. We can't change the wrongs of our past, but we can with leadership and reconciliation move forward together and I think most Australians, both white and black, agree with that line of thinking.

In the nineties there was a fearful growth in gambling, and State governments are now receiving massive revenues from gambling taxes. In April 2001 Australian Gambling Statistics put this revenue figure at $4.39 billion! Australian governments appear committed to a future tied to gambling, apparently believing that this is the best way to raise funds in the face of a shrinking taxpayer base. Never mind the studies that show that the people most likely to gamble have low incomes, less formal education, and are from non-English speaking backgrounds. As if that weren't bad enough, many of the poker machines that make the most money are concentrated in disadvantaged areas.

Unfortunately, the social consequences may be enormous, as we appear to be becoming a nation of gambling addicts. In the Productivity Commission's 1999 Interim Report on Gambling it said that women now make up half of all problem gamblers and the social problems resulting from gambling addiction, including bankruptcy, depression, family breakdown and suicide, have increased markedly.

The money that goes into gambling is ultimately siphoned away from other purchases in the economy. Rupert Murdoch has complained that sales of his newspapers are being adversely affected because people are too busy gambling their money away, and singled out the growth of casinos in Australia. For a nation of only 18 million people, we do seem to be oversupplied. There's at least one in every State and Territory, and some States have more than one.

Our addictions appear not only in gambling, but gambling may be symptomatic of our problems as a society. Adult Australians are addicted to anything from alcohol to cigarettes to hard drugs, but gambling appears to be one of our favourites. Poker machine profits are growing at the expense of all other kinds of businesses, both big and small. People just don't have the spare cash to spend on goods and services that they once did. Channel Nine economics commentator Michael Pascoe warned in 1996 that Australia was marching towards becoming 'a fully punt-based economy, with a flutter of one sort or another the solution to all problems. Need an Opera House? Hold a lottery. Health system broken? Offer odds. Can't sell beer to Australians? Bung in pokie machines'.

According to recent Government figures, the amount Australians spend on gambling has risen more than 300 per cent in real terms over the past twenty-three years. In 1972–73 when Australia's first casino, Wrest Point, opened in Tasmania, we spent $20 million on playing poker machines, lotto, horses and gaming. According to the Tasmanian Gaming Commission, total gambling losses in Australia in the 1999–2000 financial year came to a record $13.3 billion. Australians are among the biggest gamblers in the world and today our country has the dubious honour of having 21 per cent of the world's total gaming machines.

In the future, perhaps when the Government needs to build a new motorway, it will do it the old-fashioned way – and hold a chook raffle.

Some of you may be thinking that what I've written seems unduly pessimistic so far, and may be saying to yourselves: 'Surely, there will be more hope than that!' Futurists say that in this century we will win the war on drugs, and cure the common cold, cancer and many other diseases. We may even, some optimists say, win the war against ageing. Our lives will be filled with fast trains, upon which we will hurtle from station to station, city to city. There will be no crime, and children will all go to university and carry their knowledge about in pocket computers. The Golden Age, they say, will be an age of peace, health and prosperity.

Undoubtedly, the most powerful communications and marketing tool in the years ahead will be the Internet but the influential *New York Times* has warned: 'Left unfettered the Internet will eventually place so much power in the hands of the citizenry that oppressive twentieth century institutions – government, schools, the mass media – will crumble.'

Anthropologist Margaret Mead once said, 'Never doubt that a small group of committed citizens can change the world, indeed it is the only thing that ever has'. If a small group of committed citizens can change the world, imagine what a large group on the Internet could do. The potential power of the Internet is awesome and will develop in the years ahead.

I also find awesome the possibility that we might condone cloning, an issue which must pose quite a few questions in the coming years. After all, the British scientists who cloned Dolly the sheep indicated, according to a *Sydney Morning Herald* report in March 1997, that they 'could use the same technique to "photocopy" humans within two years'. Now, if this is not opening up a verit-able Pandora's box, I don't know what is. Adil Shamoo, Professor of Biochemistry at the University of Maryland's School of Medicine, said: 'The cloning of humans is coming ... the twenty-first century will be known for the biological revolution.' He argued that 'the ethical, moral and theological framework of society will be drasti-cally affected, challenged and at times, perhaps, even devalued'.

In reality, though, perhaps men will be the big losers in the long run – with cloning, will men downgrade their own role in the future? Have men really thought what cloning means? I have, and I'm against it. Why do we need cloning? Are we heading towards a world where some people will be deemed suitable for cloning and others not? Will suitable

'cloners' have to be kept in isolation until required for repro-
duction? Who will play God and decide which of us will be
replicated and for what purpose? Exactly what kind of brave
new world are we heading towards? Surely the issue of
cloning life is as worthy of debate as euthanasia? Why isn't
the debate happening?

Political correctness may be downgraded in the years
ahead. There already appears to be a movement afoot to
remove it. The Federal Government has changed 'chairperson' back to 'chairman', but who really cares? It's such a
non-issue – surely there are more urgent matters to attend
to. 'Chairman', 'chairwoman', 'chairperson', 'chair' – it doesn't
mean a thing – as long as everyone knows who is in charge,
the title is immaterial. The discussion will not be stilled, I
am sure, and there may be something of a move back to
more traditional values in the years ahead.

This could be something of a reaction to the changes
that have happened in Australia since the women's movement began its push. It is probably inescapable, as the 'Me
Generation' – having accepted that it may have lost its
bearings – seeks some kind of redefinition. As Hugh Mackay
notes in *Reinventing Australia*:

> The 'Me Generation' hasn't coped any better than
> anyone else with the Age of Redefinition and so they,
> like the rest of the community, have entered a period
> of reflection, re-evaluation and consolidation. When a
> society has come to feel that it has lost its bearings, it

is probably inevitable that the first inclination is to look back, to see whether the values of the past might have something to offer – either intact, or in recycled form.

As we move through the 1990s, certain words and themes are attracting increasing attention and support because they are so easily associated with the values of earlier times. We are going to see a growing emphasis on words and concepts which seem to be connected in some way to the idea of getting 'back to basics'. Words like responsibility; restraint; moderation; heritage; conservation; morality; integrity; balance; loyalty; decency; discipline; domesticity; the family.

In the wake of such a prevailing mood, PC language may suffer somewhat and that may not be a bad thing.

Will Australia become a Republic? Almost certainly. Even though the 1999 referendum on this issue failed, few Australians doubt that one day Australia will no longer be tied to Britain. It is a fair guess that when it happens we will have a new flag to go with it. You can also count on the Aboriginal flag as being part of it, in place of the Union Jack. As a Republic, Australia will seek new symbols of nationhood and will find them in the heritage of the first Australians.

On the health front, I remain convinced we will go from bad to worse with successive governments, State and Federal, unable to solve the problems of a flawed system.

Hepatitis C will remain a severe public health problem. Already half of all inmates in Australian prisons are infected due to sharing of needles and tattooing. As I indicated in the chapter on AIDS, who knows what sexually transmitted nightmare lies just around the corner for us?

As we move forward into the 21st century, we must avoid the danger of thinking in our typical, uncomplicated Australian way that the new millennium gives us a chance to start from scratch with a clean slate. If only life were so easy – but being the happy-go-lucky country, we tend to view things in such simplistic ways.

There really is only one thing of which we can be sure in the future – many of the problems that challenged us in the 20th century will confront us in the 21st century!

Epilogue

I can't finish this book without passing on probably one of the best pieces of advice I ever received. When I was sixteen, a journalist friend of my father's told me to save ten shillings (about $1) from my pay packet every week and to continue to do so throughout my working life. It is a matter of some regret to me that I ignored his words of wisdom.

I may not have always played it safe, but I have managed to lead what some have described as a passionate life. There is still much I want to do. I have numerous dreams. I am for the most part content with my lot. I don't mind my own company. I am happy working alone or with other people – I have a need for both. I especially want to travel and to continue to write books, both fiction and non-fiction.

I sit here in my home office in Sydney's inner-city suburb of Paddington, looking towards Centrepoint Tower, enjoying a love/hate relationship with my computer, and with Rachmaninoff's *Piano Concerto No 2* playing on my CD. In winter, Humphrey, my black labrador, sleeps on my feet. In summer, Bogart, my Siamese cat, enjoys snoozing in my desk drawer with the fan blowing gently over him. They are good companions.

Something inside tells me that the best is yet to come. I can't wait!

Ita Buttrose, Sydney, Australia
February 2001

INDEX

Index